PATERNOSTER BIBLICAL AND THEOLOGICAL MONOGRAPHS

SUFFERING AND MINISTRY IN THE SPIRIT

Paul's Defence of His Ministry in
II Corinthians 2:14–3:3

A full listing of titles in this series
will be found
at the close of this book

PATERNOSTER BIBLICAL AND THEOLOGICAL MONOGRAPHS

SUFFERING AND MINISTRY IN THE SPIRIT

Paul's Defence of His Ministry in
II Corinthians 2:14–3:3

Scott J. Hafemann

paternoster
press

This edition first published 2000 by Paternoster Press
By arrangement with Wm. B. Eerdmans Publishing Co.
255 Jefferson Ave. S.E., Grand Rapids, MI 49503, U.S.A

Paternoster Press is an imprint of Paternoster Publishing,
P.O. Box 300, Carlisle, Cumbria, CA3 0QS, U.K.
and
P.O. Box 1047, Waynesboro, GA 30830-2047, U.S.A.

03 02 01 00   7 6 5 4 3 2 1

British Library Cataloguing in Publication Data
A catalogue record for this book is available from the British Library

ISBN 0-85364-967-7

Printed and bound in Great Britain by
Nottingham Alpha Graphics

TO DEBARA,
MY PARTNER IN EVERYTHING

Contents

Chapter Three

**The Question of Paul's Sufficiency and a Working
Hypothesis Concerning Its Background in Biblical
and Jewish Tradition (II Cor. 2:16b)**

Chapter Four

**The Apologetic Function of Paul's Ministry of Suffering
in the Corinthian Correspondence (II Cor. 2:17)**

Chapter Five

Paul's Ministry of the Spirit as Corroboratory Evidence of His Sufficiency (II Cor. 3:1-3) — 180

Acknowledgments

In its present form this work is an abridged and now edited version of my doctoral dissertation, which was accepted in January, 1985, by the Protestant faculty of theology of Eberhard-Karls-Universität Tübingen. In the course of my graduate studies in Tübingen I incurred a deep debt of gratitude to so many people whom God used in various ways to make it possible for my family and me to undertake and complete this venture. Among them I would like to thank especially my parents, Jack and Gin Hafemann, and my in-laws, Harley and Nancy Jones, for their constant support and "care-packages" which met so many needs; our friends Eric Tanquist, Tom Varno, Tom and Julie Steller, John and Noel Piper, and Charlie and Debbie Cosgrove, all of whom played vital roles in our lives during this time with their friendship and support (at times even financial); the Hausens, who helped us in many practical ways during our stay in Tübingen; Frau Kienle, for her friendliness and assistance in the office; and Frau Stuhlmacher and the entire Stuhlmacher family, who opened their home to us and made our last year in Tübingen unforgettable by their warmth and kindness to us.

I would also like to express my sincere appreciation to Rotary International for the fellowship that enabled us to spend a year of study in Jerusalem, to Freundeskreis des Goethe-Instituts Blaubeuren for the scholarship that helped pay for language school, and to Professor Otfried Hofius (Dekan at that time) and the Protestant faculty of the University of Tübingen for the scholarship they granted me, which made it possible to remain in Tübingen until I was finished.

Five of my teachers also deserve my special thanks: Dr. John Piper, for his initial encouragement and personal interest in me as an undergraduate student, not to mention all I have learned from him academically and personally; Professor Daniel Fuller, for his passion in pursuit of the truth, by which he has been a role model for me; Dr. Robert Guelich, for his support and confidence in me and for recommending me to the faculty in Tübingen; and Professor Otto Betz for the many times he encouraged me with his questions and interest in my work. I owe my deepest debt of gratitude to Professor Peter Stuhlmacher, who not only gave me the opportunity to study under his guidance as my "Doctor-Father," but also gave of himself continually to help me in more ways than I can list here. He took a genuine interest in my work and family far beyond what a graduate student expects and allowed me to work as his assistant while writing my thesis. His professional, scholarly, and personal life have all been a great example to me of what scholarship is all about. Moreover, whatever strengths this work might have are due to my awareness that it would be read by him.

The publication of this American edition of my thesis, originally published in a more technical form by J. C. B. Mohr (Paul Siebeck), Tübingen, in 1986, has been made possible by a Lilly Foundation Faculty Research Support Grant awarded through the program of Gordon-Conwell Theological Seminary. I am grateful to my senior colleagues on the faculty who considered this project worthy of such support. The grant enabled me to secure the editorial services of Carol Steinbach, without whose competence and diligence this project could not have been completed. To a large degree this work is the result of her eye for what is essential for the wider audience to which this work is now available and to her willingness to do the thankless task of retyping the manuscript in its edited format. I am deeply grateful for her expertise, labor, and the cheerful way in which she takes up her tasks.

I would also like to thank Seyoon Kim for originally recommending this work to Mr. William B. Eerdmans for publication in the United States, and to Mr. Eerdmans for his interest in the project, just as I continue to be grateful to Professors Martin Hengel and Otfried Hofius for accepting the earlier version in the WUNT series. My thanks also go to the editorial staff of Wm. B. Eerdmans Publishing Co. for their careful work.

The American edition of this book is still dedicated to my wife, Debara. Her support for my teaching and writing, and her commitment to our life together, remain as constant and as vital as always.

October 3rd, 1988
S. Hamilton, Massachusetts

SCOTT J. HAFEMANN

Introduction

The Purpose and Method of the Study

*All historical writing and research must begin first with a
sense of wonder and then a clearly formulated question.*[1]

It was never my intention when I began this project to devote a
full-length study to the seven verses which now form the heart of this
investigation into Paul's self-understanding and defense as an apostle
of Jesus Christ. Rather, my original focus was on the letter/Spirit
contrast found and developed in II Cor. 3:6ff., to which II Cor. 2:14–
3:3 seemed merely to give an introduction of lesser significance. Like
most commentators, therefore, I planned simply to write an obligatory
chapter on this text in anticipation of the more weighty passage
beginning with 3:6.

But in time I came to realize that the questions raised by Paul's
argument in 2:14–3:3 were themselves of such magnitude and importance for our understanding of Paul's view of his apostolic ministry
that the letter/Spirit contrast itself could only be properly understood
once this wider contrast had been mapped out. More specifically, the
need to devote a full-length study to an investigation of Paul's thought
in 2:14–3:3 became apparent when a preliminary look at the meaning
of the image of the triumphal procession in 2:14a and the point of Paul's
argument in 2:17 led to a new understanding of the subject under
discussion in this passage. It soon became clear that II Cor. 2:14–3:3,
being part of the "theological heart" of II Corinthians, is both a

1. Cantor, *Medieval History*, 1.

1

thesis-like compendium of Paul's self-conception as an apostle, as well as a classic presentation of his corresponding apologetic for the authority and validity of his apostolic ministry.

Hence, this study attempts to investigate this self-understanding and apologetic as the important first step toward understanding the theological and hermeneutical issues raised by Paul's subsequent discussion in II Cor. 3:4-18. For it is imperative that Paul's reflections concerning the letter and the Spirit be understood within the larger context in which they are found. Thus, having investigated II Cor. 2:14–3:3, I am now writing a second work which takes up where this study ends by investigating II Cor. 3:4–4:6. In this work, besides exegeting II Cor. 3:4ff. against its relevant Old Testament backdrop, I will also provide the history of the Old Testament tradition necessary to substantiate the thesis set forth in chapter three below concerning the allusion to Moses in II Cor. 2:17. Finally, I hope to draw out the implications of these two studies for our understanding of the historical situation in Corinth at the time of the writing of I and II Corinthians, especially the age-old problem of the identity of Paul's opponents and the nature of their teaching.

The study now before us, however, is an *exegetical* study. I emphasize "exegetical" because the questions asked and pursued in this work, despite their diverse nature, all seek to understand the meaning and significance of Paul's argument as unfolded in the various texts analyzed. The "method" employed, therefore, consists of asking the simple questions of interpretation necessary to follow the train of thought of an author, ancient or modern. This study is not an attempt to apply a new method to a familiar text in order to discover something novel. Rather, it is an attempt to start with the text itself without the assumption that its meaning has already been ascertained and thus only needs to be reformulated or put within a new framework of interpretation (e.g. literary, sociological, psychological, polemical, theological, etc.). My experience has been that the Pauline texts themselves still remain to a great degree a foreign territory in need of discovery. Hence, the approach taken here is summarized well by Sean E. McEvenue, who, when attempting to describe his own "method," concluded that

> The fact is that method is nothing more than a description and systematization of acts of understanding. . . . Ultimately the re-

searcher must simply stare at his text, or fumble with it, until acts of understanding begin to take place.[2]

I also emphasize "exegetical" because, as a matter of methodology, I have consciously resisted the temptation to follow the vast majority of recent scholars in using certain aspects of the Corinthian correspondence to reconstruct a detailed picture of Paul's opponents in Corinth and their theology *from which* Paul's letters to the Corinthians are then subsequently interpreted. I have done so not because I consider the question of the identity and theology of Paul's opponents unimportant for understanding Paul's epistles or for tracing the history of the early Church in general. Quite the contrary! But the absence of direct evidence from their hands renders all attempts to *begin* with such a reconstruction as the interpretive key to Paul's writings uncontrollably circular at best, and at its worst simply a matter of historical phantasy. It will no doubt strike readers who are familiar with the history of the interpretation of I and II Corinthians in our century as surprising and strange, therefore, to discover that no attempt has been made in this work to identify Paul's opponents in Corinth or to outline what they taught. Instead, I have tried to bring to the text concerning Paul's opponents only what Paul himself reports about their criticism of him, since it is Paul's response to this criticism as he perceived it that we have before us. Thus, many important historical questions are intentionally left unanswered. My hope, however, is that these questions can be better approached once Paul's own thinking has been clarified internally as much as possible.

For this same reason (in my interpretation of II Cor. 2:14–3:3) I have also been very cautious in my use of the other Pauline epistles, not to mention the rest of the New Testament. My procedure has been to adduce interpretive parallels primarily from the Corinthian correspondence itself, since we can be sure that Paul's comments in our passage would be compared to the rest of his writings received by the Corinthians and were intended by Paul to be so compared. When I do point to another, non-Corinthian, Pauline writing, my purpose in doing so is to highlight the common structure and themes in Paul's respective

2. McEvenue, *Narrative Style,* 11

arguments as a confirmation of my exegesis of the text under consideration. If a parallel in thought between our passage and another Pauline text can be demonstrated, then we can be encouraged that our exegesis is on the right track. The only other occasion for leaving the Corinthian correspondence is when it becomes necessary to acquire some additional historical knowledge in order to determine the wider meaning of a word or implication of an idiom, etc. But again, the determination of the meaning of Paul's use of such idioms and traditions is based, in the final analysis, on internal considerations. Hence, I have also left open the question of developing a Pauline theology of the various issues raised in this study. The methodology followed in this work thus follows the basic principle outlined earlier by Nils A. Dahl in regard to I Cor. 1–4:

> In so far as they do not directly serve the purpose of philological exegesis, but provide materials for a more general historical and theological understanding, information from other Pauline epistles, Acts, and other early Christian, Jewish, Greek, or Gnostic documents should not be brought in until the epistolary situation has been clarified as far as possible on the basis of internal evidence.[3]

As a result, the respective strengths of this work are also its weaknesses. But inasmuch as the safest route historically is to begin with what one has in its specificity before drawing conclusions about the darker corners of history that surround it or about its broader intellectual, theological, and literary context, it seems most appropriate to start the unavoidable hermeneutical circle that exists between a text and its context with a particular text, rather than with a reconstruction of its broader context. For only then will we be able to establish criteria for distinguishing between the plethora of opinions already confronting us concerning the nature of Paul's opposition in Corinth, not to mention the myriad interpretations of Paul's own theology, its place within the development of the early Church, and its relationship to the biblical traditions from which it sprang. The task is a formidable one. But it is a task that is best carried out with a historical humility that is willing to admit what can and cannot be known given the evidence

3. Dahl, "Paul and the Church at Corinth," 318.

available. The results of such a "humility" will naturally be much more modest than often found in recent literature on the Corinthian epistles, but in turn, their modesty will carry with it a higher degree of certainty.

THE CHARACTER OF THE AMERICAN EDITION

This present edition preserves the content and argument of the original version published in 1986 by J. C. B. Mohr (Paul Siebeck) under the title *Suffering and the Spirit: An Exegetical Study of II Cor. 2:14–3:3 within the Context of the Corinthian Correspondence* (Wissenschaftliche Untersuchungen zum Neuen Testament, 2. Reihe, 19). But for the sake of a broader audience, I have translated all Greek and Hebrew biblical texts and quotations from foreign language secondary literature into English. Greek and Hebrew, where retained, have been transliterated. In addition, the technical discussion and history of the debate originally carried on in the footnotes, when deemed essential to the argument, have been incorporated into the body of the text. But for the most part they have been eliminated. Those who wish to follow my divergence from and interaction with previous scholars are thus encouraged to consult the previous edition. The original bibliography has nevertheless been retained in order to indicate all the scholars to whom I am indebted and without whom this work could not have been written.

Despite the appearance of English translations, I have cited the following works in their original German forms, either because the English translations had not yet been produced when I did my research or because the English translations were not available to me in Tübingen at that time: Rudolf Bultmann's *Der Zweite Brief an die Korinther* (*The Second Letter to the Corinthians,* tr. R. A. Harrisville, Minneapolis: Augsburg, 1985); Hans Conzelmann's *Der erste Brief an die Korinther* (*1 Corinthians,* tr. J. W. Leitch in the Hermeneia series, Philadelphia: Fortress, 1975); Dieter Georgi's *Die Gegner des Paulus im 2. Korintherbrief* (*The Opponents of Paul in Second Corinthians,* Philadelphia: Fortress, 1986); Leonhard Goppelt's *Theologie des Neuen Testaments* (*Theology of the New Testament,* tr. in two volumes by J. Alsup, Grand Rapids: Eerdmans, 1981 and 1982); Karl Hermann Schelkle's *Der Zweite Brief an die Korinther* (*The Second Epistle to the Corinthians*, tr. by K. Smith for the series The New Testament for Spiritual Reading, New York: Herder and Herder, 1969); Peter Stuhlmacher's *Versöhnung, Gesetz und Gerechtigkeit: Aufsätze zur biblischen Theologie* (*Reconciliation, Law, and Righteousness: Essays in Biblical Theology*, tr. E. R. Kalin, Philadelphia: Fortress, 1986); Gerd Theissen's *Studien zur Sociologie des Urchristentums* (*The Social Setting of Pauline Christianity: Essays on Corinth*, tr. J. H. Schütz, Philadelphia: Fortress, 1982); Theissen's *Psychologische Aspekte paulinischer Theologie* (*Psychological Aspects of Pauline Theology*, tr. J. P. Galvin, Philadelphia: Fortress, 1987); and Walther Zimmerli's *Ezechiel* (*Ezekiel*, tr. in two volumes by J. D. Martin [I] and R. E. Clements [II] for the Hermeneia series, Philadelphia: Fortress, 1979 and 1983). English readers should have no difficulty in finding the appropriate sections in the published English translations of these works. The English translations of Bultmann's *Theologie des Neuen Testaments* and of the articles by Ernst Käsemann do not reflect the latest German editions, which are cited here. Unfortunately, it has also not been possible to interact with the secondary literature published since 1984 when the thesis was completed. The substantiation of the argument presented here in view of this literature will be carried out in my forthcoming study on II Cor. 3:4-18.

Translations of ancient works follow the published translations listed in the second section of the bibliography, except where otherwise noted.

Chapter One

"Led unto Death": The Meaning and Function of Paul's Thanksgiving in II Corinthians 2:14a

Paul's "second"[1] letter to the Corinthians is, without a doubt, one of the strongest witnesses to the fact that "everything that Paul says, writes, and teaches is not developed in the neutral realm of a general consideration, but is a part of his work and desire, his dramatic life-struggle itself."[2] Indeed, even if II Corinthians were not "without doubt the most personal of the extant letters of Paul,"[3] the subject matter of the letter itself would force us to anchor Paul's theology as seen within this letter within the context of his apostolic ministry. Even a cursory reading of II Corinthians makes it clear that the nature of Paul's apostolic ministry provides both the input and the occasion for the epistle. Recognition of this fact is especially pertinent for any investigation of Paul's theological maxim that "the letter kills, but the Spirit makes alive," which, at first glance, seems so abstract and proverbial. For once we attempt to interpret II Cor. 3:6 within its *own* context, we are confronted with the surprising[4] fact that it is embedded

1. Regardless of the myriad of opinions concerning the literary unity of II Corinthians itself (see n. 7 below) and its relationship to I Corinthians, all are agreed on the basis of I Cor. 5:9 that the canonical II Corinthians is at least the third letter that Paul sent to the church in Corinth.

2. Von Campenhausen, *Kirchliches Amt,* 32.

3. Dinkler, "Korintherbriefe," 21.

4. It is surprising only because Paul's statement in 3:6 has usually been lifted from the context of Paul's apostolic ministry in order to relate it directly to Paul's

in "the most intricate and profound exposition of St. Paul's apostolic ministry to be found anywhere in his letters."[5] Our task, therefore, is to understand the meaning and function of the letter/Spirit contrast in II Cor. 3:6 within the context in which it is found.

A. DELIMITING THE PRIMARY CONTEXT

It has long been recognized, even by those who argue most strongly for the literary integrity of II Corinthians, that the unmistakable transitions at 2:14 and 7:5 and the internally coherent thought structure of the passage itself serve as clear indications that 2:14–7:4 comprises a self-enclosed literary unit. As such, this is the larger literary context within which 3:6 is to be understood. But within 2:14–7:4 the close parallels in thought between 2:14–3:18 and 4:1-6, combined with the introduction of the extended discussion of Paul's suffering in 4:7ff., provide a further demarcation. It thus becomes necessary to focus our attention in interpreting 3:6 on 2:14–4:6 as the *primary context* for our study. For as T. Provence has recently indicated,

> Paul answers the question of 2:16b throughout chapter 3. . . . But even more importantly, 4:1-6 summarizes Paul's answer by picking up the themes of 2:16-17 *and* chapter three. . . . Thus the section introduced by the question in 2:16b is not completed until its conclusion in 4:1-6. Indeed, the close connection between chapter three and 4:1-6 prompted Plummer to comment that "the division of the chapters is unintelligently made" because in the first part of chapter four "the Apostle is still urging the claims of his office."[6]

The limitation of the primary context of our study to II Cor. 2:14–4:6 is also necessary, however, in the light of the complex literary

---

view of the law. This is a result of the fact that 3:6 is most often related only to what immediately follows in 3:7-18 without paying close attention either to what precedes (2:14–3:6a) or to the continuation of Paul's argument in 4:1ff.

5. Bates, "Integrity," 59, on II Cor. 3–6.

6. Provence, " Who is Sufficient? " 57, quoting Plummer, *Second Corinthians,* 109.

problems surrounding II Corinthians as a whole. The apparently abrupt transitions at 2:14 and 7:5 constitute only one of four interrelated literary problems encountered in the canonical text of II Corinthians. Hence, the place of 2:14–7:4 within the larger development of Paul's thought in the epistle as we have it is also dependent upon (1) whether or not 6:14–7:1 is an interpolation, and if it is, whether its origin is Pauline; (2) whether or not 2:14–7:4 is of a piece with 1:1–2:13 and 7:5-16; (3) the internal relationship between chapters 8 and 9 and their respective places within the overall context of the epistle; and (4) the relationship between chapters 1–9 and the literary unity of chapters 10–13.[7] Thus, because of the uncertainty concerning the unit of II Corinthians, the safest path to take methodologically is to begin with an investigation of the smallest meaningful context possible. In our case this is 2:14–4:6. For as C. K. Barrett has emphasized, "all attempts to analyse 2 Corinthians and to trace out the record of Paul's dealings with the Church stand or fall by the exegesis of the relevant parts of the epistle."[8] This does not mean that the larger questions of literary and historical reconstruction can be ignored. The question is simply one of methodology. For if any progress is to be made on the complex literary and historical problems raised by II Corinthians, Barrett is again correct in pointing out that

> we are unlikely to make much advance towards their solution by surveying them as a whole and trying to think out a comprehensive hypothesis capable of explaining everything at once. If advance is to be made at all it will be made by the pursuit, and eventual integration, of a number of details.[9]

The limitation of our study to II Cor. 2:14–4:6 as the primary context for an investigation of the letter/Spirit contrast is therefore not only justified contextually, but is also the surest and most fruitful starting point methodologically.

---

7. For a discussion of the problems as well as the relevant literature cf. Kümmel, *Introduction*, 287-293; Barrett, *Second Corinthians*, 12-20; Georgi, "Corinthians, Second," 183-186, each representing one of the three main approaches to the literary problems of II Corinthians.

8. Barrett, *Second Corinthians*, 18.

9. Barrett, "Titus," 1.

B. THE FUNCTION OF PAUL'S THANKSGIVING IN II COR. 2:14-16a

Paul begins his discussion of the nature and function of the apostolic ministry in 2:14–4:6 with a characteristic *thanksgiving formula* in praise of God. The classification of the phrase "but thanks be to God" *(tō de theō charis)* plus substantival participle(s) as a stylized praise-thanksgiving formula, found not only here, but also in I Cor. 15:57 and II Cor. 8:16,[10] is based on Obrien's extensive examination of thanksgiving and blessing *(berakah)* formulas.[11] For although the formula in II Cor. 2:14-16a falls beyond the scope of Obrien's work, a comparison of its form with the thanksgiving and blessing formulas found elsewhere in Paul's writings makes it clear that the phrase "thanks be to God" also belongs to the literary genre of the "praise-thanksgiving."[12]

The significance of this observation is twofold. First, Obrien's study has demonstrated that the "thanksgiving periods" perform a very definite threefold function in Paul's letters. As he summarizes it,

> Paul's introductory thanksgivings have a varied function: *epistolary,* *didactic* and *paraenetic,* and they provide evidence of his pastoral and/or apostolic concern for the addressees. In some cases one may predominate while others recede into the background. But whatever the particular thrust of any passage, it is clear that Paul's introductory thanksgivings were not meaningless devices. Instead, they were integral parts of their letters, *setting the tone and themes of what was to follow.*[13]

Hence, rather than understanding II Cor. 2:14 as an unexpected explosion of gratitude which found its expression in a Christian hymn of praise (a typical understanding),[14] Obrien's study forces us to regard it as a carefully crafted, thesis-like statement that not only encapsulates

---

10. This formula also occurs in modified forms in Rom. 7:25; II Cor. 9:15; I Tim. 1:12ff.; and II Tim. 1:3ff.

11. Obrien, *Introductory Thanksgivings,* 233-240.

12. Cf. Obrien, *Introductory Thanksgivings,* 100f., for his conclusion concerning the "thanksgiving-period."

13. Obrien, *Introductory Thanksgivings,* 263.

14. Plummer, *Second Corinthians,* 67.

the main theme(s) of its section (i.e. 2:14–4:6 [–7:4]), but also contains an implicit paraenetic appeal to his readers.

Second, Obrien observed that although the blessing-formula, which he characterized as a "short Christianized form of the Jewish praise-thanksgiving or eulogy," is quite distinct from Paul's more common thanksgiving-formula in both terminology and structure, nevertheless the two forms are essentially synonymous in their basic meaning. In his words,

> What we are concerned to point out is that the use of *to give thanks* (*eucharisteō*) does *not necessarily exclude* the idea of praise . . . while the appearance of the blessing formula does not rule out any thought of personal gratitude.[15]

In the light of this overlap in meaning between praise and personal gratitude within the two basic types of thanksgivings found in Paul's writings, it is therefore somewhat surprising to discover that for Paul the two forms were *not* simply interchangeable. For as Obrien goes on to emphasize,

> Of far greater significance is the fact—unnoticed by almost all scholars—that although either the thanksgiving- or blessing-formulas (*eucharisteō-* or *eulogētos-*) could have been used of thanksgiving or praise to God for his blessings *either* to others *or* for oneself, Paul in the introductions of his letters, uses the thanksgiving-formula (*eucharisteō*) consistently of expressions of gratitude . . . for God's work in the lives of the addressees, and the blessing-formula (*eulogētos*) for blessings in which *he himself* participated.[16]

Similarly, when we examine the three occurrences of the formula "thanks to be God" in I Cor. 15:57; II Cor. 2:14; and 8:16 we are struck with the fact that here too it is this latter emphasis that Paul clearly has in mind. In all three instances Paul's doxology is for something he

---

15. Obrien, *Introductory Thanksgivings,* 239.

16. Obrien, *Introductory Thanksgivings,* 239 (final emphasis added). Obrien's distinction holds true in general, though it is difficult to see how Paul's praise to the Creator in Rom. 1:25 or his eulogy of God as his witness in II Cor. 11:31 could be described as relating to blessings in which Paul has participated. For clearer examples, cf. II Cor. 1:3ff.; Eph. 1:3ff.; Rom. 9:5.

himself has experienced, namely, victory over sin (in I Cor. 15:57), his experience in Troas (in II Cor. 2:14), and his relief in knowing Titus has been accepted by the Corinthians (in II Cor. 8:16), although in I Cor. 15:57 Paul's focus is on an experience he shares with all Christians (see I Cor. 15:58). As the key to Paul's concern, the thanksgiving-formula of II Cor. 2:14-16a thus alerts us to the fact that from the beginning the focus of our attention in 2:14–4:6 is to be directed toward Paul himself.

C. THE NATURE AND PURPOSE OF THE APOSTOLIC MINISTRY IN 2:14-16a

1. The Apostle Paul as the Subject and Object of 2:14-16a

The conclusion that the thanksgiving-formula found in II Cor. 2:14ff. functions not only to signal the tone and theme of the section but also to call our attention specifically to Paul himself can only be maintained, however, if the *plural* objects and subject of the thanksgiving ("us," "through us" in 2:14, "we" in 2:15) can be construed to be "literary" or "epistolary" conventions which actually refer to Paul alone and not to some larger circle of co-workers (e.g., Paul and Timothy, 1:1; Silvanus, 1:19; and/or Titus, 2:13; etc).

The vast majority of commentators in the past have in fact assumed that the first person plurals of 2:14-16a are literary devices meant to refer to Paul himself and therefore, usually without further comment, have construed the entire passage of 2:14–4:6 to be part of Paul's self-defense. Yet there has been some significant opposition to this assumption, the most extreme of which is Lightfoot's judgment that "there is no reason to think that St. Paul ever uses an 'epistolary' plural referring to himself solely."[17] Moreover, Lightfoot's judgment seems to be borne out in our context by the contrast between the consistent use of the plurals in 2:14ff. and the emphasis on the first person singular in 1:15–2:3, on the one hand, and, on the other hand, by the parallel statement to 2:14 in 1:19 in which

17. Lightfoot, *Colossians and Philemon*, 229.

"through us" is explicitly defined to include Silvanus and Timothy as well as Paul.

Nevertheless, the decision of the majority to make Paul himself the subject and object of 2:14-16a (and indeed, of 2:14–4:6 as a whole, except for 3:18) is in keeping with Paul's use of language elsewhere. For even if we assume for the moment that 2:14ff. is of a piece with 1:15–2:13, the sudden switch from the first person singular to the plural in 2:14 does not necessarily indicate a change of subject, since there are clear examples elsewhere in II Corinthians of Paul's ability to switch from the singular to the plural in referring to his *own* ministry (see II Cor. 10:11–11:6).

For example, in I Cor. 4:15 Paul had reminded the church at Corinth that although they had "a myriad of guides" he alone had become their father through the gospel. Later, in II Cor. 11, Paul again reaffirms the fact that he was their "spiritual father" by evoking the image of the betrothal tradition to describe his own relationship to the Corinthian Church. Like the father of the would-be bride, who pledged his daughter to her future husband as a guarantee of her fidelity and purity, Paul had betrothed the Corinthians to Christ. Hence, it was only fitting and natural that he feel a "divine jealousy" over their readiness to submit to "a different gospel" (cf. 11:1-6). Thus, when Paul defends the fact that he had not boasted beyond limit in the assertion of his authority over the Corinthians on the basis of this same spiritual fatherhood in II Cor. 10:14, it can hardly be doubted that what Paul has in view is his *own* ministry, *even though he speaks in the plural.* Similarly, although Paul quotes one of the charges that has been registered against him *personally* in II Cor. 10:9f., he nevertheless responds to the charge *in the plural* (10:11; cf. 10:1, 3ff.). Finally, that Paul can describe the very same set of circumstances in either the first person singular or the first person plural indicates that the distinction between "I" and "we" cannot be strictly maintained in Paul's letters. For in II Cor. 2:12f. Paul describes his anxiety over Titus, which eventually forced him to leave Troas in hopes of meeting Titus in Macedonia, in the first person singular, only to continue this report in the first person plural in II Cor. 7:5ff. Apparently then, even in the most personal contexts, Paul is able to move from the real singular to the literary plural with ease. As C. E. B. Cranfield concluded most recently, "that Paul did sometimes use the first person plural with reference simply to himself we regard as almost certain."[18] Hence, it is by all means possible that the plurals in 2:14–4:6 can be construed to refer to Paul himself.

18. Cranfield, "Changes of Person and Number," 286.

Having come this far, our results are still, however, largely negative. In other words, we have seen that there is no compelling reason to think that Paul could *not* have used the literary plural in II Cor. 2:14ff. to refer to himself as he does elsewhere in his writings in general and in II Corinthians in particular. But are there any *positive* indications that Paul was, in fact, referring specifically to himself in 2:14ff. and not to some larger group of co-workers as in 1:19?

In II Cor. 1:19f. Paul refers to the message of Jesus Christ, which was preached to the Corinthians by Silvanus, Timothy, and Paul, using the plural: "having been preached by us." In 4:5 Paul then describes this message preached to the Corinthians, again using the plural,

> for we are not preaching ourselves but Jesus Christ as Lord and ourselves as your slaves for Jesus' sake.

But the ground or reason that Paul offers in 4:6 to support his statement that "they" do not preach themselves as lord, but, in contrast, are to be considered "slaves for Jesus' sake" is a clear allusion to Paul's own conversion-call experience on the road to Damascus. Thus, although II Cor. 1:19 might lead one to broaden the plural references throughout 2:14–4:6 to include Paul's co-workers, 4:6 makes it clear that it is Paul's *own* ministry, based on his conversion-call on the road to Damascus, that he has in mind in 4:1-6.

Second, that Paul is also referring to himself in 2:14–3:18 is made evident by his statement in 3:2f., where he supports his assertion that in "their" case letters of recommendation are not necessary by pointing to the Corinthians themselves as "their" letter of recommendation. The fact that this is a reference to the founding of the Corinthian church is clear.[19] Paul's argument is simply that the very existence of the church in Corinth serves as the recommendation of "their" ministry. But in the light of I Cor. 1:17; 2:1-5; 3:6, 10; 4:14-16; 9:1-2; 15:1-3 and II Cor. 7:14; 10:13f.; 11:2-4 it is also evident that Paul considered himself *alone* to be the founder of the Corinthian community. Hence, Paul's argument in II Cor. 3:2f. holds true only if the lack of need for a letter of recommendation relates specifically to Paul and not to Paul and his co-workers, since Paul alone was the "father" of the church. This

19. See chapter 5 below for an exegesis of this passage.

becomes even more evident when we consider that Paul himself had to write a letter of recommendation for those he was sending to Corinth to settle the affairs concerning the collection for Jerusalem (cf. II Cor. 8:18-24 and 9:3). Therefore, although written in the plural, the point of the argument in II Cor. 3:2f. is that Paul, *unlike* other Christian emissaries (even his own co-workers!), does not need the customary letter of recommendation from other congregations, since he alone is responsible for the very existence of the Corinthian church. Consequently, the trustworthiness and quality of his ministry should be beyond question to the Corinthians. This means, however, that not only the plurals of 4:1-6, but those of 3:1-6 and 12 must refer to Paul himself.

Finally, the close parallels already mentioned among 2:14-17; 3:1-6; and 4:1-6 make it unlikely that in 2:14ff. Paul is referring to a wider circle of co-workers, rather than to himself alone. For nowhere throughout 2:14–4:6 is there any indication of a switch in subject, except in 3:18, when Paul momentarily includes the Corinthians in the general Christian experience of being conformed to the image of God.

But if Paul himself is the subject and object of 2:14–4:6, the question that naturally arises is why Paul chose to employ the literary plural in the first place. The answer to this question lies in Paul's conception of himself as "an apostle of Christ Jesus by the will of God" (II Cor. 1:1). For as Wendland has already emphasized, "us" in II Cor. 2:14 refers not merely to Paul as such, but to Paul *as an apostle,*[20] so that the emphasis in 2:14ff. is on the nature of the apostolic ministry. This emphasis is then made explicit in Paul's use of the "to minister / be a minister" motif in 3:3 and 6. Consequently, 2:14ff. becomes "a primary source for Paul's self-understanding as an apostle."[21] In other words, the use of the literary plural is best attributed to the fact that Paul was conscious that he represented the apostolic "office." Paul realized that his ministry carried a significance far beyond his own personal position. In fact, the man Paul becomes inseparable from his office, and indeed, is even swallowed up by it.[22] As a result, the issue

20. Wendland, *An die Korinther,* 175.
21. Ibid.
22. For Paul's representation of himself to the Corinthians as an apostle, see I Cor. 1:1, 17; 2:2ff.; 3:5-10; 4:1, 9; 9:1f.; 9:15-18; 15:8-11; II Cor. 1:1; 2:14-17; 3:4-6; 4:1–5:21; 6:3-10; 10–13.

at stake for Paul in Corinth was much greater than merely the Corinthians' disenchantment with him and his ministry. In Paul's mind, if the Corinthians were to reject Paul they would not only be turning their backs on their own "spiritual father," but would, at the same time, be rejecting the very gospel itself! For as we shall come to see, Paul views himself in his apostolic calling not only as one who *preaches* the message of good news to the world, but equally important, as one ordained by God to be an *embodiment* of that gospel, called to reveal the knowledge of God by and through his very life. It is this identification of the message with its messenger, first seen in Christ and then carried on in his apostles, that Paul develops in 2:14-16a.

2. The Roman Institution of the Triumphal Procession as the Crux Interpretum *to II Corinthians 2:14a*

a. The Problem Presented by the Image of the Triumphal Procession

The reason for Paul's praise in 2:14a is expressed in the two substantival participles "leading in triumph" *(thriambeuonti)* and "making known" *(phanerounti)* of 2:14a and b. That is, Paul praises God *because* of what God is presently doing in and through the life of the apostle. But when we turn to investigate more closely the nature of this divine activity, we are confronted with what has appeared to commentators to be an insurmountable problem. For the usual meaning of "to lead in triumph," which occurs elsewhere in the NT only in Colossians 2:15 and not at all in the LXX, seems to be impossible *theologically* in the present context. For as John Calvin pointed out over four centuries ago, if the verb is taken literally to refer to the Roman institution of the triumphal procession, one is faced with the uncomfortable realization that in the Roman triumph, "prisoners are said to be led in triumph when to disgrace them they are bound in chains and dragged before the chariot of the conqueror."[23] Inasmuch as Paul could hardly be praising God for being led as a prisoner in disgrace, Calvin felt compelled to conclude, for theo-

---

23. Calvin, *Second Corinthians, Timothy, Titus and Philemon*, 33.

logical reasons, that "Paul means something different from the common meaning of this phrase. . . ."[24] Calvin's solution to this problem was to ascribe to this verb a *factitive* sense. Instead of meaning "to lead in triumph," Calvin thus interpreted the verb *thriambeuein* to mean "to cause to triumph." In this way, Paul could be understood to be praising God in II Cor. 2:14 because he shared, in one way or another, in God's victory.

By the end of the nineteenth century this attempt to understand the verb "to lead in triumph" in a factitive sense was recognized and "pronounced on high authority" to be " 'philologically impossible.' "[25] For those verbs which do carry a secondary factitive sense are almost always *intransitive,* while the verb in 2:14 is clearly *transitive.* Furthermore, no evidence for such a factitive meaning could be found anywhere else in Greek literature. In 1879 George Findlay could therefore observe that II Cor. 2:14a was consistently being translated "triumph over us" "by nearly all the more recent critics."[26] As Meyer put it in 1870, this verb means "to conduct, present anyone in triumph," since "the accusative is never the triumphing subject, but always the object of the triumph."[27]

However, rather than solving the problem, the recognition that Paul must be seen to be the object of the triumph in 2:14 only made matters worse theologically. Since this verb invoked the image of a triumphal procession in which the vanquished foes were led through the streets of the city as a public display, the idea that Paul could portray himself as such a prisoner, and then praise God for being the one who leads the procession, seemed quite out of place, to say the least. This image simply did not conform to the popular understanding of Paul's view of his apostolic ministry as one of "triumph in Christ." As Findlay himself put it so well over 100 years ago, the metaphor appears to be

> intolerably harsh and incongruous. For it would make the Apostle *the victim of defeat.* And when the nature of a Roman triumph is considered—then it must be remembered, existing in its grim reality—with

24. Ibid.
25. Findlay, "ΘΡΙΑΜΒΕΥΩ," 404.
26. Ibid.
27. Meyer, *Epistles to the Corinthians,* 451.

the ignominious position of the captive, and the miserable death in which the exhibition usually ended for him, the figure appears most unsuitable to express the relation between the Apostle and the gracious God to whom he renders thanks. Not *so*, surely, did God 'always triumph over' his faithful servant; nor could such a triumph 'manifest the savour of his knowledge in every place!'[28]

Faced with such a problem, and with recourse to the factitive sense no longer possible, almost all commentators since Findlay have simply chosen either to ignore the significance of the meaning of the word altogether "by vague generalizations which rob the metaphor of all precision and vividness,"[29] or to modify the meaning itself in order to bring it in line with their theological convictions. But against all such attempts it must be observed that the need felt to ignore or modify the image of Paul as conquered, so that Paul becomes the conqueror (either alone or with Christ; either his own victory or sharing in the victory of God/Christ), finds its basis, not in the immediate context, but in *a priori* judgments concerning Paul's view of the nature of the apostolic ministry. For example, James I. H. McDonald responds to the translation "who always triumphs over us . . ." by pointing out that "Lexically, this is normal usage," only to go on to assert that "Contextually, it is hardly admissible." But what is significant for our point here is the fact that McDonald concludes his critique of this view by going beyond the context to a theological judgment of its appropriateness: ". . . it remains doubtful whether Paul would have grounded what appears to be an important and characteristic aspect of God's activity in the triumph of a pagan general. . . ."[30]

As a result of such *a priori* judgments, no less than ten different possibilities have already been suggested for the meaning of the verb usually translated "to lead in triumph" or "in a triumphal procession" in II Cor. 2:14:

1) to cause to triumph; 2) to present or lead a conquered and captive one in triumph; 3) to lead a captive criminal through the streets; 4) to lead someone about publicly (with no negative connotations implied);

28. Findlay, "ΘΡΙΑΜΒΕΥΩ," 404-405.
29. Ibid., 405.
30. McDonald, "Paul and the Preaching Ministry," 36f.

5) to disgrace or shame someone; 6) to parade or make a show or spectacle of someone or something; 7) to triumph over someone in the sense of having a victory over that person; 8) to lead one in triumph as partners or co-victors in the triumph; 9) to lead one in a festal of choral procession as the dithyrambic procession and dance associated with the cultic processions of Dionysos; and 10) to lead one in triumph as a metaphor of social shame and humiliation.[31]

In view of this ever-growing number of interpretations being suggested in order to bring the meaning of II Cor. 2:14 into harmony with Paul's apostolic conception, the question raised by Paul's use of "to lead in a triumphal procession" may be formulated as follows: Can Paul's use of this word be understood in such a way that it provides a suitable backdrop against which verse 14 can be interpreted, while at the same time making sense within the larger context of Paul's apostolic self-conception as presented in the Corinthian correspondence as a whole (rather than starting with some general and abstract notion of how Paul viewed himself)? Or must we agree that the only way to make sense out of Paul's thought is to modify the image of the triumphal procession itself, under the assumption that Paul used it in his own idiosyncratic manner?

In order to answer this question, we must begin by reexamining the role of the conquered in the triumphal procession. For in spite of the fact that this important Roman institution has long been recognized to be the backdrop to II Cor. 2:14 and Col. 2:15, the precise significance of the fact that Paul portrays himself as led in this procession has not been clearly applied to our text.

b. The Role of the Conquered in the Triumphal Procession and its Implications for Understanding II Cor. 2:14-16a

The institution of the Roman triumphal procession as practiced in Paul's day was the result of a long and complex development, extending back into the pre-Roman period of the Etruscan dynasties, which

---

31. Taken from the summaries of Windisch, *Zweiter Korintherbrief,* 96f., who lists six possible interpretations, and McDonald, "Paul and the Preaching Ministry," 35-39, who also lists six, three overlapping with those given by Windisch, with the tenth being that suggested by Marshall, "Metaphor."

ended late in the 6th century BCE. In fact, according to Orosius, 320 triumphs were celebrated between the founding of Rome and the reign of Vespasian.[32] Fortunately, the contours of the triumphal procession have been thoroughly investigated by scholars, so that the structure and content of the procession itself are well known. In addition, H. S. Versnel's *Triumphus: An Inquiry into the Origin, Development and Meaning of the Roman Triumph* provides a massive (409 pages!) and methodologically sound study of the more controversial issues surrounding the origin and early development of the Roman triumph.

Versnel's theory is that the Roman triumph we encounter in our literary sources was not originally a Roman institution, nor a direct adaptation of the Hellenistic processions carried out in honor of Dionysos, but instead owes its origin to the triumphal procession practiced in Etruria in the pre-Roman period; which in turn was an adaptation of an originally sacral ceremony performed as part of a New Year's Festival in which the king represented the deity in his yearly arrival and/or renewal.[33] This explains why in the Roman triumphal procession the triumphator was portrayed as a personification and epiphany of the god Jupiter, as well as a representative of the ancient *rex*, even though the idea of a human being representing, let alone embodying, the presence of a deity was offensive to the Roman religious consciousness during the period of the republic.[34] In Versnel's words

> by wearing the *ornatus Iovis*, the *corona Etrusca*, the red lead, the triumphator is characterized as the representative of Iuppiter. The exclamation *triumpe* proves that he was looked upon as the god manifesting himself. This idea, however, was no longer alive during the time of the Roman republic. It had its origin in Etruscan kingship and can be explained only against the background of Etruscan religion.[35]

Thus,

> . . . there is no doubt that the Etruscan triumph, once it had been introduced into Rome and was kept up by the republic, underwent a fundamental change of meaning. . . . [T]he scene of a man acting the part of a god, a deification, is incompatible with the truly Roman religion as we know it from the republican period.[36]

32. *Hist.*, 7.9.8.
33. Cf. Versnel, *Triumphus*, 7, 34ff., 38, 47, 55, 72, 89-91, 164, 196f., 293, 396.
34. Cf. ibid., 48, 83, 90f., 164, 305.
35. Ibid., 92.
36. Ibid., 305.

As a result, the customs remained, though their meaning was reinterpreted in the Roman period. The triumphator's former role as an epiphany of the deity is now replaced by his identity as the bearer of good fortune, i.e., the magical power of *felicitas*, who returns to bring welfare and blessing to the city. Nevertheless, although the triumphator himself is no longer identified with Jupiter in the Roman triumph, the religious significance of the procession was never lost. As Livy tells us, the triumph was intended to honor the gods as well as the valour of the victor.[37] It was a special act of worship to Jupiter and the highest honor a Roman citizen could receive. As Versnel summarizes it in the beginning of his study,

> The entire history of Rome has thus been marked by a ceremony which testified to the power of Rome, its mission of conquest and domination, and to the courage of its soldiers. Primarily, however, the triumph characterized the greatness of Rome as being due, on the one hand, to the excellence of the victorious general, and, on the other, to the favor of the supreme god, who, *optimus maximus*, ensured the continuance and the prosperity of the Roman empire. *In no other Roman ceremony do god and man approach each other as closely as they do in the triumph.* Not only is the triumphal procession directed towards the Capitolium, where the triumphator presents a solemn offering to Iuppiter O.M., but the triumphator himself has a status which appears to raise him to the rank of the gods. Amidst the cheers of *io triumphe* he enters the city via the Porta Triumphalis, standing on a triumphal chariot, which is drawn by four horses. He is clothed in a purple *toga* and a *tunic* stitched with palm-motifs, together called *ornatus Iovis*, and in his hand he carries a scepter crowned by an eagle. His face has been red-leaded. It seems as if Iuppiter himself, incarnated in the triumphator, makes his solemn entry into Rome.[38]

Our purpose is not to provide another examination of the meaning or significance of the triumphal procession as such, but merely to present the role of the captives who were led in these processions. Our aim in doing so is to highlight what it meant, in Paul's day, to be led in a triumphal procession, since, as we shall see, Paul pictured himself in II Cor. 2:14a as occupying this role. Since this aspect of the triumphal procession has been largely neglected in studies dealing with II Cor. 2:14a, it will be necessary to provide a number of representative descriptions of the fate of those led in the triumph in order to make clear what has already been recognized outside the

37. 45.39.10.
38. Versnel, *Triumphus*, 1 (emphasis added).

realm of biblical studies, namely, that the captives "led in triumph" were, in reality, being led to their death.[39] Finally, since the focus of our attention is on Paul's use of this imagery, our discussion will be limited to the relevant Greek sources from the first century BCE through the first century CE.

The first significant glimpse from this period into the nature and purpose of the Roman triumph is found in *The Roman Antiquities* of Dionysius of Halicarnassus, whose literary activity stretched from 30 / 29 BCE to 2 BCE. According to Dionysius, the Roman custom of the triumphal procession began as a spontaneous response by the people to the return of Romulus after his victory over the Caeninenses and Antemnates (II.33.2–34.2).[40] But Dionysius is quick to point out that since its early beginnings the nature of the triumph had significantly changed, if not, in his opinion, always for the better.

> Such was the victorious procession, marked by the carrying of the trophies and concluding with a sacrifice, which the Romans call a triumph, as it was first instituted by Romulus. But in our day the triumph has become a very costly and ostentatious pageant, being attended with a theatrical pomp that is designed rather as a display of wealth than as the approbation of valour, and it has departed in every respect from its ancient simplicity. (II.3)

In fact, the institution of the Roman triumphal procession had become so well-established that within the more general category of the "triumph," there had developed a clear distinction between a "greater" and a "lesser" triumph, each with its own distinct set of rituals (see V.47.2-3). Hence, in conjunction with the victories of Siccius and Aquilius over the Volscians, Dionysius records that

---

39. See ibid., 95.

40. This is, of course, legend. Versnel, *Triumphus,* 89, points out that the archaeological data we now have confirms the view presented by Livy 1.38.3 that the triumphal procession actually began in Etruria in connection with the reign of Tarquinius Priscus. For such a triumph presupposes the use of the Jupiter statue in the procession, but there is no evidence of such statues in Rome prior to the Tarquinii dynasties. "There is, therefore, every indication that the triumph is an Etruscan ceremony, which was introduced into Rome by the dynasty of the Etruscan kings" (p. 91).

When the couriers sent by the consuls arrived in Rome, the people were filled with the greatest joy, and they immediately voted sacrifices of thanksgiving for the gods and decreed the honour of a triumph to the consuls, though not the same to both. For as Siccius was thought to have freed the state from the greater fear by destroying the insolent army of the Volscians and killing their general, they granted him the greater triumph. He accordingly drove into the city with the spoils, the prisoners, and the army that had fought under him, he himself riding in a chariot drawn by horses with golden bridles and being arrayed in the royal robes, as is the custom in the greater triumphs. To Aquilius they decreed the lesser triumph, which they call an ovation (I have earlier shown the difference between this and the greater triumph); and he entered the city on foot, bringing up the remainder of the procession. (VIII.67.9-10; cf. also IX.36.3, 71.4)

The striking aspect of this account is that unlike the reports referred to above, in which only the spoils and the victorious armies were mentioned as being led through the city in the triumphal procession, we now learn that there was also an important third component in the march, namely, the prisoners of war. Although in Dionysius's earlier accounts he had specifically mentioned the taking of prisoners as part of the final stages of victory itself (II.33.2–34.1) and had told us that these prisoners were "carried off" (V.47.1), or in one case even "carried down the river to Rome" (II.55.4), he had, until now, remained silent regarding their fate. It is nevertheless clear that they too played an important role in the triumphal procession, though the exact nature of their role only becomes clear when we examine the next significant source of information concerning the nature of the triumphal procession, that of Plutarch's *Lives*.

Like Dionysius, Plutarch also knows the tradition that the Roman triumph had its origin in Romulus himself (cf. *Romulus,* XVI.5-7). But unlike Dionysius, Plutarch reports that even in the time of Romulus the prisoners of war played a decisive part in the pageant, now in the form of "captives." For in commenting on Romulus's last triumphal procession, in response to his victory over the Tuscans, Plutarach singles out the fact that

Romulus also celebrated a triumph for this victory on the Ides of October, having in his train, besides many other captives, the leader of the Veientes, an elderly man, who seems to have conducted the campaign unwisely, and without the experience to be expected of his years. Wherefore to this very day, in offering a sacrifice for victory, they lead an old man through the forum to the Capitol, wearing a boy's toga with a bulla attached to it, while the herald cries: "Sardians for sale!" For the Tuscans are said to be colonists from Sardis, and Veii is a Tuscan city. (*Romulus*, XXV.4)

Here we encounter the use of the verb "to lead in a triumphal procession" *(thriambeuein)* for the first time in our sources. Its reference is clearly to the performing of the triumphal procession. It thus functions as the verbal equivalent of the noun "triumphal procession" *(thriambos)*.

We are afforded an even better look into the nature and purpose of the triumph by Plutarch's long description of Pompey's third triumphal procession, which took place in 61 BCE after his campaign in Asia. In fact, Plutarch even lists some of the more illustrious prisoners "led in triumph" in that celebration, including "Aristobulus, King of the Jews" (see *Pompey*, XLV.1-5). But it is only in Plutarch's extensive report concerning the lavish triumph celebrated by Aemilius Paulus in 167 BCE as a result of his victory over Perseus that we learn what the role of the captives being led in the procession actually was. For after a very long and detailed description of the first two days of the three-day triumphal procession (see *Aemilius Paulus*, XXXII.1-5), and following his mention of the 120 oxen led to sacrifice and the 77 vessels of gold carried through the streets (XXXIII.1-2), Plutarch continues his report by telling us that

then, at a little interval, came the children of the king, led along as slaves and with them a throng of fosterparents, teachers, and tutors, all in tears, stretching out their own hands to the spectators and teaching the children to beg and supplicate. There were two boys, and one girl, and they were not very conscious of the magnitude of their evils because of their tender age; wherefore they evoked even more pity in view of the time when *their unconsciousness would cease*, so that Perseus walked along almost unheeded, while the Romans, moved by compassion, kept their eyes upon the children, and many of them shed tears, and for all of them the pleasure of the spectacle was mingled with pain, until the children had passed by. Behind the children and their train of attendants walked Perseus himself, clad in a dark robe and wearing the high boots of his country, but the magnitude of his evils made him resemble one who is utterly dumbfounded and bewildered. He, too, was followed by a company of friends and intimates, whose faces were heavy with grief, and whose tearful gaze continually fixed upon Perseus gave the spectators to understand that it was his misfortune which they bewailed, and their own *fate* least of all concerned them. And yet Perseus had sent to Aemilius begging not to be led in the procession and asking to be left out of the triumph. But Aemilius, in mockery, as it would seem, of the king's cowardice and *love of live,* had said: "But this at least was in his power before, and is so now, if he should wish it," signifying death in preference to disgrace; for this, however, the coward had not the heart, but was made weak by no one knows what hopes, and became a part of his own spoils. (*Aemilius Paulus* XXXIII.3– XXXIV.2, emphasis added)

Thus, the "grim reality" of the triumphal procession was even more harsh than is usually recognized by biblical scholars.[41] For as Plutarch's account makes clear, the king, his family, and their friends and personal attendants were led through the streets as representatives of the vanquished in prelude to their execution. Even the children were led as "slaves," unaware of the fate which awaited them at the end of the parade, while the king himself, as a result of his "cowardice," begged "to be left out of the triumph." It seems, however, that Perseus did, in fact, receive mercy at the hand of Aemilius. For in commenting on the fact that the deity Fortune had, as always, balanced his successes with the counterweight of a painful loss, i.e., the fact that he had lost one of his sons just prior to the celebration of his triumph and the other one just after it, Aemilius is said to conclude

that deity has sufficiently used me and my affliction to satisfy the divine displeasure at our successes and she makes the hero of the triumph as clear an example of human weakness as the victim of the triumph; except that Perseus, even though conquered, has his children, while Aemilius, though conqueror, has lost his. (XXXVI.6)

41. The idea of being "led to death" as an essential aspect of the triumphal procession has found no acknowledgement in any of the ten views that have been previously propounded for II Cor. 2:14ff.

The fact that the prisoners of the triumphal procession were being led to their death thus explains the cryptic saying in Plutarch's eulogy of Pompey that

> when it was in his power to lead Tigranes the king of Armenia in his triumphal procession, (he) made him an ally instead, saying that he thought more of the future time than of a single day; (*Agesilaus and Pompey,* III.2)

and the dilemma faced by Volumnia as she contemplated the fact that her own son Marcius was about to march against Rome, his native city, and her ensuing decision to commit suicide if he persisted in his plan, since in her dramatic words,

> it does not behoove me to await that day on which I shall behold my son either led in triumph by his fellow citizens or triumphing over his country. (*Coriolanus,* XXXV.3)

The significance of the Roman triumph is also graphically portrayed in Cleopatra's speech over the tomb of Antony, after hearing that Caesar was about to send her off to Rome to be displayed in his triumphal procession:

> After Cleopatra had heard this, in the first place, she begged Caesar that she might be permitted to pour libations for Antony; and when the request was granted, she had herself carried to the tomb, and embracing the urn which held his ashes, in company with the women usually about her, she said: "Dear Antony, I buried thee but lately with hands still free; now, however, I pour libations for thee as a captive, and so carefully guarded that I cannot either with blows or tears disfigure this body of mine, which is a slave's body, and closely watched that it may grace the triumph over thee. Do not expect other honours or libations; these are the last from Cleopatra the captive. For though in life nothing could part us from each other, in death we are likely to change places; thou, the Roman, lying buried here, while I, the hapless woman, lie in Italy, and get only so much of thy country as my portion. But if indeed there is any might or power in the gods of that country (for the gods of this country have betrayed us), do not abandon thine own wife while she lives, nor permit a triumph to be celebrated over thyself in my person but hide and bury me here with thyself, since out of all my innumerable ills not one is so great and

dreadful as this short time that I have lived apart from thee. (*Antony,* LXXXIV.2-4)

But the prospect of being put to death in the triumph and buried in Italy away from Antony was too much for Cleopatra to bear. She decided to commit suicide with an asp, her last request being that she be buried at Antony's side (cf. *Antony,* LXXXV.1-3). Thus deprived of his captive, Caesar nevertheless compensated. For as Plutarch reports, "in his triumph an image of Cleopatra herself with the asp clinging to her was carried in the procession" (*Antony,* LXXXVI.3).

The fact that the Roman triumph often meant death for the conquered prisoners who were led as slaves in the procession, or at least for a representative number of them (e.g., the defeated royalty and/or the mightiest of the captured warriors), and that their being led to death was an integral part of the institution as a whole is confirmed by Appian's (95-165 CE) parallel account of Pompey's third triumph in 61 BCE, which we saw earlier was also described in Plutarch's *Life of Pompey,* XLV.1-5. As part of Appian's account we read:

> [I]n the triumphal procession were two-horse carriages and litters laden with gold or other ornaments of various kinds, also the son of Hystaspes, the throne and scepter of Mithridates Eupator himself, and his image, eight cubits high, made of solid gold, and 75,100,000 drachmas of silver coin; also an infinite number of wagons carrying arms and beaks of ships, and a multitude of captives and pirates, none of them bound, but all arrayed in their native costumes.

(Then follows a long list of the various kings, satraps and generals, etc., who were also led in the procession).

> [But when Pompey] *arrived at the Capitol he did not put any of the prisoners to death, as had been the custom of other triumphs, but sent them all home at the public expense, except the kings. Of these Aristobulus alone was at once put to death and Tigranes somewhat later.* (The Mithridatic Wars, XII.116-117, emphasis added)[42]

The last important witness for our purposes to the nature and intent

---

42. For Appian's two other major descriptions of a triumphal procession, cf. *Roman History,* VIII, IX.66; II, XV.101-102.

of the Roman triumph is found in the writings of Josephus (37-100 CE). In the *Jewish War* VI.414-419, Josephus describes the fate of those who had held out against the Romans within Jerusalem, but had subsequently been taken prisoner when Titus entered the city in 70 CE. According to Josephus, Titus "issued orders to kill only those who were found in arms and offered resistance, and to make prisoners of the rest" (*J.W.*, VI.414). Josephus goes on to recount, however, that "the troops, in addition to those specified in their instructions, slew the old and the feeble; while those in the prime of life and serviceable they drove into the temple and shut them up in the court of women" (VI.415). The task was then given to Fronto, one of Caesar's friends, to determine what to do with the slightly more fortunate prisoners. As Josephus narrates it,

> Fronto put to death all the seditious and brigands, information being given by them against each other; *he selected the tallest and most handsome of the youth and reserved them for the triumph;* of the rest, those over seventeen years of age he sent in chains to the works in Egypt, while multitudes were presented by Titus to the various provinces to be destroyed in the theatres by the sword or by wild beasts; those under seventeen were sold. (*J.W.*, VI.417-419, emphasis added)

Our first indication of what it means to be "selected" and "reserved for the triumph" is not given, however, until some time later in Josephus's narrative, when, in describing the final search for those who were still hiding in the "mines" or secret passageways within the city after the fall of Jerusalem (VI.429ff.), Josephus reports that

> John, perishing of hunger with his brethren in the mines, implored from the Romans that protection which he has so often spurned, and Simon, after a long struggle with necessity . . . surrendered; the latter was *reserved for execution at the triumph,* while John was sentenced to perpetual imprisonment. (*J.W.*, VI.433-434, emphasis added)

Jewish War VII.119-157 is devoted to a description of Titus's actual return to Rome and the "triumphal ceremonies" which accompanied it. Unfortunately, Josephus's description of the triumphal procession itself, the most extensive and detailed that we have, is much too long to reproduce here (cf. *J.W.*, VII.123-157). Like those we have already cited, Josephus's account also focuses on the wealth of the spoils which were paraded through the city and the procession of the prisoners who had been selected for their strong statures and were now beautifully adorned for the march to their death (see *J.W.*, VII.138). Of interest to us is Josephus's narrative of the execution which took place at the culmination of the procession. As he describes it:

> the triumphal procession ended at the temple of Jupiter Capitolinus, on reaching which they halted; for it was a time-honored custom to wait there until the *execution* of the enemy's general was announced. This was Simon, son of Gioras, who had just figured in the pageant among the prisoners, and then, with a halter thrown over him and scourged meanwhile by his conductors, had been haled to the spot abutting on the Forum, where Roman law requires that malefactors condemned to death should be executed. After the announcement that Simon was no more and the shouts of universal applause which greeted it, the princes began the sacrifices, which having been duly offered with the customary prayers, they withdrew to the palace. (*J.W.*, VII.153-155)

Having thus reproduced a representative sample of the relevant evidence from both the early Greek historians and Josephus, it is now possible to draw a fourfold conclusion concerning the nature and purpose of the Roman triumphal procession in relationship to the fate of those "led in triumph" and to draw out the implications of this study for our further investigation of II Cor. 2:14-16a.

1. The *explicit* purpose or goal of the triumphal procession, from beginning to end, was twofold: First, to render thanks to the deity who had granted the victory in battle (in Rome, Jupiter, and in Egypt, Dionysos; see below), and second, to glorify the general or consul who had achieved it. (The *implicit* sociological and politico-religious function need not concern us here, since our purpose is merely to highlight one particular aspect of the procession.) These two goals were by no means independent of one another, but inextricably interwoven so that the political and religious aspects of the triumphal procession combined to form an indistinguishable unity. In the texts we investigated, this unity was evident in the emphasis on the songs of praise to the

deity which formed an integral part of the procession itself, as well as in the fact that the Roman triumph culminated at the temple of Jupiter, where sacrificial offerings and prayer provided the concluding climax to the parade. Thus, although the focus of the procession itself was on the triumphator, with its displays of the spoils of war, the recounting of the high points of the decisive battle through dramatic presentations and paintings, the army's praise for its general, and the parade of the vanquished foes, the procession *itself, as a whole* was intended to be an act of worship to the god who had granted the victory. Furthermore, as both Versnel and Wallisch have emphasized, this "unification of the religious with the political"[43] was not a late adaptation of an earlier, purely secular institution, but a continuation of the function which the triumph always had. Moreover, Wallisch has pointed out that the corresponding Hellenistic triumphs, as celebrated among the Ptolemies and the Seleucids, also preserved this religious dimension. Unlike the Roman triumphs, however, these celebrations were interpreted in terms of the legend of the god Dionysos's triumphal procession after his successful military campaign in India, which Alexander is said to have imitated in his march through Carmania, portraying *himself* as the successor of Dionysos.[44] The sources make it clear, therefore, that by the second century CE, the legend of Dionysos's "discovery" or establishment of the triumphal procession as the basis of the institution was widespread. Thus, whereas in Rome Jupiter became the deity of the triumph, in Egypt it was Dionysos. At this point it is thus once again appropriate to recall what Versnel has said concerning this dual aspect of the Roman, and by extension also the Hellenistic, triumph, namely, that "In no other Roman ceremony do god and man approach each other as closely as they do in the triumph."[45]

2. The fact that the triumphal procession was a well-known and well-established Roman institution is evidenced by the various stereotypical rituals which were involved (e.g., the manner of clothing, the order of the procession itself, the prescribed activities of the triumpha-

43. The phrase is Wallisch's; cf. "Name and Herkunft," 252.

44. Cf. Arrian, *Anabasis*, VI.28.1-3; Diodorus of Sicily, Book III.65.8; and Wallisch, "Name und Herkunft," 251.

45. Versnel, *Triumphus*, 1.

tor, the fixed parade route), the detailed conditions which had to be met before such a triumph could be celebrated, its relationship to the other Roman ceremonies, and by the corresponding *terminus technicus* nature of the "triumph" word-group itself. For although the verb and adjective forms occur less frequently than the noun, it is clear that all three refer specifically to the institution of the triumphal procession, and not to the more general idea of a triumph in battle, for which the word-group "to win a victory" / "victory" *(nikaō [nikeō]–nikē)* was most often used.

3. The use of "to lead in a triumphal procession" with prepositional phrases to indicate its object or with a direct object alone, *always* refers to the one who has been conquered and is subsequently led in the procession, and never to the one who has conquered or to those who have shared in his victory (e.g., his army, fellow officers, etc.).

4. Finally, the role of those thus "led in triumph" was to reveal the glory and might of the victor by illustrating the *strength* of those conquered. In other words, the function of the captive led in triumph was to provide an *a fortiori* argument for the military strength of the victor: the greater the stature of those conquered, the greater the stature of the conqueror. And, as we have seen, this illustration often, or *even normally* culminated, as did the procession as a whole, with the execution of these prisoners (or a representative selection of them). *To be led in triumph could thus mean, in a word, to be led to one's death in the ceremony of the triumphal procession as a display of the victor's glory and, by implication, of the benevolence of the deity in granting this victory to the victor.*

In conclusion, therefore, there is, to my knowledge, no external evidence for the suggestion that "to lead in a triumphal procession" in Col. 2:15 and II Cor. 2:14 could refer either to Christ's act of victory in triumphing over the principalities and powers in a battle (Col. 2:15), or to God's triumph over Paul at his conversion (II Cor. 2:14), since this verb refers *only* to the specific Roman ceremony of the triumphal procession, which *presupposes* this prior conquest, but is by no means identified with it. Rather, the triumphal procession, which took place in Rome, was the result and expression of the victory which had *already* taken place on the battlefield. This temporal relationship and semantic distinction between the victory and the triumphal procession is explicitly indicated in Col. 2:15. The rulers and authorities are disarmed and then led in a triumphal procession, the result of which is God's public display of their defeat and destruction (death). In II Cor. 2:14, Paul's prior defeat, i.e., his conversion-call on the road to Damascus, although not explicitly referred to, is thus also presupposed, even though the verb "to lead in a triumphal procession" *itself* does not refer to Paul's conversion. For a triumphal procession without a prior triumph is inconceivable.

In addition, there is also no lexical evidence that to be led in triumph could refer either to the idea of somehow sharing as a co-victor in the triumphator's victory, or for the factitive meaning of being "caused to triumph." Rather, the evidence demands that we first attempt to understand both Col. 2:15 and II Cor. 2:14 in the light of the one, common meaning which is attested for the time of Paul before we conclude, as C. K. Barrett has concerning II Cor. 2:14, that

> *notwithstanding the lack of supporting lexical evidence* it is right to follow Liddell and Scott, Allo, and Kümmel in taking Paul to represent himself as one of the victorious general's soldiers sharing in the glory of his triumph.[46]

Nor should we assume that Paul employed this verb in any other, non-attested, idiosyncratic manner.

Instead, the starting point for understanding Paul's view of his apostolic ministry in II Cor. 2:14-16a is the supposition that Paul pictured himself as one of God's *previously* conquered enemies. In the light of Paul's conception of all Christians as "enemies" before their reconciliation "by the death of his Son" (Rom. 5:10), his ability to picture those Jews who were rejecting the gospel as "enemies of God" (Rom. 11:28), and his judgment that those who reject his example and gospel "live as enemies of the cross of Christ" (Phil. 3:18), it seems very natural to find this same predicate applied by Paul, by implication, to himself as he was prior to his Damascus road experience.

It is as a conquered enemy, then, that Paul, as a "slave of Christ," was now, to take the image in its most specific meaning, *being led by God to death* in order that he might display or reveal the majesty, power,

46. Barrett, *Second Corinthians,* 98.

and glory of his conqueror. Or, as Paul puts it, "thanks be to God who always leads us in his triumphal procession." Only if this meaning can be shown to be inappropriate, may we look for another. In other words, as startling as this may sound at first, our exegetical hypothesis is that in II Cor. 2:14 Paul is rejoicing precisely because God, like a victorious general after his victory, is leading him *as a slave to death.*

Unfortunately, commentators have been aided in their attempt to avoid this meaning by the ambiguity which exists in the two major Greek lexicons available today. Liddell-Scott-Jones lists no less than four possible meanings for this verb, three of which are asserted to be current in the NT period. Moreover, they suggest the meaning "to lead in triumph as a general does his army" for II Cor. 2:14—a meaning which is unattested in the literature. On the other hand, the Bauer lexicon is even more misleading, suggesting three different possibilities for II Cor. 2:14 alone! The inadequacies of both treatments have already been shown in detail by Lamar Williamson, Jr., and need not be repeated here. What must be emphasized, however, is that all the evidence points to the conclusion that there is only *one* basic and common meaning for this term available in the time of Paul, namely, that of the triumphal procession in which the conquered enemies were usually led as slaves to death, being spared this death only by an act of grace on the part of the one celebrating the triumph.

This conclusion seems to be called into question, however, by Rory B. Egan's study, "Lexical Evidence on Two Pauline Passages." Egan attempts to offer a completely different and independent meaning for *thriambeuein* in the time of Paul (i.e., "display," "reveal," "noise abroad," "show," "manifest," "divulge," "publicize") on the basis of the fragmentary 14 BCE papyrus from Roman Egypt listed as number 1061 in *Ägyptische Urkunden aus den königlichen Museen zu Berlin.*[47]

Egan's plea is unconvincing because BGU 1061 does not refer to *thriambeuō* at all, but to *ekthriambizō* (the semantic relationship between *thriambeuō* and *ekthriambizō* is by no means clear—they are not necessarily synonyms). In addition, Egan offers no detailed exegesis of II Cor. 2:14 in its context, or in the Corinthian correspondence as a whole. But his study is helpful in pointing out that the only

47. I/4: *Griechische Urkunden.*

possibility for interpreting *thriambeuein* with any lexical support at all in the Pauline period (discounting his own suggestion) is its attestation as a reference to leading the previously defeated enemies in a triumphal procession[48]

It appears, however, that my study has made the attempt to take the triumphal procession background seriously even more problematic, since it hardly seems possible to picture Paul as actually intending to say that he praises God for leading him to death. What must be demonstrated, therefore, is that the common understanding of "to lead in a triumphal procession" as outlined above, with its emphasis on being led to *death*, makes sense in this context, rather than being "scarcely tenable" as Egan believes,[49] or an example of an inappropriate attempt "(to press) the full extent of the triumph relationship" as Peter Marshall cautions.[50] Indeed, it is my contention that once the introductory thanksgiving in II Cor. 2:14ff. is understood against the backdrop of the "triumphal procession," with its emphasis in our context on Paul as the conquered slave of Christ who is led to death, that this meaning not only fits the context, helping to solve the other exegetical and theological problems of II Cor. 2:14-16a, but that it also corresponds to Paul's apostolic self-conception as developed throughout the Corinthian correspondence as a whole.

The goal of chapter two is to provide the necessary exegetical support for this assertion. As a result, it will become clear that the key to understanding Paul's thought in II Cor. 2:14-16a, as well as its place within the Corinthian correspondence as a whole, is the realization that to be "led in triumph" means, in fact, to be "led to death."

48. See Egan, "Lexical Evidence," 37f.
49. Ibid.
50. "Metaphor," 312.

Chapter Two

The Apostle Paul as the Sacrificial Aroma of Christ (II Cor. 2:14-16a)

In the past, the problem of understanding II Cor. 2:14-16a has been compounded by the sudden switch in metaphors in these verses. It has often been assumed that if Paul intended "fragrance" (vv. 14b, 16a) and "aroma" (v. 15) to evoke the Old Testament cultic image of the sacrificial aroma which arises to God from the acceptable offering (see below), then the connection with verse 14a, understood as a reference to the triumphal procession, becomes tenuous at best. In fact, though it did not affect their interpretations of v. 14a, most commentators in the past confessed that the switch in metaphors from the imagery of the triumphal procession to that of the cultic sacrificial offering was impossible. Faced with this difficulty, the only way out seemed to be to posit a drastic discontinuity within the thought of Paul, or to assign a completely different meaning either to "lead in triumph (to death),"[1] or to "fragrance" and "aroma."[2] The first indication that our exegetical hypothesis from chapter one is correct, therefore, is that once we see that the triumphal procession imagery involves the idea of Paul being led to *death*, the inner connection between the imagery of 2:14a and 14b becomes apparent, if not less abrupt.

---

1. So Egan, "Lexical Evidence," 38, who rejects the idea of the triumphal procession partly because "any attempt to construe the image of the military triumph here is not really corroborated *by the second part of the verse*" (emphasis added).

2. See Barrett, *Second Corinthians,* 98; Lietzmann, *An die Korinther,* 108; Wendland, *An die Korinther,* 176; Windisch, *Zweiter Korintherbrief,* 97; Friesen, *Glory,* 26.

A. THE MEANING OF II CORINTHIANS 2:14-16a

1. The Logical Structure of 2:14-16a

Paul's explanation for his burst of praise in v. 14a continues with a second participial phrase joined to what precedes by the simple conjunction "and":

> and through us reveals the fragrance of the knowledge of him in every place.

Yet there are two reasons for regarding Paul's thought in v. 14b as a logical progression from v. 14a. First, the *internal relationship* between verses 14a and 14b makes the need for a progression in thought from the participle "leads in triumph (to death)" *(thriambeuonti)* to "reveals" *(phanerounti)* evident. For if the two ideas represented by these participles are conceived to be logically coordinate, then Paul's reason for rendering praise to God ought to be clear on the basis of v. 14a alone. But the thought of v. 14a, "thanks be to God because he always leads us to death in Christ," remains incomplete and unintelligible in and of itself. It thus becomes necessary to construe v. 14b as a continuation of Paul's argument in order to complete the sense of v. 14a.

Second, the *external relationship* between v. 14b and v. 15 also demands that we interpret v. 14b as a logical progression in Paul's thought. The clause introduced by "for" *(hoti)* in v. 15 makes sense only as a ground for v. 14b, not as a support for both 14a and 14b, which would be expected if the two statements were intended to be read as separate coordinate ideas:

> for we are the aroma of Christ to God among those who are being saved and among those who are perishing.

Paul then completes his description of the apostolic ministry with a statement of its twofold effect among those whom he encounters—

> on the one hand to some a fragrance from death to death, on the other hand to others a fragrance from life to life.

The flow of Paul's logic in II Cor. 2:14-16a may thus be reconstructed in the following manner:

v. 14a   Thanks be to God
          because he always leads me as his conquered slave to death

v. 14b   *and in so doing* reveals through me as an apostle the fragrance
          of the knowledge of him in every place.

v. 15   *That God reveals himself through me is evident because* as an
          apostle I am the aroma of Christ to God among those who are
          being saved and among those who are perishing.

v. 16a   *As a result, my ministry as an apostle is* a fragrance from death
          to death among those who are perishing and a fragrance from
          life to life among those who are being saved.[3]

In order to understand the meaning of Paul's argument, however, the nature of the imagery evoked by Paul in his use of "fragrance" and "aroma" in verses 14b-16a, through which he not only completes the thought of v. 14a, but also supports his contention that as an apostle he functions as God's revelatory agent, must now be determined.

2. The Sacrificial Imagery of 2:14b-16a

The problem of understanding the imagery suggested by these terms is twofold. First, there is the difficulty of determining the precise meaning of the terms "fragrance" and "aroma" themselves. Second, there is the problem of determining what relationship, if any, exists between the ideas that they represent, i.e., whether or not the meaning of "aroma" *(euōdia)* can, or should be, extended to "fragrance" *(osmē)* in our present context. In response to this twofold problem three solutions have been suggested, which can be summarized as follows:

1)   v. 14b: Hellenistic reference to incense
     v. 15a: Jewish reference to sacrifice

     Therefore discontinuity between vv. 14b and 15a, but continuity between 14a and 14b.[4]

---

3. Italics are used here to make Paul's logical connections explicit.
4. For example, Windisch, *Zweiter Korintherbrief,* 97-98.

2)   v. 14b: Jewish reference to sacrifice
     v. 15a: Jewish reference to sacrifice

Therefore continuity between vv. 14b and 15a, but discontinuity between vv. 14a and 14b-15a.[5]

3)   v. 14b: non-sacrificial reference to fragrance
     v. 15a: non-sacrificial reference to fragrance

Therefore continuity throughout vv. 14-15, but only at the expense of the sacrificial imagery.[6]

At first glance it does appear as if Paul intends to evoke two distinct images by his use of "fragrance" and "aroma," since the referents with which the two terms are associated appear to be quite different. In v. 14b "fragrance" is associated with the knowledge of God, whereas in v. 15 "aroma" is associated with Christ. (Although grammatically "of him" in v. 14b could also refer to Christ, the fact that the praise is directed to God for what he does "in Christ" indicates that the referent is, indeed, God.[7]) This is confirmed by the parallels to 2:14b in II Cor. 2:17 and 4:6. For in 2:17 Paul describes a second[8] characteristic of the genuine apostles, i.e., that they are not engaged in "hawking the word *of God*" but speak "in Christ." The "through us" of v. 14b is thus further explicated by the apostolic activity of v. 17: God reveals the knowledge of himself *through the apostle* (v. 14b) who speaks his word "from sincerity" (v. 17, for the meaning of this statement, see below, chapter four). Hence, the subject of both v. 14b and v. 17 is the revelation of the knowledge of *God;* in the former by means of the display of the apostle in the triumphal procession as one led to death, and in the latter by means of his preaching. Similarly, in 4:6 the content of the revelation which is made known by God is described as "the light of the knowledge of the glory of God in the face

---

5. So Lietzmann, *An die Korinther,* 108.

6. E.g., Wendland, *An die Korinther,* 176.

7. This was the main point made earlier by Manson in "2 Cor. 2:14-17"; see esp. pp. 157 and 159f.

8. For the point that 2:14 ought not to be read in the light of 2:17, so that 2:14 also becomes a statement primarily concerning Paul's ministry of preaching, see below.

of Christ," so that the "knowledge" portrayed in 2:14, "with the image of the fragrance" is now pictured in 4:6 "with the image of splendor."[9] But in both cases it is the knowledge of *God* which is in view.

Nevertheless, in spite of this difference, the unity of the two images becomes clear in view of the fact that in v. 15 the support for Paul's assertion that he reveals the knowledge of God is precisely that he is the aroma of *Christ*. Thus, the "fragrance of the knowledge of God" in v. 14b must be equated with the "aroma of Christ" in v. 15 in order for the logic indicated by the "for" of verse 15a to make sense. The reason Paul is confident that God is revealing the knowledge of himself "through us" is because ("for") *he* is the aroma of Christ who, in the light of II Cor. 4:6, is the manifestation of the knowledge of the glory of God. In other words, since it is Paul who reveals the knowledge of God in v. 14b and Paul who, at the same time, is the fragrance of Christ, the fact that this latter statement functions to support or ground the former one demands that the two be equated, the latter functioning to define the former, and in so doing, to provide the reason for Paul's confidence in v. 14b. T. W. Manson was right, therefore, in observing that the *entire* phrase "the fragrance of the knowledge of him" must refer to Christ, although "him" itself refers to God.[10] But even more importantly, the fact that "among those who are being saved and among those who are perishing" modifies the predicate "we are the *aroma* of Christ" in v. 15, while its corresponding relative pronouns "to some . . . to others" provide the link to the *parallel* phrases "fragrance . . . fragrance" in v. 16a, demonstrates that the two concepts must be equivalent in meaning in II Cor. 2:14-16a.[11]

This conclusion is confirmed by the use of the word-pair "fragrance/aroma" *(osmē/euōdia)* elsewhere in the New Testament. It can

9. The quotation as well as this last insight are from Bultmann, *Zweiter Korintherbrief,* 67.

10. Manson, "2 Cor. 2:14-17," 157. Manson missed the point of the imagery in v. 14 as a whole, however, concluding that what Paul intended to express was that, in spite of his anxiety over the Corinthian church (2:12f.), "we must be thankful to God, who does not leave us a prey to our cares and anxieties but carries us along in victorious progress of the Messianic triumph, which is sweeping the world" (p. 161).

11. So too Lietzmann, *An die Korinther,* 108.

be no mere coincidence that in the other two instances in which "aroma" *(euōdia)* occurs in the NT it also appears in conjunction with "fragrance" *(osmē;* see Phil. 4:18 and Eph. 5:2). In addition, in both cases the terminology is exactly the same. In Phil. 4:18 Paul describes the gifts he has received from the Philippians at the hand of Epaphroditus as literally *"a fragrance of aroma,* an acceptable sacrifice, pleasing to God," while Eph. 5:2 refers to the fact that Christ gave himself up for us, as literally, "an offering and sacrifice to God for a *fragrance of aroma."* Thus, the two terms appear to have been merged in meaning and in both contexts function together as a metonymy for the idea of sacrifice, as evidenced by their use as a parallel to the word "sacrifice" *(thusia)* in these texts.[12]

Finally, this merging of "fragrance" *(osmē)* and "aroma" *(euōdia)* to produce a metonymy, witnessed to in the NT, finds its origin in the Old Testament,[13] where the terms "fragrance" and "aroma" are the

12. The only other occurrence of either term is John 12:3, where *osmē* occurs alone and retains its literal meaning. Stumpff, εὐωδία, 809, also notices that this terminology "is both linguistically and materially connected with the sacrificial context well known from the O.T."

13. Cf. Delling, ὀσμή, 494, though he himself rejects this as the background to II Cor. 2:14f. For an opposing view, cf. Windisch, *Zweiter Korintherbrief,* 98, who postulates the possibility of seeing the background to *osmē* in v. 16 in the fact that incense worked fatally on several different kinds of animals, as attested to by Aristotle and Aelian (see p. 98 for his list of sources). He proposes that this idea was then taken up by the Rabbis of later times and applied to the twofold effect of the law. This same rabbinic background was already suggested by Moore, "Conjectanea Talmudica" and then once again taken up by Manson, "2 Cor. 2:14-17," 157-161 on the basis of the rabbinic parallels assembled in Wettstein's *Novum Testamentum Graecum* II, 182 and Strack/Billerbeck, *Kommentar* III, 498f. The contention is that 2 Cor. 2:14-16a parallels the rabbinic conception of the Torah as a drug which brought either benefit or harm (cf., e.g., Dt. Rabbah 1.6; b. Shab. 88b; b. Yoma 72b, etc.).

But this parallel in *function* between the law and the gospel in these texts ought not to be taken as an indication that *osmē* itself in v. 16a is intended to be equivalent in *meaning* to this "medicine of Life" *(sm ḥyym).* For there is no evidence that *osmē* was ever used either as an equivalent to the idea of a medicine or linked directly with the Torah. On the other hand, it is questionable if the Hebrew term *sm* ever meant "odor" (cf. Kümmel's addition to Lietzmann, *An die Korinther,* 198), though Barrett, *Second Corinthians,* 102 points to Ex. 25:6 and 30:7, where it is associated with anointing oil and incense respectively "and this might have helped Paul to form the connection." In this regard, cf. too II Baruch 67:6 where we read of "the vapour

standard LXX renderings of Hebrew *ryḥ* and *nyḥḥ* respectively.[14] *Ryḥ* is a derivative from the very common root *rwḥ* ("breath," "wind," "spirit") and normally means "scent" or "odor." As such, it can be used concretely of plants and fields (Gen. 27:27; Song Sol. 1:12; 2:3; 4:11; 7:14; Hos. 14:7), ointments (Song Sol. 1:13; 4:10), persons and/or their garments (Song Sol. 4:11; 7:9), and water (Job 14:9); or figuratively of one's influence or reputation (Ex. 5:21; Jer. 48:11). In a similar manner, when *nyḥḥ* is used alone as a derivative of the verb *nwḥ* ("to rest"), it usually means a "quiet," a "soothing," or a "tranquilizing" (cf. Job 36:16; Num. 28:2; Lev. 26:31 and Ezek. 20:28).

But when the two terms are combined in the construct phrase *ryḥ nyḥḥ*, both lose their usual meanings and take on instead the nature of a *terminus technicus* meaning "a soothing, tranquilizing odor of sacrifices acceptable to YHWH."[15] It is this new meaning which is then rendered in the LXX with the phrase "fragrance of an aroma" *(osmē euōdias)* exactly as it is found in Phil. 4:18 and Eph. 5:2.[16] Gen. 8:21 is a classic example of this phenomenon. On the other hand, Ezek. 20:40-41 is a good example of the fact that the *terminus technicus* could also be used figuratively: Israel is portrayed as a pleasing sacrifice which YHWH will one day accept as his own, despite their present wickedness. It thus becomes clear that the phrase *osmē euōdias* is a rendering of the Hebrew *terminus technicus ryḥ nyḥḥ* ("a soothing odor").[17]

---

of the smoke of the incense of the righteousness which is by the law" (as translated in Charles, *Apocrypha*, 516). It is entirely possible, therefore, that Paul was associating the twofold effect of his own gospel with the twofold function of the law in order to build a parallel between the effect of his own ministry and the ministry of Moses!

14. As a translation of *ryḥ*, *osmē* occurs 55 times in the Greek translation of the Hebrew canon and *euōdia*, which always renders *nyḥḥ*, 47 times. *Ryḥ* is otherwise translated by *osphrasia* ("smell") in Hos. 14:7 and *nyḥḥ* by *thusia* ("sacrifice") only in Lev. 26:31.

15. Cf. Brown-Driver-Briggs, *Hebrew and English Lexicon*, 629, 926.

16. This observation is confirmed by John 12:3 where *osmē* ("fragrance") occurs outside of the *terminus technicus osmē euōdias* ("fragrance of an aroma"). Here it reverts back to its usual meaning of "fragrance" in reference to the smell of the ointment which Mary used to anoint the feet of Jesus.

17. Besides those texts listed by Barrett (*Second Corinthians*, 99) this same phenomenon can be seen in Ex. 29:25, 41; Lev. 1:13, 17; 2:2, 9, 12; 3:5, 11, 16;

Of most significance for our study, however, is the fact that the technical term *osmē euōdias* as a metonymy for sacrifice seems to have been so well established by the post-exilic period that not only could the term "aroma" *(euōdia)* be used alone to designate the odor of the acceptable sacrifice, but when used in the same context, the two terms could also be *separated* and used as *synonyms.* In contrast, when "fragrance" *(osmē)* was used alone it retained its usual meaning of "scent."[18] The fact that "aroma" *(euōdia)* had itself taken on a sacrificial meaning is demonstrated by its use in the synonymous parallelisms of the following wisdom sayings from Sirach:

The offering of the righteous maketh the altar fat,
and its sweet savour *(euōdia)* cometh before the most high. (35:5)

Give the aroma *(euōdian)* of sacrifice and a memorial of the finest grain,
and make fat an offering as if you no longer existed. (38:11)[19]

It is Sir. 24:15 which then provides the crucial link for understanding Paul's use of this terminology in II Cor. 2:14ff. For here, as in 2:14ff., the *terminus technicus* has been split up, but the two terms have nevertheless retained their sacrificial meaning:[20]

As cinnamon and aspalathus have I given "a fragrance" *(osmēn)*
and as choice myrrh I spread abroad "an aroma" *(euōdian).*
As galbanum and onyx and stacte
and as the smoke of incense in the tabernacle.[21]

4:31; 6:15, 21; 8:20, 27; 17:4, 6; Num. 15:5, 7, 10, 13, 14, 24; 28:2, 6, 8, 13, 24, 27; Ezek. 6:13; 16:19; 20:28.

18. See above, p. 41 n. 16 and below, n. 22.

19. This translation is my own; G. H. Box and W. O. E. Oesterly, in Charles, *Apocrypha,* 450, attempt to represent the Hebrew original at this point in their translation.

20. Stumpff, εὐωδία, 809 n. 5, points out that the speaker in Sir. 24:15 is a personified wisdom, and from this draws the conclusion that *osmēn* and *euōdian* in this context are simply recalling "a figurative intermingling of the old idea that Paradise . . . is full of fragrance with the association of sweet fragrance with the self-declaration of the Godhead."

21. Box and Oesterly, Charles, *Apocrypha,* 398, render this line : "(I was) as the smoke of incense in the Tabernacle."

This is precisely the same pattern found in II Cor. 2:14-16a.[22] Here Paul also splits the *terminus technicus*, using the two terms "fragrance" *(osmē)* and "aroma" *(euōdia)* as synonyms. Objections such as the one raised by Plummer[23] that "it is worth noting that the sacrificial phrase *osmē euōdias*, so frequent in LXX, is not used here, and this makes any allusion to sacrifice doubtful" thus lose all their force. Moreover, although it is certainly true that in the mystery religions and later Gnostic Christianity the idea of fragrance came to denote "a sign of divine presence and a sign of divine life,"[24] there is no evidence that this meaning is at play in II Cor. 2:14-16a—but even if it were somehow implied, G. Barth is correct in emphasizing that this more general meaning does not exclude a connection with the "sacrifice-motif."[25] The burden of proof thus rests on those who want to deny the sacrificial backdrop to 2:14-16a. For there is no compelling reason to interpret the meaning of "fragrance" *(osmē)* and "aroma" *(euōdia)* against any other background than that of the cultic sacrifice of the Old Testament.

It is also significant for understanding II Cor. 2:14-16a that this terminological development takes place in conjunction with the wisdom tradition found in Sir. 24:15. For on the one hand, in Sir. 24:15 the wisdom which offers the sacrificial fragrance is *itself* identified with this fragrance.[26] On the other hand, in the Wisdom of Solomon wisdom is not only equated with the power and glory of God (see especially Wisd. 7:25), but can also be said to be filled with an

22. Of course, the regular form of the technical term *osmē euōdias* still occurs; cf., e.g., Judith 16:16. The Hatch and Redpath concordance of the Septuagint also lists Sir. 20:9; 38:13; and 43:26 as possible examples of the occurrence of *euōdia*, but in each case the textual variant *euodia* seems more probable. Thus, the only other example is Sir. 50:15. When *osmē* occurs alone it always carries its usual meaning of "scent," as in Tobit 8:3; Sir. 39:14; and II Macc. 9:9, 10, 12. As an exception, in Baruch 5:8 *euōdia* also seems to carry this meaning.

23. Plummer, *Second Corinthians*, 71.

24. Bultmann, *Zweiter Korintherbrief*, 68. Cf. Bornkamm, *Paul*, 114.

25. "Eignung," 261 n. 17.

26. Cf. Lev. 16:13 LXX. For an examination of a similar spiritualization of the sacrificial cult found in Qumran and in the NT view of the Christian(s) as the temple of God, see Klinzing, *Umdeutung des Kultus*, and the earlier work of Wenschkewitz, "Spiritualisierung."

"understanding spirit, which is holy" (Wisd. 7:22), or even equated with the Holy Spirit itself (see Wisd. 9:17b in comparison with 9:17a and 9:10). In addition, one of the primary functions of wisdom's power or the Holy Spirit in this context is to enable one to understand God's ways and in so doing to make one a friend of God (cf. Wisd. 7:22, 27; 9:2, 5, 9-18, especially vv. 15-18), something which remains impossible otherwise (cf. Wisd. 9:14-17).

It is precisely this threefold constellation of ideas— (1) wisdom as the personified giver and substance of the sacrificial odor before God, (2) who is at the same time the power, glory, and Holy Spirit of God, (3) whose function it is to enable one to understand the ways and revelation of God—that provides the background to Paul's understanding in I Cor. 1:18–2:16 of his own role in relationship to the sacrificial death of Christ on the cross, now itself identified with the power, glory, and wisdom of God (see 1:18, 23, 30; 2:7f.).[27] For in the light of this tradition concerning the revelatory function of wisdom = Holy Spirit, Paul's emphasis that only those who have received the Spirit are able to understand = accept (cf. I Cor. 2:14) the wisdom of God in the cross of Christ (see 2:10-12) and his corresponding emphasis that his own ministry in Corinth therefore consisted in preaching the gospel of this divine wisdom *in the power of the Spirit and in words taught by the Spirit* (cf. 2:4, 13) become understandable, since it is the Spirit alone which can reveal the wisdom of God in the cross. Furthermore, the inner connection between Paul as a bearer of the Spirit and the Corinthians' own reception of the cross/death of Christ as the wisdom of God becomes manifest: the Corinthians have come to know the crucified Christ as the wisdom and power of God precisely *because* Paul came to Corinth as the bearer of the Spirit whose preaching was carried out "in demonstration of the Spirit and power" (2:4). Hence, they owe their very existence as Christians to the fact that Paul preached the wisdom of God in the power of the Spirit, a power which was manifest even though he himself came to them "in weakness and

---

27. I owe this insight to a seminar and colloquium discussion led by Peter Stuhlmacher and to personal conversations with him. For a detailed development of the wisdom tradition as the backdrop to Paul's argument in I Cor. 1:18–2:16 see Theissen, *Psychologische Aspekte,* 341-363.

in fear and in much trembling" (2:3). With this contrast between Paul's personal weakness and his role as the bearer of the Spirit firmly in mind, we can now turn our attention to the meaning of II Cor. 2:14-16a itself.

3. The Meaning of II Cor. 2:14-16a

Having come this far, our hypothesis from chapter one, i.e. that in 2:14a Paul is picturing himself as a conquered slave who is led to his death in the triumphal procession, can now be brought together with our conclusion that in 2:14b-16a Paul completes his thought by picturing himself in terms of the sacrificial imagery of the Old Testament, especially as this culminated in the post-exilic wisdom tradition. For although the origin of the imagery in vv. 14b-16a has certainly shifted from the Roman-Hellenistic backdrop of the "triumphal procession" to the OT cultic backdrop of the "sacrificial aroma," the two images nevertheless form a coherent picture of Paul as the medium of the revelation of the knowledge of God manifested in Christ: Paul is always being led to death as an apostolic slave of Christ and, through the display of Paul as the bearer of God's Spirit in this triumphal procession (v. 14b), God is revealing the knowledge of himself in every place (2:14).

Moreover, rather than presenting a problem for the appropriation of the imagery of the triumphal procession,[28] Paul's emphasis that God is *always* leading him to death underscores that this revelation is something to be identified with his very being and continual experience as an apostle. In other words, Paul's use of "always" in II Cor. 2:14 indicates that he views his entire life as one long triumphal procession. This is confirmed by the parallel passage in II Cor. 4:10, where Paul again emphasizes that his call to "carry in (his) body the death of Jesus" is something which constantly characterizes his life as an apostle (for the parallels between the two texts, see below pp. 64ff.). For here too he does so by stressing that this process of carrying in his body the *death* of Jesus goes on "always."

28. For the most recent example of this objection see McDonald, "Paul and the Preaching Ministry," 36f.

It is not surprising, therefore, that the "knowledge of God" revealed through Paul in II Cor. 2:14 is then further defined and made concrete as that revelation of God which took place in the cross and is now made known in Paul's ministry of the Spirit carried out in and through his own weakness = "death" (2:15-16a). Thus in II Cor. 2:14-16a Paul asserts that the sacrificial aroma of the crucified Christ, which is itself the knowledge and wisdom of God, is being made known to all in every place *through Paul's own experience of being led to death,* since *Paul himself,* as an apostle entrusted with the Spirit of the crucified Christ (= the wisdom of God) *is* the sacrificial aroma of Christ to God (v. 15).

Hence, the continuity between the triumphal procession and the cultic sacrifice is established by Paul's conception of his *own* "being led to *death*" as the *revelatory vehicle* through which the Spirit makes known to all the significance of Christ's *death* on the cross. There is, of course, no explicit mention of the Spirit in 2:14-16a, but the parallels between II Cor. 2:14f. and I Cor. 1:17f.; 4:8-13; II Cor. 4:7ff.; 12:9f., etc., which will be investigated below, as well as Paul's argument in 3:3 (see chapter five), make this connection manifest. Paul's revelatory function is grounded in the fact that *in his suffering* he preaches and acts *in the Spirit,* and that in the midst of his being led to *death* the Spirit is poured out on others to bring them to *life* in Christ. The thread that ties the two images in 2:14f. together, which at first seem so disparate, is therefore Paul himself (cf. "us," v. 14a; "through us" v. 14b; "we are," v. 15). For from start to finish the focus of attention in 2:14ff. is on Paul's revelatory role as the apostolic slave of Christ, who in his being led to death is spreading the knowledge of God by means of the Spirit.[29] As a result, the attempt to posit a distinction

29. It is difficult to decide whether the imagery of II Cor. 2:15 implies that Christ himself is to be pictured as a (burnt offering) sacrifice as Barrett, *Second Corinthians,* 99, has suggested when he interprets the meaning of Paul's imagery to be that "the apostles are the smoke that arises from the sacrifice of Christ to God. . . ." For on the one hand, although Lev. 4:31 does speak of such an atoning burnt offering (cf. Lev. 1:4; 16:24), the sin atonement was usually performed outside the camp and was distinguished from such a burnt offering (see Lev. 4:12, 21 and Heb. 13:13). Moreover, the Passover lamb was not presented as a burnt offering, so that the identification of Christ as the paschal lamb in I Cor. 5:7 (see Mk. 14:12; Lk. 22:7; John 1:29, 36; Heb. 9:13f., 23-28) does not seem to provide a suitable

between v. 14b, taken to refer Paul's ministry of preaching the word, and v. 15, taken to be a reference to Paul himself, is unjustified.[30]

In the light of the continuation of Paul's thought in 2:17, however, it must also be emphasized that Paul's apostolic role of *"being led to death" (in Christ)* in order to reveal the knowledge of God spoken of in 2:14-16a cannot be separated from his call to *preach the word of God (in Christ)* spoken of in 2:17. For although the two aspects are distinct and ought not to be collapsed into one another, they nevertheless do interpenetrate and confirm each other as the essential hallmarks of the genuine apostolic calling. The apostolic message is embodied in the life of the apostle itself, and in both cases this twofold apostolic activity takes place "in Christ." Paul's emphasis in 2:14-17 that his role of suffering and call to preach as an apostle are anchored "in Christ" is merely an extension of his fundamental conviction that he has been called to be an apostle "of Christ Jesus" (I Cor. 1:1; II Cor. 1:1) and as such ought to be regarded as a servant of Christ and steward of the mysteries of God (I Cor. 4:1). Being called by Christ to be his apostolic servant, Paul's life and message can naturally be said to take place "in Christ."

Moreover, given the nature of this apostolic calling and its fruits, Paul's relationship to the Corinthians as *their* apostle can also appropriately be described in the same manner: he became their father through the gospel "in Christ Jesus" (I Cor. 4:15); he has a boast or pride in them "in Christ Jesus" (I Cor. 15:31) and extends his love to them "in Christ Jesus" (I Cor. 16:24).

Conversely, since the church in Corinth came into existence as a result of Paul's apostolic life and message "in Christ," it too can be described in the same terms. The Corinthians have been set apart "in Christ Jesus" (I Cor. 1:2), they have been given specific gifts of grace "in Christ Jesus" (I Cor. 1:4f.), and they thus find their life "in Christ Jesus" (I Cor. 1:30; cf. 15:19, 22; II Cor. 5:17). In short, the church is the "body of Christ" (I Cor. 12:27), even though certain members of it are still babes

---

background to II Cor. 2:14f. But on the other hand, cf. Eph. 5:2. We can, however, leave this question open for our purposes.

30. The classic example of this attempt is Bultmann's treatment of this passage in *Zweiter Korintherbrief,* 67, 70, 97f.

"in Christ" (I Cor. 3:1), since the status of being "in Christ" is based on the work of God "in Christ," as described in II Cor. 5:19.

Fourthly, Paul's awareness of the fact that as an apostle of Christ he speaks "in Christ" (II Cor. 2:17; 12:19) is the foundation for his confidence that Christ is speaking "in him" (see II Cor. 13:3), just as the Corinthians' new existence "in Christ" (II Cor. 5:17) is the foundation for their confidence that Christ is in them if they maintain their faith (see II Cor. 13:5). For Paul to emphasize in II Cor. 2:14 that as an apostle he is being led to death "in Christ", or in 2:17 that he speaks "in Christ", is thus another example of his essential self-understanding that his very existence as such is part and parcel of God's continuing self-revelation "in Christ." As J. H. Schütz has pointed out,

> taking *en Christō* ("in Christ") in its adverbial sense, with *thriambeuein* ("lead in triumphal procession"), we see that Paul is describing God's activity in Christ by making the focus of that activity the life of the apostle himself. In the apostle is the manifestation of God's activity.[31]

For it is Christ whom Paul imitates (I Cor. 11:1), the suffering of Christ which Paul shares (II Cor. 1:5), and the power of Christ which rests upon him in that weakness (II Cor. 12:9).

Finally, although Paul himself does not highlight them, the coherence between the two images in 2:14 and 15 is supported by the inner connections which exist between the two motifs themselves. As we saw in chapter one, the triumphal procession was itself an act of worship through which the benevolence of the deity was glorified and revealed. Moreover, the captives who are led to death in the procession were intricately linked to the sacrifices which played such an integral role in the celebration. The thoroughly religious nature of the triumphal procession thus provided a conceptual basis for an association of the two motifs. And, as we will see below, the act of being rescued from this death in the triumphal procession as an act of grace by the emperor also seems to picture an essential aspect of Paul's own understanding of how God's glory and power are manifested through his suffering. Furthermore, Paul's understanding of himself as the conquered slave of Christ

---

31. Schütz, *Anatomy of Apostolic Authority,* 210-211.

implicit in the triumphal procession imagery in 2:14 is surely the counterpart to his understanding of himself as one who now labors and lives only by God's grace or the life of Christ in him (cf. I Cor. 15:10; Gal. 2:20). Hence, in his life as an apostle he becomes the "fragrance of Christ," i.e., what he accomplishes *and suffers* (!) (see Phil. 3:10) is an outworking of the grace of God on his behalf. Unfortunately, it is not possible to go beyond these general observations in determining the implicit link which Paul had in mind and which led him to wed these two images together. For as we have already seen, the only explicit point of contact is the *revelatory function* which Paul himself performs as *both* the captive and the sacrificial aroma in these two metaphors.

4. The Significance of the Parallel between II Cor. 2:14-16a and I Cor. 1:17-18.

The interrelationship between Paul's experience as an apostle *under the cross* and his apostolic message *of the cross*, which, as we saw above, comes to light in the transition from 2:14-16a to 2:17, is also made evident by the "well-known parallels" which exist between I Cor. 1:17f. and II Cor. 2:14-16a.[32] For in I Cor. 1:17 Paul explains the goal of his having been sent by Christ to preach the gospel "not with eloquent wisdom" in terms of a negative purpose, namely, "in order that the cross of Christ might not be emptied." He then proceeds in v. 18 to support this purpose by providing the rationale behind his mandate from Christ to conform the mode of his message to the content of the message itself (cf. I Cor. 2:1-5): Even Paul's manner of preaching must conform to the cross since it is specifically the *cross* of Christ which is the power of God.

Thus, when we compare I Cor. 1:17f. to II Cor. 2:15-16a three important results follow. First, it becomes clear that Paul considered both the style of his proclamation, as well as that of his life, to be

32. So Eicholz, *Theologie des Paulus,* 58, though he takes both passages as referring to the preaching of the gospel. Cf. also Schlatter, *An die Korinther,* 497 and Windisch, *Zweiter Korintherbrief,* 99. But although all notice the parallel between the *apollumenois . . . sōzomenois* complex, they do not mention the parallels between I Cor. 1:17-18a and II Cor. 2:14-15a.

determined by the cross and not vice versa (I Cor. 1:17 and II Cor. 2:14, cf. I Cor. 2:1, 4, 5). For as U. Luz has pointed out, "the Pauline theology of the cross . . . cannot be separated from the characteristic essence of the apostle itself. . . . There is no indication in Paul that his theology of the cross was a product, or in the same way a projection, of his sufferings."[33] Second, Paul's rationale for this, in *both* cases, resided in the fact that it was the cross which provided the foundation and content of his apostolic preaching and existence (cf. the "for" [*gar*] in I Cor. 1:18a and the "because" [*hoti*] in II Cor. 2:15a). Finally, the "horrifying truth,"[34] which for Paul undergirded both the message and existence of the apostle, was the function his ministry played in furthering the process either of one's salvation (life), or of one's damnation (death; I Cor. 1:18bc and II Cor. 2:15b-16a). For whether one thinks that the "from . . . to" structure in 2:16 refers to the Pauline concept of predestination or not,[35] what is clear in *both* contexts is that for Paul one's eschatalogical fate was already being realized. To reject Paul's message of the cross as foolishness, or to be offended by his personal "sacrificial aroma of Christ" was, for Paul, a confirmation that one was already perishing. Conversely, to accept Paul and his message was a demonstration that the power of God (I Cor. 1:18c) was already at work within (and without, cf. Rom. 8:28-39) to save.[36] Finally, and most significant for our study, a comparison of II Cor. 2:14-16a with I Cor. 1:17f. makes particularly clear that everything Paul could say

---

33. U. Luz, "Theologica crucis," 128.

34. Barrett's appropriate response to 2:16 in *Second Corinthians,* 102.

35. For examples of those who do see a reference to predestination in 2:15-16a, cf. Schlatter, *An die Korinther,* 497; Windisch, *Zweiter Korintherbrief,* 99; and Wendland, *An die Korinther,* 176. Against this view, see Bartling, "God's Triumphant Captive," 890-891; Lietzmann, *An die Korinther,* 109; Hughes, *Second Corinthians,* 81 n. 18; and Kümmel's additions to Lietzmann, p. 198. Bultmann, *Zweiter Korintherbrief,* 71, takes a mediating position, denying the sense of predestination to the construction itself, but granting it to the participles. In my opinion this text does not address the question of predestination at all, but rather simply assumes the already existing states as such. The fact that predestination is, nevertheless, a Pauline concept (contra Bartling) seems clear (cf. Rom. 8:29; 9:11f., 16f.).

36. Moreover, as Bartling has correctly pointed out, the chiastic structure of 2:15-16a (ABBA) places the emphasis on *life* as that result of Paul's ministry which was intended to be stressed.

about the message of the cross which he preached, he could also say about his *experience or way of life* as the apostolic slave of Christ who was "being led to death."[37] The parallels between I Cor. 1:17-18 and II Cor. 2:14-16a may thus be represented as follows.

I Cor. 1:17f.	**II Cor. 2:14-16a**
1. Paul is sent to preach in a mode which corresponds to the cross of Christ (1:17, cf. 2:1, 4).	1. Paul is "being led to death," which is a mode of existence that reveals the cross of Christ (2:14).
2. For *(gar)* (18a)	2. For *(hoti)* (15a)
3. the word of the cross	3. we are an aroma of Christ to God (15a)
4. is foolishness to those who are perishing (18b)	4. among those who are perishing . . . to those a fragrance from death to death (15c, 16a)
5. to us who are being saved it is the power of God (18c).	5. among those who are being saved . . . to those a fragrance from life to life (15b, 16a).

A study of II Cor. 2:14-16a has thus led to the conclusion that Paul understood his own experience of being "led to death" as an apostle to be the "flip side" of his apostolic mandate to preach the word of the cross.[38] The question that remains to be answered, however, is *how*

37. Unfortunately, this point is often missed by commentators because they make the subtle shift of substituting Paul's proclamation of the gospel, which is not introduced until 2:17, for Paul himself as the subject and object of 2:14-16a. Cf., e.g., Schelkle, *Zweiter Korintherbrief,* 59; Eichholz, *Theologie des Paulus,* 58; Wendland, *An die Korinther,* 176; Käsemann, "Heilsbedeutung," 91; and, most recently, McDonald "Paul and the Preaching Ministry," 42ff. But, as we shall see below, Paul's life as an apostle itself does function as evidence for the truth of the gospel on the one hand (contra Käsemann), while the focus of Paul's attention throughout this section is on his own apostolic lifestyle as an essential aspect of his ministry of the gospel (cf. Phil. 1:20).

38. This conclusion corresponds to the central point of Güttgemanns, *Der leidende Apostel,* but is not an endorsement of his entire program. For example, Güttgemanns links Paul's view of his suffering to a reconstruction of Paul's opponents as Jewish-Christian Gnostics, which need not be the case (cf. pp. 97ff.). For his main point, however, with which I am in basic agreement, i.e., that Paul's

Paul's "being led to death" actually functioned, in his view, to reveal the knowledge of God. In order to answer this question we must place II Cor. 2:14-16a within the context of the Corinthian correspondence as a whole. By doing so, we will, at the same time, further confirm our exegetical hypothesis concerning the meaning of II Cor. 2:14a and our interpretation of 2:14-16a in general.

B. THE APOSTOLIC "SENTENCE OF DEATH" IN THE CORINTHIAN CORRESPONDENCE

Once II Cor. 2:14-16a is recognized to be a statement of Paul's apostolic role in the salvific plan of God as the one who is "lead to death," its place within the Corinthian correspondence as a whole becomes clear. Read in this way, II Cor. 2:14a functions as one of four thesis-like summaries of Paul's understanding of the significance of his suffering as an apostle, a significance which is otherwise expressed in the so-called "tribulation lists" found in I Cor. 4:8-13, II Cor. 4:7-15, 6:1-10, and 11:16–12:10.[39]

1. I Cor. 4:8-13

It has long been recognized that I Cor. 1:10–4:21 is the *locus classicus* for the development of the Pauline theology of the cross. But as Nils Dahl has so clearly pointed out, Paul's *theologia crucis* actually serves a penultimate purpose within I Cor. 1–4. For as Dahl observed, it is rather the nature of Paul's apostleship and his relationship to the church at Corinth, and not the meaning and significance of the cross in and of

---

suffering is an "epiphanie of the Lord," cf. pp. 111 n. 100; 112-124, esp. 116-119, 123-124; 134; 140f.; 153; 195f.

39. Paul's view of his suffering as expressed in these catalogs has been the subject of intensive study in the last twenty years. Cf. Güttgemanns, *Der leidende Apostel*, esp. 94-198, 304-328; Schrage, "Leide, Kreuz und Eschaton"; Schütz, *Anatomy of Apostolic Authority*, 165-248; Hodgson, "Paul the Apostle"; and now Kleinknecht, *Der leidende Gerechtfertigte*, 208-304.

itself, which occupies all the important points of transition in 1:10–4:21 (i.e., 1:13-17; 2:1-5; 3:1-2; 3:10-11; 4:3-4) and which serves, therefore, as the focal point and key for understanding the structure of the entire argument.[40]

a. The Purpose of I Cor. 1–4

Given Dahl's insight, the primary purpose of I Cor. 1:10–4:21 is not to provide a theological reflection on the meaning and significance of the crucifixion. Rather, it is to reassert the authority of Paul as the founder and spiritual father of the *entire* church at Corinth (cf. 4:14-17), while at the same time preparing for the answers to be given to the Corinthians' questions in the rest of the letter by indicating the *theological criterion* which determines both the nature of Paul's apostleship (cf. 1:17-19) and his evaluation of the church's problems (cf. 3:1-4).[41] In other words, I Cor. 1–4 is best understood as an "apology for the Pauline apostolate,"[42] which finds its focal point in Paul's own theological understanding of the significance of the cross, first for his own ministry, and then, by extension, for the life of the Corinthian church in general (cf. 4:16).

The point of the apology in I Cor. 1–4, however, is *not* to re-establish Paul's authority per se, but rather to reassert that the authority of Paul, which is still recognized by some, or perhaps even by most of the Corinthians (cf. 1:12; 3:4f.), ought to be maintained as the *foundation* for the *entire* church. Hence, the work of the other "guides" (4:15) must be measured by the character and message of Paul and not vice versa (cf. 3:10-15)—i.e., by the cross. At this point the problem in Corinth was not that Paul's authority was no longer being accepted, but that the Corinthians had forgotten that his was the *primary* authority

40. Dahl, "Paul and the Church at Corinth," 320-321.

41. This is my own expansion and reworking of the main point of Dahl's article (see previous note), pp. 333-334, which I take to be sound. For if "Christ crucified" was the heart of Paul's Christology, then it is only natural that this would become the criterion for Paul's own apostleship and the basis for his evaluation of the problems he encountered.

42. So Vielhauer, "Paulus und die Kephaspartei," 171. Dahl, "Paul and the Church at Corinth," 317, makes this same point.

to be followed. Hence, the focus of the argument in I Cor. 1–4 is not to justify Paul's apostleship, but to correct the Corinthians' attitudes and behavior. This can be seen in the fact that the contrast between wisdom and the cross first introduced in 1:18-19 to support the nature of *Paul's* apostolic preaching is then reintroduced in 2:1f., together with a description of Paul's appearance in Corinth in 2:3f., to support Paul's intention for the *Corinthians,* namely, "in order that your faith might not be in the wisdom of men but in the power of God" (2:5). Conversely, the contrast between wisdom and the cross first "verified empirically," i.e., "by the sociological structure of the community" itself in 1:26-31[43] is then verified on the basis of the *apostolic* experience in 4:8-13, the "summarizing high point of the first four chapters of I Corinthians."[44] As a result, the interplay between Paul's theology of the cross and its significance for his ministry and the life of the Corinthian church is expressed in a chiastic structure (ABBA) which once again serves to emphasize the foundational and paradigmatic role of Paul's apostleship (cf. I Cor. 1:23f.; 2:1f.; 3:6, 10f; 4:1, 16):

(A) The Nature of Paul's Ministry (1:17, 2:3f.)	SUPPORTED BY	The Theology of the Cross (1:18-19)
(B) The Life of the Church (1:26–3:1)	SUPPORTED BY	The Theology of the Cross (1:21-25)
(B) The Life of the Church (2:5–4:5)	SUPPORTED BY	The Theology of the Cross (2:1f.)
(A) The Nature of Paul's Ministry (4:8-13)	SUPPORTED BY	The Theology of the Cross (4:6a)[45]

Having thus determined the overall structure of Paul's argument in I Cor. 1–4, we can now turn our attention to the meaning of 4:8-13 and its relationship to II Cor. 2:14-16a.

---

43. The idea that 1:26-31 is an empirical verification of 1:18-25 I owe to Kleinknecht, *Der leidende Gerectfertigte,* 210. Kleinknecht does not make the connection, however, between 1:26-31 and 4:8-13.

44. Kleinknecht, *Der leidende Gerechtfertigte,* 222.

45. For an explanation of 4:6a as a reference to the theology of the cross, see below, p. 59 nn. 52-53.

b. The Meaning of I Cor. 4:8-13 and its Relationship to I Cor. 2:14-16a

As Kleinknecht has already argued, I Cor. 4:8-13 is the "high point" or climax of chapters 1–4. More specifically, the description of the apostolic experience in 4:8-13 functions as the final step in Paul's argument against the Corinthians' propensity to boast "in men" (3:21; cf. 1:29, 31; 3:18-20; 4:6), which Paul saw to be the basic problem lying behind the dissensions (1:10), quarreling (1:11, cf. 3:3) and jealousy (3:3) which were threatening to split the church. This boasting had recently manifested itself in the form of a party-spirit (1:12f.; 3:4) which was based on the Corinthians' inflated view of their own spiritual wisdom (3:1-4, 18; 4:18f.) as a result of their over-realized eschatology (4:8).

To counter this trend, Paul had already pointed to the message of the cross (1:17-19; 2:1-5) and to the nature of the Corinthians themselves (2:26-31) as a demonstration of the fact that "God chose what is foolish in the world to shame the wise and what is weak in the world to shame the strong; i.e., God chose what is low and despised in the world, even things that are not, to bring to nothing things that are, so that no human being might boast in the presence of God" (1:27-29), neither in one's own particular spiritual gifts (1:7; 3:18; 4:7), nor in one's own particular spiritual leaders (3:7, 21f.; 4:1). That the problem of the party-spirit in Corinth was closely related to their boasting in their spiritual gifts and/or spiritual leaders is also evident when the thesis statements of 1:7 and 4:7 are brought to bear on Paul's discussion in chapters 12–14. For if, on the one hand, the opposite of boasting in one's own particular leaders is to be "united in the *same* mind and the *same* judgment" (1:10), the opposite of boasting in one's own particular gifts is the recognition that "to each is given the manifestation of the Spirit for the *common good*" (12:7, cf. 12:21-26). This ability to use one's gifts as a member of the *one* body of Christ for the *other's* good is then, in a word, love, which *by definition* is "not boastful . . . not arrogant . . . does not insist on its own way" (13:4).

Finally, in support of his disavowal of the Corinthians' attitudes and in direct opposition to their mistaken eschatology, Paul then concludes his argument by comparing the Corinthians to the "apostles" themselves in I Cor. 4:8-13. The point of Paul's comparison is clear. In contrast to the Corinthians, who consider themselves to be filled, rich, and reigning with Christ already (4:8), stands the apostle "sentenced to death" (4:9). If they are "wise," Paul is a "fool"; if they are "strong," Paul is "weak"; if they are "held in honor," Paul is "despised" (4:10).

But the significance of Paul's comparison in I Cor. 4 only becomes clear in the light of his earlier statements in 2:1-5. For there Paul has called attention to the fact that his decision to preach only "Jesus Christ and him crucified" was confirmed and supported not only by the way he preached (cf. vv. 1, 4), but also by his very *mode of appearance* in Corinth itself, i.e., by the fact that he had come to Corinth "in weakness and in fear and in much trembling" (v. 3). As "the corollary of his knowing only Christ crucified,"[46] Paul's weakness in appearance, together with his refusal to preach "in persuasive words of wisdom" (v. 4), had worked to ensure that the faith of the Corinthians "might not be in the wisdom of men, but in the power of God" (v. 5). Against this background, I Cor. 4:8-13 functions as the needed explanation of *how* it is that Paul's "weakness," in its various expressions, actually functions to support his message of the cross. In so doing it not only completes the thought of I Cor. 2:1-5, but of II Cor. 2:14-16 as well.

Paul's answer to this question is twofold. First, the very fact itself that the apostolic life is characterized by weakness is an indication that the eschaton has *not yet* arrived in its fullness, but that the power of God, once displayed in the cross, is still to be found *in the midst* of the suffering of this world.[47] At the same time, however, the kingdom of God *has* come "in power" (cf. I Cor. 2:4; 4:20). Hence, Paul's own "sentence to death" (4:9) not only corresponds to his preaching of the

46. Schütz, *Anatomy of Apostolic Authority,* 202. Cf. also Ellis, "Christ Crucified," 70-71, who argues that "Christ crucified" "refers primarily to the exalted Lord who, in his exaltation, remains the crucified one." As a result, the cross of Christ can be equated with God's power so that the weakness of Paul becomes "the ethical corollary, and indeed the proof, of the wisdom 'that is from God.' "

47. So also Bornkamm, *Paul,* 161, who in commenting on I Cor. 4:9-13 writes, "For Paul apostleship meant being branded by the 'word of the cross' and *not yet* being delivered from the hardships of daily life and death."

cross as its verification, but also functions through Paul's *positive responses and acceptance* of the suffering which he must undergo "as the scum of the world" and "the dregs of all things" (4:13) to affirm and in this way to proclaim his message of the cross. For since the call to suffer in this way implies a corresponding rejection of the "wisdom of men" (2:5), the fact that Paul responds *positively* to this suffering thus testifies to the power and wisdom of God which have been displayed in the cross (1:18, 24). In this way God has made the wisdom of the world foolish (1:20), both through the cross itself and through the life of his apostle. Paul not only proclaims the message of the cross (1:18, 21, 23, 25) and experiences the corresponding suffering of this world (4:9), but he also becomes himself "a fool for Christ's sake" (4:10) in his acceptance of that suffering in the positive endurance of faith (4:11-13a; 2:5).

For Paul, therefore, his suffering is not mere circumstance, nor simply fate, but an integral part of God's plan to "destroy the wisdom of the wise" (1:19), on the one hand, and to exhibit the power of God in the cross, on the other. It is this divine intention which is then expressed in I Cor. 4:8-13, specifically in 4:9, which, as the central assertion of the passage, functions to support Paul's critique of the Corinthians' attitudes described in 4:8. Verses 10-13 then provide a further explication of 4:9 by spelling out *what* Paul's "sentence to death" consists of (namely, his suffering as an apostle) and *how* God's power is actually made known through it (i.e., through Paul's acceptance and positive response to his suffering).

It is thus especially instructive for our study, and by no means coincidental, that Paul's *central point* in I Cor. 4:9 forms an exact parallel to Paul's statement in II Cor. 2:14:[48]

---

48. To my knowledge, the similarity between I Cor. 4:9 and II Cor. 2:14 has been noticed in the past only by Hughes, *Second Corinthians,* 78 n. 10, and Schütz, *Anatomy of Apostolic Authority,* 247. But because both scholars have not seen the full implication of the triumphal procession imagery in II Cor. 2:14, the parallel itself has not been noticed, though Schütz's comment is especially insightful: "This parallelism of Paul's 'making manifest' what the gospel also makes manifest is hinted at in II Cor. 2:14 and made explicit by the unusual language in I Cor. 4:8ff." As we have seen, however, this idea is much more than hinted at in 2:14!

I Cor. 4:9	**II Cor. 2:14**
1. God	1. Thanks be to God
2. exhibited last as sentenced to death	2. who leads to death in the triumphal procession
3. us apostles	3. us in Christ
4. because we became a spectacle	4. and through us reveals the fragrance of the knowledge of him
5. to the world, that is, to angels and to men.	5. in every place.

In both passages God is the author of the "death sentence." And in both contexts the apostles are the objects of God's activity. In I Cor. 4:9 God exhibits/displays[49] the apostles last of all like men sentenced to death in the arena,[50] while in II Cor. 2:14 God leads the apostle like one sentenced to death by his captors. Finally, the reason for Paul's vivid imagery in I Cor. 4:9 is to illustrate the fact that the apostles have become a "spectacle" to the whole world, to angels and to men.[51] Similarly, God's purpose in leading the apostle to death in II Cor. 2:14 is to reveal himself in every place. Thus, in both passages, the role of the apostle is characterized by "death," a death which reveals the knowledge of God.

The parallels between II Cor. 2:14-16a and I Cor. 1:10–4:13, especially 1:17f. and 4:8-13, make it clear, therefore, that for Paul the "knowledge of God" to be revealed in the apostolic ministry is the

49. Bauer, *Lexicon* (1979²), 89, even translates *apedeixen* in I Cor. 4:9, "he has made, or exhibited us (as) the last ones perh. in a triumphal procession."

50. On the phrase "as sentenced to death" as a reference to those "wretches" brought on to die at the close of a display in the arena, cf. Barrett, *First Corinthians*, 110-111; Hughes, *Second Corinthians*, 143; Conzelmann, *Erster Korintherbrief*, 115, 116 n. 39, who interprets it to mean "condemned to death" so that the image is that of "the Roman theatre performance of those condemned to death." Baumert, *Täglich Sterben*, 196, connects this imagery with the rest of the Pauline corpus, i.e., with I Cor. 15:32; Gal. 2:19; Rom. 8:17; Phil. 3:10; II Cor. 1:5.

51. For the Roman custom of using prisoners as a "spectacle" to show off the glory of the conqueror by "displaying" them in various ways in the arena, a display which usually ended in the death of the captives, cf. Josephus, *Jewish War*, VII.23-24, 38-40, 96.

power and wisdom of God found in the cross, while the way in which it is revealed is not limited to the apostolic preaching, but also includes the apostles' own "sentence of death." Finally, I Cor. 4:8-13 also makes it clear that Paul's "sentence of death" (I Cor. 4:9; II Cor. 2:14) refers specifically to the *suffering* which he is called to endure as an apostle to the crucified Christ (cf. 4:12). Paul's ability to speak of his suffering as "death" is also confirmed by I Cor. 15:30-32, where in reflection on his "peril every hour" he can exclaim, "I die every day!" And Kleinknecht's recent study[52] has demonstrated that in Paul's conception, the experience of the apostle, pictured in terms of the suffering righteous of the Bible, functioned as a demonstration of the fact that God's righteousness, and hence his power (cf. Rom. 1:16f.), is displayed in the lives of those who, like God's son, suffer at the hands of the world. Paul's suffering in I Cor. 1–4 is therefore both a confirmation (I Cor. 2:1-5) and display (I Cor. 4:9) of the meaning of the cross. "Paul was convinced that he presented men with Christ crucified both in the gospel he preached and in his own life."[53]

2. II Cor. 4:7-12

a. The New Situation behind II Corinthians

As we have seen, Paul's suffering as an apostle functioned in I Cor. 1–4 both as a warning to the Corinthians not to "boast" in anything other than the cross of Christ as the source of their spiritual power and wisdom (1:24) and as a critique of the eschatology upon which this false boasting was based. What remains to be made explicit, however, is that the strength of Paul's entire argument in I Cor. 1–4 rests in the fact that, although a "myriad of guides" now existed in Corinth, Paul's own authority as their "spiritual father" nevertheless still remained basically intact, though perhaps it was now being rejected by some as relevant for the *entire* church (cf. I Cor. 4:14-16). This point is supported not only by I Cor. 4:17, but also by the fact that Paul himself

52. See Kleinknecht, *Der leidende Gerechtfertigte,* 193ff.
53. Bornkamm, *Paul,* 171.

remains the object of one of the factions (cf. 1:12f.; 3:4, 21). Moreover, the tone and purpose of the rest of the letter, i.e., to answer the Corinthians' questions and straighten out their misunderstandings, are also predicated on this assumption. Thus, for example, 7:12, 25 assume that Paul's commands will be considered authoritative without further justification. It is this presupposition that allows Paul to assume in I Corinthians that his suffering and weakness as an apostle, the very suffering and weakness that marked Paul's ministry when the church was founded (cf. 2:1-5), could also be appealed to as that characteristic of an apostle which was accepted as genuine and true by both Paul and the Corinthians. For without this common ground, Paul's argument, both in structure and content, collapses.

There is no indication in I Cor. 1:10–4:21 that Paul's suffering was being rejected by the Corinthians as illegitimate *for Paul as an apostle*, though certain members of the church may have been critical of Paul for other reasons (see I Cor. 4:3-5, 18-21). Rather, Paul seems to have been confronted with the opposite problem. Although *Paul's* suffering had always been accepted as legitimate, some of the Corinthians had nevertheless recently been persuaded, most likely on the basis of a misunderstanding of Paul's own teaching,[54] that Paul's life under the cross no longer applied to them! At the same time, on the basis of I Cor. 4:18-21 (cf. 5:3f.), the objection was also being raised by some that although Paul was the founder of the church at Corinth, his absence now meant that his authority was no longer valid for the entire church, but only for those whom he personally had won to the Lord. As for the rest, they owed their allegiance to their own particular "guides."

In response, the purpose of Paul's argument in I Cor. 1–4 is twofold: to "remind" the Corinthians of "his ways in Christ" (4:17),[55]

---

54. Following Conzelmann, *Erster Korintherbrief,* 34.

55. Schütz, *Anatomy of Apostolic Authority,* 209f., argues convincingly on the basis of the transition in v. 14 and the use of "way" (*hodos*) in the LXX in a figurative sense that Paul's "ways" in I Cor. 4:17 refer not to his travel plans but to his conduct in 4:9-13: "It is not impossible that his 'ways' are both taught and illustrated by his life . . . so we should probably connect *hodoi* with vv. 9-13 and assume that his example there is also what he 'teaches.'" In order to stress this unity, I have consciously chosen to translate Paul's "ways" in 4:17 in my discussion with a collective singular, since his teaching and his apostolic lifestyle are, in reality, one "way," the way of the cross.

and, in so doing, to call their attention to the fact that as their "father in Christ Jesus through the Gospel" (4:15), it is *his* "way," i.e., the way of the cross, that is to be imitated (4:16, cf. 11:1).[56] The appropriateness of Paul's apostolic suffering, in and of itself, is thus nowhere defended, but is *itself* the foundational premise for his argument, based, as it is, on his parental relationship to the Corinthian church. For if suffering and weakness are the essential characteristics of the apostolic ministry, upon which the Corinthians' very lives as Christians were based, then as children of their spiritual father, their lives also ought to be characterized by the power of the cross, and not by boasting in their own spiritual attainments or leaders. The significance of the cross for Paul's life as an apostle was therefore not in question—though its significance for his church was. Hence, Paul could simply respond, "Be imitators of me" (4:16).

It is beyond the scope of this study to develop this point further. Nevertheless, it should be pointed out that Paul's apostolic experience in I Cor. 4:8ff., which provides an essential part of Paul's "ways" in Christ and, as such, also forms the backdrop to Paul's command in 4:16 that the Corinthians become imitators of Paul, does not seem to be intended to be the basis for a command or call to suffering itself. Rather, Paul's apostolic experience in I Cor. 4:8ff. is intended to support Paul's emphasis throughout chapters 1–4 on the *attitude* towards one's experience as a Christian which is appropriate this side of the parousia. The problem in Corinth was not that the Corinthians were not suffering enough (!), but that they were using their spiritual experiences as a ground for boasting in themselves, as if everything they had were not a gift (cf. I Cor. 4:7). As a result, it is not entirely correct to interpret the reality of the present participation in Christ's resurrection life *only* in terms of actualizing the crucifixion (so Ellis, "Christ Crucified," 74), or to understand Paul's paradigmatic function in I Cor. 4 as implying that his experience of suffering is "the *only* way (power) can be appropriated before the end," (as Schütz, *Anatomy of Apostolic Authority,* 203, concludes), nor does it seem appropriate to describe the glory of the Church as exclusively "veiled," (as Dahl, "Paul and the Church," 332, posits), or to select suffering as "the . . . necessary consequence" for both the life of the apostle and the life of the church "in the same way" (so Kleinknecht, *Der leidende Gerechtfertigte,* 196-197). For there is no "martyr-theology" hidden within Paul's application of the theology of the cross to the life of the Church,

56. Again see Schütz, *Anatomy of Apostolic Authority,* 210: "His ways in Christ are to be their ways in Christ."

such as we find a generation later in the writing of Ignatius (cf. his *Romans* IV-VII, in which he interprets his suffering in the Pauline categories of I Cor. 15:32 and 4:4, while at the same time using them to express part of his longing for martyrdom).

By the time II Corinthians was written, however, the situation had changed. As a result of the influence of some of Paul's opponents, who had recently arrived,[57] the Corinthians had now taken the additional step of rejecting the nature, and hence, authority, of Paul's apostleship itself. In turn, the purpose of the tribulation lists in II Corinthians has also changed. Rather than functioning as a warning to the Corinthians, Paul's catalogs of sufferings now form an essential part of his *self-defense* as an apostle. For the meaning and necessity of Paul's suffering as an apostle are no longer common ground between Paul and his church, but are the very points of contention in the Corinthians' growing distrust of the legitimacy of Paul's apostolic claim. This becomes evident when we compare I Cor. 4:8-13 to II Cor. 4:7-12.

b. The Two Essential Differences between I Cor. 4:8-13 and II Cor. 4:7-12

The first thing that strikes one's attention in reading II Cor. 4:7-12 is its remarkable similarities to I Cor. 4:8-13. As in I Cor. 4:8ff., here too Paul's point is that the power of God (cf. I Cor. 1:18, 24; 2:5 and II Cor. 4:7) is made known *through or by means of* the adversative relationship expressed in the apostolic experience of suffering, with its various manifestations (compare I Cor. 4:12f. with II Cor. 4:8-9). Moreover, in both passages Paul portrays his apostolic suffering as a divinely-orchestrated "death" which performs a revelatory function (compare I Cor. 4:9 and Paul's use of "to reveal, make known" in II Cor. 4:10-11). Finally, in both cases, not only the texts themselves, but also

---

57. Although Dahl's observation ("Paul and the Church at Corinth," 316-317) that "no clarity has been reached with regard to the relation between the situation reflected in I Corinthians and in 2 Corinthians" is still true (cf. Conzelmann, *Erster Korintherbrief*, 32), there is now almost universal agreement that the situation reflected in II Corinthians is a result of the opponents who figure so predominantly in chs. 10–13.

the wider context make it clear that Paul pictures this suffering in terms of the biblical tradition of the suffering of the righteous; in the case of I Cor. 4:8-13 by the four Scripture quotations in I Cor. 1:19, 31; 2:9; and 3:19f., and in the present context by the reference to Psalm 116 (LXX 114-115) in II Cor. 4:13.[58]

But once these parallels have been noted, the two essential differences between the texts become apparent. First, the *purpose* of Paul's argument has changed, as evidenced by the corresponding change in focus. In I Cor. 4 not only the larger context (cf. vv. 7f., 14), but also the comparison which stood at the heart of the "catalog" itself (see v. 10), made it clear that Paul's primary purpose was *hortatory,* since his attention was focused on the Corinthians. In contrast, that Paul's attention in II Cor. 4:7ff. is focused on himself indicates that his primary purpose is now clearly *apologetic.* Instead of establishing a comparison between Paul and his readers, II Cor. 4:7-12 is an explanation of *why* the glory of Paul's ministry of the new covenant, a glory which is so exceeding in its magnitude (cf. 3:7-11), *must,* nevertheless, be contained in "earthen vessels," i.e., in "his weak, frail body."[59]

Second, the *context* within which Paul interprets his suffering has also significantly changed. In contrast to I Cor. 1:1–4:13, where Paul's apostolic ministry of suffering was the means by which the wisdom and power of God *in the cross* (1:24; 2:5, 6-16) was both attested (1:17f.; 2:1-5) and made known (cf. 4:9-13), in II Cor. 2:14–4:6 Paul's ministry of suffering now functions to attest (4:7) and reveal (4:11) "the knowledge of the *glory of God in the face of Christ*" (4:6; cf. 3:18; 4:4f.). Thus, instead of Paul's "sentence to death" being linked to the

58. For the influence of Ps. 116 on II Cor. 4:13 and an analysis of the traditions behind II Cor. 4:7-18 as a whole, see Kleinknecht, *Der leidende Gerechtfertigt,* 257-263.

59. Brun, "Auslegung," 212. This does not mean, however, the "body" in contrast to the soul, but the person as bearer of the message; cf. Schrage, "Leid, Kreuz und Eschaton," 151 n. 28; Maurer, σκεῦος, 358-367, esp. 359. For the opposing position, cf. Güttgemanns, *Der leidende Apostel,* 115. As Kleinknecht, *Der leidende Gerechtfertigte,* 272, puts it, 4:7ff. functions as the "counterpoint" to the glory of Paul's ministry so that the "treasure" refers to "the ministry itself, which has just shown itself as so 'glorious' " (this is also the view of Bultmann, contra Lietzman and Windisch). That 4:7 is a continuation and extension of the thought of 3:4– 4:6 is also one of the central points made by Baumert, *Täglich Sterben,* 39-40.

death of Christ as its "corollary," Paul now emphasizes that he is being "given up to death" in order that the *life* of Jesus might be manifested or revealed in Paul's mortal flesh (4:11). In short, if Paul's suffering in I Cor. 1–4 was inextricably linked to his "theology of the cross," in II Cor. 2:14–4:12 it is of a piece with his (paradoxical) "theology of glory." As a result, the *symmetry* between Paul's message and his apostolic suffering, which we saw to be at the heart of I Cor. 1–4, has seemingly been replaced by an insoluble *contradiction*. Hence, as a matter of *self*-defense, Paul must now explain what in I Cor. 4:8-13 was taken for granted, namely, why the apostolic treasure can only genuinely be carried in "clay pots." Paul's answer to this question is contained in the three purpose ("in order that") clauses of verses 7b, 10b, and 11b. Of course, the twin emphases of Paul's theology of the cross and theology of glory are not to be seen as contradictory to one another. Paul's whole point in II Corinthians, in fact, is to demonstrate their unity as found in his apostolic ministry. The apparent conflict is rather between his suffering and his theology of glory—Paul's task is therefore to show *how* his apostolic experience of being "led to death" can support *both* his *theologia crucis* and his *theologia gloriae*.

c. The Meaning of II Cor. 4:7-12 and its Relationship to I Cor. 4:8-13 and II Cor. 2:14-16a

II Cor. 4:7-12 is therefore best interpreted as a carefully structured argument designed to elucidate the connection between Paul's suffering and his (paradoxical) "theology of glory." It accomplishes this through an interrelated series of three statements, each of which supports a purpose clause, and which together combine to support the conclusion of verse 12.

As we have already noted, the first statement and its purpose clause in vv. 7-9 repeat the themes familiar to us from I Cor. 4:8-13, though in an entirely different context. For as in I Corinthians, so also in II Cor. 4:7, Paul's suffering, now pictured in terms of the "earthen vessel," functions to call attention to the fact that the power evident in the gospel belongs to God and not to the apostle (cf. I Cor. 1:17; 2:1-5). Now, however, the reference is not to the power of God in the cross, but to the power of God seen in the "face of Christ" (II Cor. 4:6), i.e., to God's glory. According to 4:7, therefore, the treasure is thus carried in a simple pot, *in order that* the "extraordinary quality" of the treasure, i.e., the "power," will in no way be confused with its container, but be recognized for what it is: the power "of God."[60] Consequently, although II Cor. 4:7 restates the same "corollary" or "attesting" function that we saw in I Cor. 1:17f. and 2:1-5, the change in subject matter from the *cross* of Christ to the *glory* of God has significantly altered the *way* in which Paul's suffering attests to his message. In a word, as an earthen vessel, Paul now confirms his message not by being its corollary, but by becoming its *antithesis*.

In a similar way, the eight participles in verses 8 and 9, which are grouped in four pairs, each exhibiting an adversative relationship, all modify the statement of 4:7, thus illustrating the *means by which* Paul's suffering confirms that the glory or (treasure)-power belongs to God. Hence, in terms of function, 4:8 relates to 4:7 in much the same way as I Cor. 4:8-13, especially vv. 11-13, related to I Cor. 2:1-5. But whereas the focus in I Cor. 4:11-13 was on *Paul's* response to his suffering, in II Cor. 4:8 the focus has changed to the ways in which *God* responds to Paul's suffering—namely, by rescuing him again and again from his peril.[61] This means, therefore, that the suffering of the apostle does not serve as a disconfirmation of his ministry, but is rather an integral part of it. For Paul's suffering not only provides the *occasion* for the manifestation of God's power/glory as the one who rescues the apostle from his suffering, but also ensures that the power thus displayed is recognized to be God's alone.

60. Hence the purpose of 4:7 is not to prevent Paul, or the Corinthians for that matter, from boasting, contra Tannehill, *Dying and Rising*, 90. The problem with this view is simply that it is neither Paul's faith nor his own personal struggle not to boast that is in view, but the gospel of the glory of Christ in Paul's ministry. Paul need not be reminded of his weakness—he is weak, that is precisely the problem! Tannehill thus makes the common mistake of reading the different emphasis of I Cor. 4 and II Cor. 12 into II Cor. 4.

61. This essential difference, attested to not only by the passive nature of the passage in general, but also by the widely recognized parallel in II Cor. 1:8-10, has often been observed—cf. most recently, Moxnes, *Theology in Conflict*, 280: "The passage from 1:8-11 with its strictly theological language has a parallel in 4:7-15. With its Christocentric language this paragraph serves almost as an interpretation of the earlier one. . . ."

The second statement[62] in verse 10 is a further interpretation of this basic principle, a principle which plays such a crucial role in the biblical and Jewish tradition of the suffering of the righteous,[63] in terms of the suffering of *the* Righteous One, Jesus. Using the categories of the "death of Jesus" and the "life of Jesus" Paul is thus able to interpret his own experience of being delivered from situations of suffering in terms of the death *and* resurrection of Christ. As John Schütz has observed,

> The point of contact between Christ's death and Paul's weakness is in Paul's suffering. In Phil. 3:10 Paul speaks of the "sufferings of Christ" when he actually refers to Christ's death. The reference to suffering is unusual, for Paul never describes Christ's death as a suffering, nor does he speak of any other sufferings of Christ. Since this connection is made elsewhere only in conjunction with Paul's own sufferings, it must be his device. *In order to understand the death of Christ working in himself Paul connects his death with his sufferings* and then speaks of Christ's sufferings, by which he actually means Christ's death. This is clearly what has happened in II Cor. 1:3ff. . . . *paraklēsis* is an eschato-logical-soteriological term denoting what Paul often calls "life." . . . It is noteworthy here that Paul understands his tribulation/suffering as Christ's suffering (Christ's death) and his comfort as the equivalent of the new life in Christ. *The death and resurrection of Christ inform the life of the apostle with perfect analogies.* The actual specification of tribulation/suffering is given in vv. 8-11. Paul means that his physical hardships and persecutions are to be understood as the equivalent of Christ's weakness (i.e. Christ's death) in this parallelism. This identi-fication is also made in II Cor. 4:7-12.[64]

62. Although syntactically v. 10 is a continuation of the string of participles which modify "we are being delivered over" in v. 7, two factors justify taking it as its own independent statement: (1) the absence of the adversative structure found in the first four pairs and (2) the fact that this verb *(peripherontes)* also supports its own *hina* (purpose) clause in v. 10b.

63. This principle is ably summarized in Ps. 116 (114–115 LXX), where in verses 3f. (LXX 114:3f.) the Psalmist describes being in a situation of death, only to be rescued by the Lord (cf. vv. 6 and 8). The Psalmist's response is therefore to fulfill his "vow" of praise to the Lord (116:14, LXX 115:9), his "sacrifice of praise" (116:17, LXX 115:8; cf. II Cor. 4:15; 1:11!)—which is the intent of the Psalm itself (cf. 116:1, LXX 114:1; 115:1). The parallels to II Cor. 1:8-11 and 4:7-15 are both clear and instructive.

64. Schütz, *Anatomy of Apostolic Authority*, 242-243.

Moreover, that Paul's revelatory role (that of "carrying around the death of Jesus in the body" in order that the life of Jesus might also be revealed in his body) is a *continuous* one taking place in the *present* reflects his conviction that in the death and resurrection of Christ the new age has already begun, though, of course, not in its fullness (cf. II Cor. 4:14).

This Pauline (and early Christian in general) "already-but-not-yet-in-its-fullness" modification of the traditional apocalyptic, two-age conception is, of course, well-known and widely recognized.[65] But it is important to notice that it is precisely this tension between the present and the future in Paul's eschatology which enables him to interpret his *own* suffering and deliverance in terms of the decisive eschatological events of the death and resurrection of Christ. Thus, in Paul's view, because the kingdom is not yet present in its fullness it becomes necessary for him to continue to carry in his body the "death of Jesus." Nevertheless, because the new age has already decisively broken into the present aeon in the resurrection of Christ, it is also possible for Paul's *present* suffering to be at the *same time* a *present* revelation of God's resurrection power, i.e., "the *life* of Jesus." For as II Cor. 1:8-11 illustrates, God's deliverance of Paul from his suffering is intended to be interpreted as an expression of God's ability to raise the dead.

Paul's third statement in v. 11 then provides the theological basis for his interpretation of his apostolic suffering as a mediation of the new age in the midst of the old (v. 10). It is not surprising, therefore, that we encounter in v. 11 the *same* idea that we have already discovered in I Cor. 4:9 and II Cor. 2:14, namely, that Paul's afflictions and persecutions, i.e., his "death," are not mere circumstance, but instead are the outworking of God's plan to spread the gospel. For in II Cor. 4:11 Paul once again asserts, this time through the use of the divine passive "we are being delivered over,"[66] that God himself is the

65. For two classic treatments of this theme, cf. Cullmann, *Christ and Time*, and Ladd, *Presence of the Future*.

66. For other examples of this verb (*paradidōmi*) as a divine passive, cf. Lk. 4:6; Rom. 4:25; and possibly Rom. 6:17. It is also possible that the tradition found in Mt. 17:22 / Mk. 9:31 / Lk. 9:44 and Mt. 20:18 / Mk. 10:33 / Lk. 18:32 ought to be construed as a divine passive, though of course Judas is clearly identified as the one who "hands Jesus over" throughout the synoptic tradition and John. For this

one who has delivered the apostle up to death "for Jesus' sake," in order that the life of Jesus might also be revealed in his mortal body. This is confirmed by a comparison of these three texts, which reveals the following parallels:

II Cor. 4:11a	II Cor. 2:14a	I Cor. 4:9a
1. divine passive	1. Thanks be to God	1. God
2. Constantly (cf. "always" in v. 10a)	2. always	2. (cf. "until the present hour," v. 11 and "until now," v. 13)
3. we the living	3. us	3. us apostles
4. are being handed over to death	4. leads us in a triumphal procession to death	4. exhibited last of all as those sentenced to death
5. on account of Christ	5. in Christ	5. (cf. "on account of Christ," v. 10)

II Cor. 4:11b	II Cor. 2:14b	I Cor. 4:9b
1. in order that the life of Jesus might be revealed	1. and reveals the fragrance of the knowledge of him	1. because we became a spectacle
2. in our mortal flesh	2. through us	2. ———
3. ———	3. in every place	3. to the world, that is, to angels and to men

Hence, Paul's bold assertion that the same eschatological events that took place in the death and resurrection of Christ are now being expressed in his own apostolic ministry (v. 10) is supported and legitimized by the fact that he too, like Jesus, is being "delivered over to

---

verb in the active with God as the subject, cf. Acts 7:42 and its close parallel in Rom. 1:24, 26, 28. Especially instructive is Rom. 8:32, where God is said "to hand over Jesus," while in Gal. 2:20 Jesus gives himself up. Cf. also Eph. 5:2, 25.

death" (v. 11a). For Paul's own suffering and being rescued, first interpreted as an expression of the "death" and "life" of Jesus in his own
body in verse 10, is now given its own independent status as his *own*
death and life in verse 11a. In other words, while in v. 10 Paul merely
"carries" the death of Jesus in his own body, in v. 11a Paul *himself* is the
one who is both living and delivered up to death. Yet, in *both* verses the
purpose remains the same, as is clearly shown by the almost exact
parallels between the two purpose-clauses of vv. 10b and 11b:

v. 10b: in order that the life of Jesus might also be revealed in our
          body
v. 11b: in order that the life of Jesus might also be revealed in our
          mortal flesh

The fact that Paul's own "death" also functions as a revelatory agent
in v. 11a thus does not lead Paul to the conclusion that the "life"
revealed through it is also his own—this remains, of course, the "life
of Jesus."[67] One must be careful, therefore, not to extend the identification between verses 10b and 11b back into verses 10a and 11a. Verses
10a and 11a are parallel, but not identical. Verse 11a must be given its
more usual sense of indicating a ground or support, rather than an
interpretation. Verse 11 is therefore, in this sense, better interpreted as
a restatement of Paul's first assertion in v. 7. Although he is the one
being delivered up to death as an earthen vessel, the life/power revealed
through his suffering belongs to God. Consequently, it must once again
be emphasized that the relationship between Paul's apostolic experience and its result is antithetical. This self-understanding of Paul leads,
then, to the conclusion in verse 12, which in the light of Paul's earlier
argument in I Cor. 4:14-17 is, at first glance, somewhat surprising.

Earlier, Paul's suffering as the *corollary* of the cross was coupled
with the conclusion in I Cor. 4:14-17 that the Corinthians, as his
spiritual children, ought to become "imitators" of Paul (see v. 16). For
in their own apostle the Corinthians could see the embodiment of the

---

67. For the association of the life of Jesus with divine power, i.e., the power
of the resurrection, cf. Rom. 1:4; I Cor. 6:14; II Cor. 13:4; Phil. 3:10, especially the
last two, in which Paul shares in the power of Christ's resurrection. Cf. Tannehill,
Dying and Rising, 85, for these parallels. This then establishes the connection
between the power / resurrection / life of Jesus which links vv. 7 and 11 together.

gospel of the cross and thereby be reminded that their own boast was only in the cross of the Lord, which, in turn, would solve the problem of the party-spirit in the church (cf. 4:6f.).

Now, however, when Paul's apostolic role of suffering is pictured as the *antithesis* of "the glory of God in the face of Christ," Paul goes on to conclude that there is an essential and valid *distinction* between himself, *in his role as an apostle,* and the Corinthians, which is different from the illegitimate and pejorative contrast in I Cor. 4:8ff. (see above). For now the contrast is between the "death" at work in Paul and the "life" at work in the Corinthians. In other words, as a result (cf. v. 12a) of Paul's being led to death in the pattern of Christ, the resurrection power, i.e., the "life of Jesus," is revealed in such a way that those who accept Paul's message and apostleship (cf. I Cor. 1:18 and II Cor. 2:15f.) already begin to experience this "life" in the present (note the present tenses in II Cor. 4:12 and 2:15f.). Paul, however, *as an apostle,* experiences "death" in the present.

This is not to deny, of course, that Paul also experienced the "life of Jesus"—just the opposite is asserted in II Cor. 4:7-11 and 4:16–5:5. Instead, the point to be made is that v. 12 concerns the specific *apostolic* role assigned to Paul over against the Church, and not the general Christian experience. In a *derivative sense,* therefore, it is appropriate to describe Paul's conception of his suffering as being endured *for the sake of* the Corinthians: Paul is delivered over to death, a death which he interprets in terms of the death of Jesus, in order that the Corinthians might experience the "life of Jesus."

Again the parallel to II Cor. 1:3-11 is instructive. Paul had received "the sentence of death" in order that he might trust only in God, who raises the dead (v. 9). Yet, like the Psalmist (see above, n. 63), Paul too was delivered and is thus filled with the hope that God will continue to deliver him in the future (v. 10). God's purpose in establishing this "death" and "resurrection" pattern within Paul's life, however, is not primarily to strengthen Paul's faith, though that too is intended, but rather to provide a basis in Paul's life from which he may "comfort" the Corinthians (cf. vv. 3-5). Thus, Paul understands both his "afflictions" and his "comfort" to be for the Corinthians in order that they might be saved and comforted enough to endure the same sufferings (v. 6).

It is important to note, however, that in II Cor. 1:3ff. the roles are not reversed, which would be expected if Paul conceived of his suffering to be equivalent to that of the Corinthians not only in kind, but also in purpose—especially when Paul's intent is to explain the relationship between the apostle and his church. The relationship between Paul and his church cannot be described as reciprocal when it concerns the apostolic call to share abundantly in the sufferings of Christ (v. 5). As Paul puts it in 4:15: "It is all for your sake, so that as grace extends to more and more people it may increase thanksgiving, to the glory of God" (cf. also 5:13).

Yet here, too, Paul's self-conception remains derivative, since it is *Jesus'* death and resurrection which provide the pattern for Paul's experience, and it is *God's* comfort which is made manifest.[68] Paul's conception of his suffering is therefore derived from his understanding of the nature of Christ's death, but is not intended to be understood as a repetition of it, even in some sort of modified form, that is, as some sort of "second atonement." For both II Cor. 1:3-11 and 4:7-12 demonstrate that Paul conceived of his own "death" as merely a mediation of the significance of the death and life of Jesus. Paul remains, in a word, a "minister" of the new covenant (II Cor. 3:6) whose task is to reveal or mediate the "gospel of the glory of Christ" both in his preaching (2:17; 4:5f.) and in his suffering (2:14; 4:7ff.).

In conclusion, as a minister of the new covenant, Paul stands *between* the death and resurrection of Christ, i.e., the glory of God, and the "life" of his church in the apostolic role of *mediatory agent* (II Cor. 4:12; cf. 3:7-18!).[69] Thus, in the context of the mediation of the "life

---

68. Paul thus derived his apostolic self-conception concerning his suffering from his understanding of the death and resurrection of Christ—*not* from his understanding of the nature of general Christian experience, as Ellis, "II Cor. 5:1- 10," 215-216, and Schütz, *Anatomy of Apostolic Authority,* 245, posit. Ellis does this because he mistakenly applies II Cor. 4:11; Phil. 3:10; and II Cor. 1:5 to *all* Christians and not primarily to Paul as an apostle; while Schütz fails to see that Paul's uniqueness as an apostle includes his call to suffer as well as his commission to preach. For although Schütz is correct in concluding on p. 206 that "Paul does not *repeat* what Christ has done. He *reflects* what Christ has done. In him, the account of that action is made manifest" (cf. p. 230 for the same point), he nevertheless fails to recognize the unique role as *mediatory agent* that Paul does occupy (see below).

69. I have chosen "mediatory agent" to describe the function of Paul's apostolic ministry, instead of the seemingly more appropriate term "mediator," in

of Jesus" / "glory of God in the face of Christ," Paul's apostolic suffering functions as an antitype which cannot, in the strict sense, be imitated, but only accepted or rejected. For Paul's apostolic ministry is now the means *through* which God makes his appeal to the world (cf. 5:20). It is this last point that Paul makes explicit in II Cor. 6:1-10 and chapters 10–13.

3. II Cor. 6:1-10 and 10–13

In II Cor. 5:18 Paul once again asserts that God has entrusted him with his "ministry" (cf. 3:6; 4:1, 6), so that as an "ambassador of Christ" his ministry occupies the mediating role between God and the world (see 5:20).[70] But having done so, Paul must again stress the unique nature of his apostolic experience. Although his appearance as an apostle is certainly not what one might expect of God's ambassador, Paul's point is that it is precisely his weakness and suffering that "commends" him (cf. 6:3f. and 3:1), being both the "corollary" to the cross of Christ and the revelatory "antithesis" to the glory of God in the face of Christ, i.e., to the twin aspects of the gospel which he has just summarized in the classic formulation of 5:14-21. By incorporating the themes of I Cor. 1–4 (see 6:4-8a) *and* those of II Cor. 4:7-12 (see 6:8b-10), II Cor. 6:1-10 thus provides an appropriate capstone for Paul's self-defense as

---

order to avoid confusion with Paul's own statement in Gal. 3:19f. and the christological statements in I Tim. 2:5; Heb. 8:6; 9:15; 12:24. Nevertheless, this is precisely the function whch best captures Paul's ministry as portrayed in II Cor. 2:14ff. By "agent" I thus do not mean someone who arranges something (like a "travel agent"); rather I am using it in the technical sense of "means" or "instrument," i.e., one who acts "as an intermediary agent in bringing, effecting, or communicating"; so *Webster's Seventh New Collegiate Dictionary* under "agent" and "mediate," pp. 17 and 526. For this point see too Beker, who has referred to Paul as "mediator" in his *Paul the Apostle*, 6. But Beker does not develop this notion. Although the noun itself is not used, Paul's role as a mediator is also emphasized strongly by Kamlah, "Wie beurteilt?" 225, who saw Paul's "mediatory role" to be "the key to understanding his apostolic self-consciousness," and most recently see Marshall, "Metaphor," 316, who also takes 2:14 to be "thoroughly consistent" with Paul's self-conception as "the medium of the message."

70. See now Hofius, " 'Gott hat unter uns.' "

an apostle. As K. Prümm so aptly put it, "the section is therefore intended to be read as an apostolic identification card."[71]

Moreover, Paul's self-understanding and interpretation of his weakness as an apostle are once again derived from the biblical tradition of the suffering of the righteous as confirmed and given its decisive formulation by the death of Jesus. For the "strikingly compact reference to the context of deutero-Isaiah,"[72] which already exists in Paul's summary of his ambassadorship and its message in 5:20–6:1, is then made explicit by the quotation in 6:2 from the suffering servant tradition of Isaiah 49:8a.

Now however, since the themes of II Cor. 6:1-10 are already familiar to the Corinthians, it is rather the structure of the passage which serves to highlight Paul's point. Syntactically, the negative disclaimer in v. 3 and the positive catalog of commendation in vv. 4-10 are both participial phrases intended to modify the finite verb "we urge" of v. 1, the only finite verb of the entire section other than the parenthesis of v. 2. The catalog itself is a long list of phrases linked to the participle of v. 4 "commending ourselves" by the prepositions "in" and "through" (vv. 4b-8a) and the comparative participle "as" (vv. 8b-10c). The catalog is thus divided into two main sections. As a result, the argument of 6:1-10 is very compact and abbreviated, forcing the reader to fill in the important logical relationships between the propositions.

The meaning of the first section of the catalog (vv. 4b-8a) further depends on how the punctuation of v. 4 is construed:

> but in everything commending ourselves as servants of God in much endurance in afflictions in hardships in distresses. . . .

Although no less than five different possibilities have been suggested,[73] the central issue is whether the phrase "in much endurance" ought to be

---

71. Prümm, *Diakonia Pneumatos* II/1, 184. Cf. Bornkamm, *Paul*, 169f.

72. Kleinknecht, *Der leidende Gerechtfertigte*, 280. For his discussion of the tradition of the suffering of the righteous which stands behind this passage, see pp. 263-268.

73. The Textus Receptus, Bover (4th ed.), Nestle-Aland (26th ed.), Authorized Version, Revised Version (1881), and the American Standard Version all place a minor stop before and a minor stop after "in much endurance." The Zurich ed. of

considered part of the preceding clause so that the catalog which follows would, in effect, modify the nature of this endurance, or whether the phrase is simply one of the members of the catalog itself, all of which would then directly modify "commending ourselves." In other words, there are two possible ways to construe Paul's thought in v. 4:

1. We commend ourselves in every way as servants of God by means of much endurance; an endurance in the midst of afflictions, hardships, calamities, etc.

2. We commend ourselves in every way as servants of God; namely, in much endurance, in afflictions, hardships, calamities, etc.

But the addition of the adjective "much," which distinguishes the phrase "in much endurance" from the catalog of one-word phrases which follows; the contrast between the positive quality of "endurance" and the list of adverse circumstances in vv. 4b-5, which parallels the concessive relationships established in 8b-10c; and the difficulty of understanding how afflictions, hardships, calamities, etc., in and of themselves serve to commend the apostle, all combine to suggest that the first alternative is preferable (cf. Rom. 5:3f.).

Therefore, according to 6:4-10, the true apostle commends himself (and at the same time disqualifies his opponents) in two ways:

1. *by actively* exhibiting great endurance in the midst of the most adverse circumstances, an endurance which manifests itself in a demonstration of those qualities befitting a servant of God (6:4-8a; i.e., Paul as the "corollary" to his theology of the cross) and

2. *by passively* displaying the power of God as he is delivered by God from his afflictions, so that his "sentence of death" mediates life to the Church (6:8b-10; i.e., Paul as the "antithesis" to his theology of glory).

Consequently, in reading II Cor. 6:1-10 we are again made aware of the fact that the problem which now faced Paul in Corinth was the growing rejection of his authority as an apostle because his suffering

---

Die Heilige Schrift has no punctuation at this point at all, while Westcott and Hort (1881), the RSV, and Luther's Bible place a major stop before and a minor stop after the phrase. The Jerusalem Bible reads only a major stop before the phrase.

seemed to disqualify his claim to be a "minister" as that role was currently being defined by his opponents and accepted by the Corinthians. For although the exact reasons remain unclear, it is nevertheless apparent that the criteria now being accepted in Corinth *excluded* weakness as an appropriate sign of God's commission. This brief look at II Cor. 6:1-10 makes it evident, however, that Paul's response to this criticism is still the same: his suffering is not an obstacle to the gospel, but in fact is an essential part of it. For the *true* apostle verifies (i.e., Paul as "corollary") and reveals (Paul as "antithesis") the gospel of Christ by his suffering. Rather than being a cause for his rejection, it is Paul's weakness *itself* which "commends" him and, by implication, disqualifies his opponents as genuine ministers of Christ.

The new element in 6:1-10 is the note of appeal and urgency which accompanies Paul's description of his apostolic role (cf. 5:20b; 6:1, 11ff.). Paul's conviction that his weakness and afflictions are the true characteristics of the apostolic office and his assurance that God is thus "making his appeal through us" (5:20) carry with them the awareness that to reject his ministry is, in effect, to reject the gospel of Christ as well. Consequently, in Paul's mind, the Corinthians now stand in danger of having "accepted the grace of God in vain" (6:1). Paul's battle for the legitimacy of his apostolic ministry is, in reality, a battle for the truth of the gospel which he bears, and the life of the Corinthians to whom he brought it. This becomes evident in the light of the connection between II Cor. 2:15f.; 6:1; and 13:1-10. Paul's conviction that a person's reaction to his ministry acts to signify and further his or her destiny (2:15f.) leads quite naturally to the entreaties of 6:1 and 13:1-10. As a result, the "test" of faith becomes whether or not the Corinthians will remain loyal to Paul, not because Paul somehow stands independent of or above the gospel, but because he is convinced that he is its true and genuine representative and embodiment. Hence, for Paul, it is not *his* ministry that is presently being called into question, but the genuineness of the faith of the Corinthians themselves.

This explains why Paul's begging the Corinthians to be reconciled to God in 5:20 and his entreating them not to accept the grace of God in vain in 6:1 can become an appeal for the Corinthians to reaffirm their loyalty to him in chapters 10–13 (cf. the same verbs, "entreat" in

10:1 and "beg" in 10:2). Paul's self-identification with his gospel, which was the implicit presupposition behind all three of the previous "catalogs," is now made explicit in chapters 10–13 (cf. 11:1-6). It is a fitting conclusion, therefore, that when forced to boast about the "signs" of his apostleship, Paul does not take refuge in the "signs and wonders and mighty works" which he had performed in Corinth (cf. 12:12), but in those things that show his weakness (cf. 11:30). For like his opponents, Paul too is interested in manifesting the "power of God" in his ministry. But unlike his opponents, Paul is convinced that the same pattern displayed in the Christ who "was crucified because of weakness, but lives because of the power of God" (13:4), is also to be the distinguishing characteristic of his apostles. As he himself puts it,

> Most gladly, therefore, I will rather boast about my weakness, that the power of Christ may dwell in me. Therefore I am well content with weakness, with insults, with distresses, with persecutions, with difficulties, for Christ's sake; for when I am weak, then I am strong. (12:9b-10, NASB)[74]

For as we have seen, part of the "mystery of God" which Paul preached and cared for as its steward (cf. I Cor. 2:1; 4:1) was the revelation that God was making himself known not in the outwardly flamboyant, self-confident display of "spiritual" power so characteristic of the spirituality of the Corinthian church and of the false apostles which they had come to accept, but through the "weakness" and "death" of his genuine apostles. The good news of the revelation of God's power in the deliverance and vindication of those who trust in him in spite of their suffering, first declared in the biblical and post-biblical tradition of the suffering of the righteous, and then proclaimed and embodied in the ministry, death, and resurrection of God's own son, "the Lord of glory" (I Cor. 2:8), was *now* being made known to the world through

---

74. For an outline of the various interpretive possibilities for this text, cf. O'Collins, "Power Made Perfect," 528-530. O'Collins emphasizes that Paul's stress in 12:9f. is on the simultaneity of the weakness and power (cf. I Cor. 2:3f.). Hence, this text also points to the "Christological setting in which Paul sees his ministry" (p. 536). "Far more important than any moral education he undergoes is the fact that his apostolic activity involves participation in the weakness and power of Calvary and Easter" (p. 536).

Paul's "ministry of the new covenant." Thus, as a revelatory agent of the gospel of the power of God, Paul's "sentence to death" could become both his "boast" (II Cor. 12:5, 9) and the ground for his thanksgiving (II Cor. 2:14).

4. Summary

Paul's answer to the question of *how* his "sentence to death" as an apostle, expressed in the parallel statements of I Cor. 4:9; II Cor. 2:14; and II Cor. 4:11, spread the knowledge of God in Christ (and its corresponding implications for the church at Corinth) is now clear. When forced in I Cor. 1–4 to respond to the boasting of the Corinthians, Paul could point to his suffering as an apostle as the necessary *corollary* or *verification* of his gospel of the cross. Here, Paul's acceptance of his suffering, manifested through his endurance of faith, functioned to affirm that the power of God found in the cross was still being made known through and in the midst of the tribulations of this world. Furthermore, by responding *positively* to the suffering he encountered Paul became a "fool for Christ's sake," who, as the spiritual father of the Corinthian church, could urge the Corinthians to "imitate him" in his active affirmation and acceptance of the fact that the *cross* is the power of God. In other words, to imitate Paul was to "boast *only* in the Lord" (1:31), thus becoming a "fool" in the eyes of the world (3:18), since "the Lord of glory" in whom one was to boast was the *crucified* Christ.

On the other hand, when Paul is forced to defend the very nature of his apostolic ministry itself in II Corinthians, he is able to point to his suffering as an apostle as the necessary *antithesis* to his "gospel of the glory of Christ" (II Cor. 4:4). For since the knowledge of God being revealed through the apostles, which was defined as the "*power* of God in the cross" in I Corinthians, was now being defined in II Corinthians in terms of the "*glory* of God in the face of Christ" (4:6, cf. the link to "power" in 4:7), this change in focus necessitated a corresponding change in Paul's depiction of how his suffering revealed God's power.

This new situation in II Corinthians, whether a further development of the old problems or an entirely new constellation, was no doubt instigated by the arrival of Paul's opponents and had as its center of gravity a denial of the legitimacy of Paul's apostleship. It is probable, therefore, that not only the "minister" *(diakonos)*-terminology, but also the "theology of glory" motif itself was originally introduced by Paul's opponents. Nevertheless, Paul does not reject either, but instead strives to show the genuineness of his own ministry using the categories supplied by his opponents.

Hence, although the agenda is set by Paul's opponents, the interpretation of the themes of the true "minister" / "ministry" and of the glory of Christ is Paul's own. Consequently, in response to this new apologetic context, Paul's *active* role in affirming the power of the cross by accepting his suffering in faith is now replaced by his *passive* role in revealing God's glorious power through the rescuing activity of God as manifested again and again in Paul's situations of suffering. Moreover, as the parallels to II Cor. 1:3-11 make clear, Paul's experience in his suffering is now interpreted in terms of the death and resurrection of Jesus himself. Paul's suffering, like the death of Christ, also becomes a platform for the display of God's resurrection power.

Nonetheless, despite the difference in emphasis and in the role which Paul's suffering actually plays, it is Paul's conviction that the new age or "new covenant," which forms the foundation of his thinking in both I and II Corinthians, has already been inaugurated. Thus, whether as the "active corollary" to the cross (I Corinthians) or the "passive antithesis" to the glory of Christ (II Corinthians), Paul understands his role as an apostle to be the mediation of the *power* of the new age in the midst of the old. Paul regards himself as the eschatological and mediatory agent who stands between God in Christ and the Church and who, as the minister of the new covenant (cf. II Cor. 3:6), is entrusted with the task of revealing the gospel of the glory of Christ in his preaching and suffering. As such, Paul's role as an apostle or minister of the new covenant, as this is fulfilled in his apostolic suffering, cannot be imitated, but only accepted or rejected. This is the point of II Cor. 6:1-10 and chapters 10–13.

Finally, this identification of Paul with his gospel creates an urgency in his self-defense which can only be explained by Paul's corresponding conviction that his ministry and gospel were the true and genuine expressions of the death (cross) and resurrection (glory) of Christ. Over against his opponents, in Paul's ministry the cross and glory of Christ do not stand in opposition or exclude one another, but are, in fact, necessitated by each other. That is to say, it is precisely Paul's suffering as an apostle which ties together these two aspects of the proclamation of the gospel of Christ. Hence, as the affirmation of the cross *and* the revelation of God's glory, Paul's suffering, rather than calling into question the legitimacy of his apostolic calling, becomes an essential aspect of his apostolic ministry. It is only natural, therefore, that from Paul's perspective, to reject the nature of his apostolic ministry is to reject the true and only gospel itself and to indicate that one's own eschatological fate has already been determined (cf. II Cor. 2:15f.).[75]

C. CONCLUSION: THE APOSTLE PAUL AS THE MEDIATORY AGENT OF THE GLORY OF GOD

The implications of our study thus far for an understanding of the letter/Spirit contrast in II Cor. 3:6 can now be drawn.

1. The Letter/Spirit Contrast as an Expression of Paul's Apostolic Self-Understanding

Our study has shown that II Cor. 2:14-16a is an essential part of the theme of Paul's weakness as an apostle which runs throughout the Corinthian correspondence. As one of the three thesis-like statements in I and II Corinthians which express the role of Paul's apostolic "sentence to death" in the salvific plan of God (cf. I Cor. 4:9; II Cor. 4:11), II Cor. 2:14-16a thus makes it clear that the context in which the

---

75. This same urgency is also reflected in Gal. 1:6-24, where Paul's need to defend his gospel cannot be separated from his need to defend the genuine nature of his apostleship. Hence, Paul's *first* response to the Galatians' rejection of the gospel (see 1:6-9) is not to defend his message per se, but to defend himself (see 1:10ff.).

letter/Spirit contrast is to be understood is Paul's apostolic *self-conception* as the one who is called to reveal the knowledge of God by means of his suffering. More specifically, the use of the triumphal procession imagery in 2:14 prepares for Paul's thought in 4:7ff. by highlighting the *passive* role of Paul's apostolic agency, inasmuch as the captive "led to death" in the triumphal procession was at times rescued from his fate of death by the grace and power of the conqueror (see above, chapter one, p. 25). Moreover, it also anchors Paul's statement in II Cor. 3:6 within a very specific thematic context in the Corinthian correspondence as a whole. Hence, the introduction of the theme of Paul's suffering in II Cor. 2:14-16a necessitates that we also understand the letter/Spirit contrast as an essential aspect of Paul's apologetic, rather than as a detached and dogmatic theological maxim.

2. The Relationship Between 2:12f. and 2:14-16a

Moreover, once II Cor. 2:14-16a is understood as an assertion of the legitimacy of Paul's suffering as an apostle, its function within II Cor. 1–7 also becomes evident. The fact that Paul bursts into praise in 2:14 in the midst of a description of his trials and tribulations as they culminated in his experience of anxiety over Titus in Troas has led many recent commentators to posit a literary break between 2:12f. and 2:14, with the original train of thought being picked up in what is now 7:5. II Cor. 2:14–7:4 thus becomes a fragment of a lost letter which was later introduced into this strange new environment. However, once the *cause* of Paul's praise in 2:14-16a is recognized to be precisely these trials and tribulations, i.e., his being "led to death," of which his "sentence of death" in 1:3-11, his prior "affliction and anguish of heart" in 2:4 and his anxiety in 2:12f. (cf. 11:28) are certainly a part; and once 2:14 is anchored firmly within the polemical situation behind II Corinthians as a whole, the logical relationship between 2:12f. and 2:14ff. is manifest. For inasmuch as Paul's legitimacy as an apostle was now being called into question precisely *because* of his sufferings, Paul's reference to yet another change in his plans as a result of his anxiety over Titus (cf. 1:15-22) makes it necessary to remind the Corinthians immediately of the essential role his suffering plays in his apostolic ministry.[76] Not to do so would simply supply more ammunition for his opponents' attack. Paul counters this possibility by praising God for the very thing which the Corinthians are being led to believe disqualifies Paul as an apostle, namely, his suffering. The burst of praise in II Cor. 2:14 is therefore not a premature response to his recollection of the joy and relief he felt at meeting Titus in Macedonia as reflected in 7:5ff.,[77] nor the beginning of a lost letter now retained only in the fragment 2:14–7:4. It is the necessary and logical response to the suffering of Paul reintroduced in 2:12f. "Always" and "in every place" in II Cor. 2:14, as the parallels in I Cor. 4:9 and II Cor. 4:11 confirm, are thus best interpreted as relating back to the anxiety Paul felt in Troas. For as II Cor. 11:28 makes clear, part of Paul's suffering and weakness as an apostle includes "the daily pressure upon me of anxiety for all the churches." There is thus no compelling reason to split II Cor. 1–7 into one or more fragments, except perhaps for the notoriously difficult text of 6:14–7:1.[78]

76. Hickling, "Sequence of Thought," 383, has also stressed the unity between 2:12f. and 2:14-17 by taking 2:14-17 as a response to the reproach that Paul's sudden change of plans in 2:12f., as in ch. 1, indicates instability or a wanderlust. In Hickling's view, 2:14 counters this charge by emphasizing that as part of the triumphal procession Paul is led and does not decide himself the route he is to take—i.e., he travels "dictated by the needs of that gospel or by supervening pastoral necessity." But Hickling's view does not take into account the full force of the triumphal procession metaphor, nor the problem of Paul's anxiety, which is clearly the focus of 2:12f. The problem is not just that Paul changed his plans, but rather *why* he was forced to do so.

77. This has been the most common explanation among those who try to link 2:14 to something other than 2:12f. For only a few typical examples, cf. Schelkle, *Zweiter Korintherbrief*, 57; Bartling, "God's Triumphant Captive," 886; Barrett, *Second Corinthians*, 97 (Barrett sees 2:12f. itself as already reflecting relief!); and Plummer, *Second Corinthians*, 67, who is so certain of this position that he can conclude: "to seek for any other explanation is an unintelligent waste of time." The inappropriateness of reading 2:14 in the light of 7:5ff. has been strongly argued by Thrall, "Second Thanksgiving." For a good critique of those who posit splits between 2:13 and 14 and between 7:4 and 5, cf. Thrall, 107-111.

78. In a very important, but often overlooked article, Price ("Aspects of Paul's Theology," esp. pp. 96-99, 103, 104f.) has argued that the key to the unity of the sections 1:1–2:13 and 2:14ff. is to be found in an understanding of the role of affliction in Paul's thinking. He emphasizes in particular the link between 1:6f. and 4:8-11 on the one hand, and 3:1-3 on the other hand. He also relates 3:5f. and 3:1ff.

Once the meaning of the triumphal procession becomes clear, so that II Cor. 2:14-17 can be located within Paul's statements concerning his suffering as an apostle, the connection between 2:12f. and 2:14 is patent. Indeed, the contrast between his suffering as an apostle as reflected in 2:12f. and his being used by God to reveal the knowledge of God becomes the very heart of his apostolic self-understanding. Hence, when "to be led in triumph" *(thriambeuein)* is understood to refer to Paul as the prisoner who is being led to death by God, it becomes the *crux interpretum* of 2:14-16a by solving the three interpretive problems encountered in this text:

1. It makes the "abrupt" transition between 2:13 and 14 understandable;

2. it allows the meaning of the verb *thriambeuein* ("to lead in triumph") itself to be understood against the backdrop of the "triumphal procession," without having to do damage either to the image itself or to the context; and

3. it provides the missing link conceptually between the images of v. 14b and vv. 14c-16a.

3. The Relationship Between 2:14-16a and 2:16b–4:6

On the other hand, as the necessary apologetic response to Paul's suffering in 2:12f., II Cor. 2:14-16a also exercises a specific and important threefold function in relationship to what follows.[79] First, Paul's use of the introductory thanksgiving formula in 2:14 signals *literarily* his intention to introduce the significant train of thought which runs from 2:14–4:6, and then to the end of chapter 7. In addition to this *epistolary purpose*,[80] the parallels to I Cor. 4:9 and II Cor. 4:11

---

to 1:21 and 4:14f. to 1:13f., while at the same time stressing the connection between the theme of suffering in 1–7 and the "weakness" theme of 10–13, concluding that it is the theme of Paul's suffering that ties the various sections of the letter together.

79. On the threefold function of introductory thanksgivings, see above, chapter one, p. 10.

80. As in I Cor. 15:57 and II Cor. 8:16, the introductory thanksgiving formula in II Cor. 2:14 differs from its normal usage as an introduction to an epistle in that

make clear that II Cor. 2:14-16a also performs a clear *didactic function* in reminding the Corinthians that the suffering that Paul endures is an inextricable part of the divine intention for his apostleship. And finally, in the light of the new polemical situation which existed in Corinth, II Cor. 2:14-16a also performs a *paraenetic function* as an implicit appeal not to reject, but to accept Paul's interpretation of his apostolic role as the aroma of Christ.

It is apparent, therefore, that the "tone and themes" of 2:14–4:6 are already clearly outlined in II Cor. 2:14-16a.[81] The tone is apologetic. The thesis to be defended is the genuine nature of Paul's apostolic role as the mediatory agent between God and his new people. Moreover, Paul's first point has already been established: Paul's suffering as an apostle is an essential part of God's plan, functioning to affirm the cross and reveal God's glory. Therefore, rather than calling into question his legitimacy as an apostle, Paul's suffering is *itself* evidence of his authenticity.

But it is not the only evidence to support the integrity of Paul's apostolic calling. A second, and even more compelling, proof is the spiritual existence of the Corinthian church itself. This becomes the main point of II Cor. 2:16b–3:6 and the bridge between Paul's self-defense and his paradigmatic statement that "the letter kills, but the Spirit makes alive."[82] But, as we shall see below, *both* Paul's description of his apostolic ministry of suffering in II Cor. 2:14-16a *and* his emphasis on his ministry of the Spirit in II Cor. 3:1-3 are anchored in his understanding of his *sufficiency* to be an apostle—a sufficiency derived from his call and modeled after the sufficiency of Moses himself. This, then, is the subject of our next chapter.

---

here the thanksgiving relates equally well both to what follows and to what precedes. Thus, II Cor. 2:14 might just as well be described as a transitional thanksgiving formula because of its location within Paul's train of thought.

81. This is the twofold purpose of the introductory thanksgivings as summarized by Obrien. See above, chapter one, p. 10.

82. In A. D. Nock's classic work, *St. Paul*, 202, he observed concerning II Cor. 1–9 that it was here that "Paul sets forth his deepest reflection on the Christian ministry in its relation to those who hear its message and to those whose minds are closed, in relation again to the ministry of the law. Suffering is of the essence of this vocation."

Chapter Three

The Question of Paul's Sufficiency and a Working Hypothesis Concerning Its Background in Biblical and Jewish Tradition (II Cor. 2:16b)

As we have seen in chapter two, Paul contended in II Cor. 2:14-16a that his suffering was the vehicle through which the knowledge and glory of the crucified Christ was now effecting salvation and judgment in the world. This tightly knit apologetic was meant to *commend* his apostolic ministry to the Corinthians within the church, as well as to *defend* it from the onslaught of his opponents, who had recently arrived from without.[1] In order to accomplish these goals Paul painted a picture of his apostolic ministry which could hardly be more profound in its theological meaning, nor more important in its practical significance. For in 2:14-16a, Paul portrayed himself as an eschatological mediatory agent in the salvation/damnation of the world (see 2:15-16). As G. Barth expressed it, "with the preacher, the life- and death-bringing power of the gospel itself is present."[2]

---

1. Since this study was originally completed, this point has also been made by Lambrecht, "Structure and Line of Thought," 347. In commenting on all of 2:14–3:6 Lambrecht writes, "the tone of the passage is at the same time apologetic (an apology directed towards the Corinthian Christians) and a polemic (a counter-attack against the intruders and opponents)."

2. Barth, "Eignung," 262. See too Jones, "Second Moses," 17-20, who emphasizes that in 2:14-16 the gospel is expressed in Paul's lifestyle with the apostle and the gospel being identified. In his words, "Paul is aware of having been made the human vehicle or medium of the gospel" (p. 20).

Having reminded the Corinthians of the meaning and significance of his apostleship, Paul now continues his apologetic by posing the question: "And who is sufficient for these things?" (2:16b). It is to this question and its "answer" that we now turn our attention.

A. THE UNRESOLVED PROBLEM CONCERNING THE "UNANSWERED" QUESTION OF 2:16b

The first and most important observation to be made concerning Paul's question in II Cor. 2:16b is that Paul nowhere directly answers it. It is not surprising, therefore, that scholars have understood Paul's question and its implied answer in various, and often contradictory, ways. For example, the "sudden" polemical tone of 2:16b created for Windisch an irresolvable tension in Paul's logic.[3] As a result, this tension led Windisch to posit the existence of a lacuna between 16a and 16b due to a pause in Paul's dictation, or even to suggest, following Volker, that 2:16b–4:5 be eliminated as a post-Pauline gloss. Moreover, since Paul had already assumed that he was in God's service in 2:14-16a, and had even praised God for it, in Windisch's opinion the question of 2:16b was moot. The real question ought to have been, "Who belongs to us?" Nevertheless, when confronted with the text as it now stands, Windisch viewed verse 17 as *implying* that Paul and his co-workers were to be understood as the only legitimate answer to the question of 2:16b.[4] Windisch emphasized, however, that this answer could only be implied, since the normally expected enumeration of the qualities demanded for the acceptance of the apostolic office, or a direct indication of its appointments, are not given in response to the question. As it stands, therefore, the question can be perceived as a question of *resignation,* as in Joel 2:11; Rev. 6:17; Mk. 10:26; Rom. 11:34, etc. Hence, Windisch also posited the possibility of a second answer to Paul's question, namely, "no one except whom the Lord makes sufficient."[5]

3. Windisch, *Zweiter Korintherbrief,* 99-100.
4. Ibid., 100.
5. Ibid. We will return to these possibilities below.

On the other extreme, C. K. Barrett's emphasis on the unity between 2:16a and b and his belief that "Verse 16a makes the question of 16b readily intelligible" led him to posit a *negative* answer to Paul's question.[6] For in Barrett's view, the question of 2:16b was to be seen as the logical response to the overwhelming responsibility outlined in 2:14-16a. Hence, again taking verse 17 as his clue to the answer of 16b, Barrett's logic ran as follows: Since "those who handle the word of God in its purity know how inadequate they are for the task" (i.e., as outlined in 2:14-16a), the unanswered question of 16b must be understood to mean: "I make no claims to *self*-sufficiency, for we are not, like the majority, watering down the word of God."[7] In a similar way, R. V. G. Tasker argued that if the unexpressed answer were, in fact, "we apostles," then

> such a note of *self*-satisfaction would seem ill-fitted to the context. The logic of the passage seems to demand the answer that *no one* is sufficient for such a high calling in his own unaided strength, for it does not mean carrying the gospel about like a hawker, who adulterates his goods and gives bad measure for the sake of his own personal gain.[8]

In yet a third solution, Dieter Georgi employs his understanding of Paul's opponents as "divine men" to forge a middle position between the views of Windisch and Barrett.[9] Like Windisch, Georgi also sees the introduction of the question in 2:16b as abrupt and unexpected. But unlike Windisch, Georgi does not see in this "jump in thought" a lacuna of some sort, but rather an indication that Paul is now moving to discuss the position of his opponents, who must have said, "we are sufficient."[10] Hence, although for Georgi Paul has already asserted his sufficiency in 2:14-16a, his failure to give a *direct* answer to the question of 2:16b is a sign that Paul is comparing himself to his opponents in their *self*-affirmation. As a result, like Barrett, but for different reasons, Georgi takes Paul's refusal to answer the question of

6. Barrett, *Second Corinthians,* 102-103.
7. Ibid. (emphasis added).
8. Tasker, *Second Corinthians,* 58.
9. Georgi, *Gegner,* 220-225.
10. Ibid., 224.

2:16b to be, in reality, a *negative* answer in opposition to the position of his opponents.[11]

But Georgi also wishes to emphasize that the key to Paul's thought is to be found precisely in the fact that the question in 2:16b remains unanswered. For Georgi's interpretation of 2:16ff. is not only derived from his view of the opponents' claim of "sufficiency," but also from his understanding of the *eschatological* context of Paul's question itself. Georgi sees a parallel between II Cor. 3:4ff. and I Cor. 4:1-5, with I Cor. 4:3 understood as a paraphrase of what Paul intends in II Cor. 2:16f. and 3:4ff. This leads him to suggest that, for Paul, the question of his own sufficiency as an apostle can only be decided by God's eschatological judgment. II Cor. 2:16f. thus becomes a statement of Paul's *present resignation* as he awaits the final eschatological evaluation of his apostolic ministry, as well as a statement of his confidence in the future judgment of God itself (cf. I Cor. 4:4/II Cor. 3:4f.).[12] That this is the point of Paul's argument in 2:16b, i.e., that Paul "awaits everything from the judgment of God," is then further confirmed for Georgi by the alleged parallel between II Cor. 2:16b and the LXX version of Joel 2:11. For when faced with the reality of having to pass before the eschatological judgment of God, Joel too responds with the unanswered question: "And who will be sufficient for it?" In Georgi's words,

> When we bring the perspective represented in Joel 2:11 together with II Cor. 2:16, Paul would then be saying, through the fact that he states this question but then gives no direct answer: If no one can stand before the divine judgment, how can a person be a mediator of precisely this judgment at all? I understand the question (in II Cor. 2:16b), just like the one in Joel 2:11, to be a *question of resignation.* The answer has not fallen out.[13]

For Georgi, therefore, the unanswered question in 2:16b is meant to be Paul's critique of his opponents' confidence that they are already sufficient, a confidence which no one can claim before the just God.

---

11. Ibid.
12. Ibid., 223.
13. Ibid., 224 (emphasis added).

In posing this question, Paul is rejecting the attempt of his opponents to appropriate for themselves the characteristics of God, which they are only able to do because of their self-conception as "divine men" on the one hand, and their lack of eschatological perspective on the other hand.[14]

Finally, as a fourth alternative, Hans Lietzmann and Rudolf Bultmann are examples of those who not only assume the *unity* between 2:14-16a and 16bff., but who, at the same time, also stress that Paul's question is to be answered *positively*.[15] Again, both scholars also point to verse 17 for a confirmation of their view. Thus for Lietzmann the question is, in reality,

> And how can the person be created who will be the bearer of so high a task? Answer: just as I am! Paul does not say this; he leaves the response to the reader and presupposes it in what follows, "For we are not, etc."[16]

Or as Bultmann puts it,

> The question has indeed this sense: who can be such a bearer of the word; or how can I be such a bearer? Therefore also the answer of verse 17 . . . does not list off the required characteristics, but is rather a self-confession. . . . [V]erse 17 is linked to verse 16 with "for," which grounds an unexpressed "I." The answer to the question of verse 16 . . . thus runs: Me! and at the same time says indirectly: the one who preaches the word selflessly.[17]

From this survey of the interpretive possibilities usually represented in the literature four observations may be made. First, the relative strengths and weaknesses of the four basic positions become clear in their mutual critique of one another. Hence, on the one hand, those who

---

14. For a slight variation of this position, see Barth, "Eignung," 262-263. Like Georgi, Barth also sees 2:16b as Paul's response to his opponents, though unlike Georgi, Barth recognizes that 2:16b follows directly from 2:16a as the natural response to the contrast between the lowliness of the apostle and the greatness of his office (cf. p. 263).

15. Lietzmann, *An die Korinther,* 109; Bultmann, *Zweiter Korintherbrief,* 72-73.

16. Lietzmann, *An die Korinther,* 109.

17. Bultmann, *Zweiter Korintherbrief,* 72-73.

stress the unity between 2:16a and b (e.g., Barrett, Tasker, Lietzmann, Bultmann) have, in my opinion, shown that it is unnecessary to posit additional external hypotheses in order to explain the logical transition between Paul's elevated description of his apostolic ministry in 2:14-16a and the natural response of raising the question of sufficiency for this ministry in 2:16b. Moreover, my own study in chapters one and two has shown that the polemical tone of 2:16b is neither new, nor in tension with 2:14-16a. Thus, the need to posit an abrupt break in Paul's thought between 2:16a and b, which must then be explained by some external hypothesis (à la Windisch, Georgi), does not exist.

This point has recently been emphasized by T. Provence, who also sees v. 16b as occasioned by the bold statement of vv. 15-16a.[18] Nevertheless, Provence too must bring to the text the assumption of a certain reader-response in order to explain v. 16b:

> Were Paul not to ask the question of 2:16b, those who opposed him would have had grounds to accuse him (as some may have done) of the most repugnant sort of arrogance. Paul had no choice but to raise and answer the question of his qualification to preach a message which may bring about salvation for some, but which may, on the other hand, "prove fatal to those who come in contact with it."[19]

But it is not necessary to assume that 2:15-16a would lead Paul's readers to react in a certain way in order to explain v. 16b, especially when in v. 16b, in contrast to 3:1, Paul gives no indication that he is anticipating a certain response. As we shall see below, it is rather Paul's *answer* to v. 16b which provides his adversaries with grounds for their accusation. Furthermore, once the biblical and Jewish background to Paul's question is clarified, additional evidence can be adduced to support the contention of those who have argued that the occasion for the question of 2:16b is Paul's understanding of his apostolic ministry in 2:14-16a.

On the other hand, Windisch, Bultmann, and Lietzmann have pointed out that the logical relationship between vv. 16b and 17 ("for" or "because"!) only makes sense when Paul's question in 2:16b is under-

18. "Who is Sufficient?" 56-57.
19. Ibid.

stood to imply a *positive* answer.[20] The weakness of the alternative position is further confirmed by the fact that both Barrett and Tasker must import into 2:16b the pejorative theological construct of "*self*-sufficiency" from Paul's statements in 3:4f. in order to construe v. 17 to mean that Paul, unlike "the many," is disavowing all claims to self-sufficiency or adequacy. But the idea of "sufficiency," in and of itself, carries no such pejorative connotations,[21] and v. 16b simply does not pose the question "And who is sufficient for these things *from himself?*" Moreover, Paul's statements in 3:1 and 3:5 ought not to be read back into 2:16b since they make sense *only* if the question of 2:16b has *already* been answered positively. In other words, Paul's assertion in 3:5 that his sufficiency is not "in himself" or "from himself" makes sense only if this sufficiency has already been implied. For in 3:5 Paul does not *assert* his sufficiency, he *assumes* it. That is to say, 3:5 does not answer the question of 2:16b; it clarifies the answer which has already been given, albeit indirectly.

Similarly, if Paul had answered the question of 2:16b negatively, then the implied criticism of Paul reflected in 3:1 would lose its force. No one would accuse someone of commending himself who had just disavowed all claims to sufficiency! Therefore, although Provence is again right in emphasizing that "one of the most important keys to understanding 2 Cor. 3 lies in grasping its connection with 2:15-16 . . . ," it is not entirely accurate to say that "Paul intends 3:5-6 to be an answer to the question raised in 2:16 . . . ," though in a broader sense it is true that "Paul answers the question of 2:16b throughout chapter 3."[22] Those who argue for the internal coherence of the text as well as for an implied positive answer to the question of 2:16b on the basis of verse 17 (e.g., Lietzmann and Bultmann) do the most justice, therefore, to the text on *internal* grounds.

---

20. So too already Hodge, *Second Corinthians* (1859), 47, and the classic work of H. A. W. Meyer, *Epistles to the Corinthians,* on 2:17.

21. One need only check the 48 times *hikanos* ("sufficient") appears in the LXX, or its widespread use in Josephus (over 80 times) and Philo (over 150 times), to see that when used alone it connotes a purely neutral sense of "sufficiency," "adequacy," or "capability." This is also true for the New Testament, where it appears 39 times (or 40, depending on the reading of Rom. 15:23) but, as Rengstorf, ἱκανός, 293, has emphasized, carries no particular moral connotation.

22. Provence, "Who is Sufficient?" 56, 57.

This brings us to our third observation, an observation occasioned by the work of Dieter Georgi, inasmuch as Georgi's attempt to develop the significance of the parallels among our text, I Cor. 4, and Joel 2:11 points to a weakness in the other positions. For only Georgi has felt the need not only to explain the internal function of 2:16b, but also to take the important additional step of attempting to clarify the traditional background necessary to understand the broader theological significance of the text. Thus, although Georgi's own internal analysis of the text, which necessitates that he posit the theology of Paul's opponents in order to explain the "abrupt" introduction of Paul's question in 2:16b and its "negative" answer, is inadequate, his observation that Paul's question cannot sufficiently be understood merely on the basis of its internal function in Paul's argument is correct. For even when the question is seen as a natural response to Paul's description of his apostolic ministry in 2:14-16a and as implying a positive answer on the basis of 2:17; 3:1, 4-5, one is still left exegetically troubled by Paul's *form* of argumentation itself. The fact that Paul introduces the theme of his adequacy for the apostolic ministry in the form of an indefinite question which is never directly answered, but whose answer is intended to be so unmistakably clear that Paul can later assume it in his argument (cf. 3:5), raises not just the question of *what* Paul said, but also forces us to ask *why* he said it in the particular way he did.[23] In other words, what is the reason for this seemingly circuitous mode of argumentation, if Paul's point is simply to stress that he is sufficient for the apostolic task outlined in 2:14-16a (cf. I Cor. 15:9f.)? To answer this question, we must, like Georgi, look outside our immediate context for a parallel Pauline or non-Pauline tradition which might shed some light on Paul's argument.

The fourth and final observation to be made, therefore, is that although Georgi has indeed raised an important question, his own attempt to answer it on the basis of the alleged parallels among II Cor. 2:16b; I Cor. 4:1-5; and Joel 2:11 is nevertheless not compelling for several reasons. First, the link between I Cor. 4 and II Cor. 2:16ff. cannot be

---

23. This is not meant, however, to be an exercise in reading Paul's mind, thus falling prey to the so-called "intentional fallacy," but is simply to pose the question of form to the text itself as a clue to a further aspect of Paul's *expressed* intention.

maintained. For in contrast to I Cor. 4:1-5, the context of II Cor. 2:16b–3:6 nowhere indicates that Paul is thinking of God's *future* eschatological evaluation of his ministry as an apostle. Instead, the consistent emphasis in this text is on Paul's past and present sufficiency *to be* an apostle.[24] While in I Cor. 4:1-4 the issue is whether or not Paul has faithfully exercised his office as a servant and steward, in II Cor. 2:16ff. the issue at stake is now whether or not Paul even has a right to occupy the office at all. In I Cor. 4 Paul is *primarily* on the offense, while in II Cor. 2:16ff. he is on the defense. In I Cor. 4 Paul's purpose is *primarily* hortatory, in II Cor. 2:16ff., apologetic. I emphasize *primarily* because I do not want to deny that already in I Corinthians Paul's role as an apostle was being questioned in relationship to the other "guides" in Corinth (cf. I Cor. 4:15). But the debate in Corinth had taken a significant turn by the time II Corinthians 2:16ff. was written. In I Corinthians Paul merely needed to reestablish his role as the Corinthians' "father" among the "guides," in II Corinthians he now has to fight for his right even to be considered an apostle at all.[25]

This basic distinction between I Cor. 4:1-5 and II Cor. 2:16ff., which we have already seen in chapter two as characteristic of the difference between I and II Corinthians elsewhere,[26] together with Paul's emphasis on the present in 2:16ff., make it difficult to use I Cor. 4 as an interpretive key to II Cor. 2:16ff., except by way of *contrast*. Georgi's attempt to build a case for a parallel between I Cor. 4:1ff. and II Cor. 2:16ff. on the basis of the existence of the same verb, to "reckon" or "consider," in the two passages (cf. I Cor. 4:1; II Cor. 3:5) thus remains unconvincing.[27]

Second, the alleged parallel between II Cor. 2:16b and Joel 2:11, which Georgi sees as a confirmation of his eschatological interpretation

---

24. Cf. 2:17; 3:3; 3:4; 3:5; 3:6.

25. Bailey, "Structure of 1 Corinthians," 160, comes to this same conclusion based on his study of the structure of I Cor. 1:4–4:16: "[I]n this essay [i.e., 1:4–4:16] Paul is not *primarily* defending his position as an apostle." He too thus concludes, "We grant that in the process Paul defends his apostleship. But his theological method (as seen here) indicates that the primary topic is the proper attitude for Christians in regard to their leaders."

26. See above, chapter two, pp. 59ff.

27. Cf. Georgi, *Gegner*, 223.

of 2:16b,[28] is also tenuous. For not only is the context of eschatological judgment lacking in reference to Paul's ministry in II Cor. 2:16ff., but the link between the subject matter of the two texts is also missing. The premise found in Joel needed for the argument, i.e., Joel's resignation before God's judgment, is absent in Paul. Rather than resignation in the light of God's coming judgment, Paul consistently expresses an unreserved hope based on the atoning work of Christ, both for the salvation of those "in Christ," and for the effectiveness of his own apostolic ministry.[29] In this context, it is also significant that even though Paul never assumes without question that his converts will continue in their faith and can even call into question the genuineness of certain members of his congregations,[30] he nevertheless never seems to doubt that his own call to be an apostle and its results are from God. Thus, when faced with the prospect of God's judgment of the believer or God's eschatological evaluation of Paul's ministry (cf. I Cor. 9:24ff.), Paul's response is not one of resignation, but of confidence.

Moreover, Windisch's attempt to draw a parallel between 2:16b and other examples of questions of resignation in the NT also breaks down.[31] The question in Rev. 6:17 is not posed by the faithful, but by those who are faced with "the wrath of the Lamb" (cf. 6:15f.). In contrast, the faithful do not shrink from the final judgment, but look forward to it (cf. 6:10f.; 19:1-9). The same holds true for Mk. 10:26. In response to the disciples' question, Jesus' simple reply is that "all things are possible with God." Finally, the link suggested between the questions of Rom. 11:34 and II Cor. 2:16b is difficult to establish. The resignation one feels when faced with God's wisdom, knowledge, and mercy, if the questions of Rom. 11:34f. are even meant to be so interpreted,

28. As we saw above, Georgi is following Windisch, *Zweiter Korintherbrief*, 100, for this point, who in turn referred to Loesner, *Observationes ad NT e. Philone Alex.* (1777), 301ff.

29. One need only think of the basic principle applied to believers in Rom. 1:16f.; 5:1f.; 6:3-8, 9-11; 8:1, 28-30; 1 Cor. 15:21f., 49, 57; II Cor. 4:13-17; 5:14-21; Phil. 1:6; 3:20f.; Col. 2:9-16; 3:4; I Thess. 3:11-13; 4:14-17; 5:9f. and of Paul's own attitude to his work as an apostle in Rom. 15:5b-19; I Cor. 3:1-10; 4:4a (!), 15f.; 7:10, 12, 17, 25; 9:1-2, 18-27; 11:1; II Cor. 5:20; 6:1; 10:7f.; 11:5; 12:11f.; 13:4, 6 (!); Gal. 1:10-12; 2:8f.; 4:14; Col. 1:24-29.

30. Cf. Rom 11:20-22; 14:10-12; I Cor. 10:1-12; 15:2; II Cor. 1:24; 6:1f.; 13:5f.; Gal. 3:1-4; 4:11; 5:4; Phil. 2:15f.; Col. 1:21-23; I Thess. 3:6-8.

31. Cf. Windisch, *Zweiter Korintherbrief*, 100.

has little, if any, bearing on the context of II Cor. 2:16b. In II Cor. 2:14-16a Paul may be marveling that in God's wisdom he has chosen to display his glory through the suffering of his apostle, but this only makes the question of 2:16b more necessary; it does not change the question itself into one of resignation. For in 2:16b Paul is asking a question not about God but about himself.

Georgi's (and Windisch's) attempt to interpret Paul's question in II Cor. 2:16b as one of resignation runs aground, therefore, not only on the basis of the alleged parallels themselves, but also because it stands in opposition to Paul's consistent confidence for the future because of his understanding of the salvific work of the cross of Christ. We are thus left with the unresolved problem of whether or not a background in Paul's tradition can be found which will help explain the significance of Paul's mode of argumentation in II Cor. 2:16b-17, while at the same time remaining true to his apostolic self-conception as evidenced not only in the immediate context, but elsewhere in the Pauline corpus as well.

B. THE SUFFICIENCY OF MOSES: A WORKING HYPOTHESIS

In the light of the conscious effort in the past to determine an OT background to Paul's question in II Cor. 2:16b, it is surprising that more attention has not been focused on the only other possible parallel besides Joel 2:11 in the LXX to the "sufficiency"-theme of 2:16b, namely Ex. 4:10. In fact, although it has been overlooked by recent scholarship, this solution to the problem of the background to II Cor. 2:16b was pointed out, but not developed, over forty years ago by Austin M. Farrer. Farrer observed that when called at the burning bush, Moses responded with the confession, "I am not sufficient" *(hikanos)*, but was nevertheless "made sufficient by the All-sufficing (El Shaddai, interpreted as *theos ho hikanos*)."[32] Taking this as the antitype to Paul's statements in II Cor. 2:16; 3:4f.; and I Cor. 15:9,[33] Farrer posited that Paul was casting his

32. Farrer, "Ministry," 171, 173.
33. The meaning of I Cor. 15:9f. and II Cor. 3:4f. will be dealt with in my forthcoming study of II Cor. 3:4–4:6. Cf. too the related texts of Gal. 1:11ff.; Eph. 3:8; and I Tim. 1:15f.

own question in terms of this tradition, thus paraphrasing Paul's question and its "answer" in 2:16: "Who then, says the apostle, is sufficient *(hikanos)* for the second and greater ministry? We are: but our sufficiency also is infused by grace."[34] Farrer then goes on to combine this insight with the contrasts between the apostolic and Mosaic ministries in II Cor. 3:7–4:10 and concludes that "the fulfillment of Moses, St. Paul says, is found not in Christ but in the apostles . . ."[35] and that the apostle can be described as a "new Moses."[36]

Farrer's insight concerning the parallel between II Cor. 2:16b and the call of Moses has been taken up and extended by Peter Ronald Jones in his unpublished dissertation, *The Apostle Paul: A Second Moses According to II Corinthians 2:14–4:7.*[37] As his title indicates, Jones takes the additional step of arguing that the parallels and contrasts between the call and ministry of Paul and Moses in II Cor. 2:14–4:7 indicate that Paul consciously understood and portrayed himself as the eschatological fulfillment of the hope for a non-messianic "second Moses" found in the OT and developed in Jewish literature, the most distinct example being the conception of the Teacher of Righteousness found in the Qumran writings.[38] In Jones's words,

> in the exercise of his apostolate Paul is not only following the terms of his "commission" and the leading of the Spirit, but is consciously determined by a prior common tradition of the second Moses.[39]

More specifically, in

> II Cor. 2:14–4:7, Paul's description of his apostolic task is radically shaped and conditioned by an already existing second Moses tradition.[40]

---

34. Farrer, "Ministry," 173.

35. Ibid., 172.

36. Ibid., 173.

37. For his reference to Farrer, see pp. 40-41. The main points of Jones's dissertation have been summarized in his article "Second Moses," 224-233. He again handles II Cor. 2:16b by pointing to Farrer (p. 226).

38. See esp. *The Apostle Paul: A Second Moses,* 6, 33f., 40f., 59-69, 187-202, 252-255, 257, 316ff., 351, 374-376; "Second Moses," 220, 233.

39. *The Apostle Paul: A Second Moses,* 109. He then outlines this tradition on pp. 110-255.

40. Ibid., 255.

But regarding II Cor. 2:16b itself, Jones is content merely to refer to Farrer's earlier study and to observe that

> the terminology which is characteristic of the call of Moses is also an appropriate term for Paul, for whom the notions of grace and apostleship are intimately tied.[41]

Or in the words of Jones's later summary,

> It is significant, and perhaps more than coincidental, that the account of Moses' own vocation at the burning bush contains the pregnant term *hikanos*.[42]

Having accepted Farrer's assertion, Jones then incorporates it into his overall thesis as another example of the Moses / Paul = Second Moses parallel in II Cor. 2:14–4:7.

Without entering into a detailed critique of Jones's interpretation of II Cor. 2:14–4:7,[43] his methodology, or his basic thesis that Paul conceived of himself as the "second Moses" promised in Jewish tradition, suffice it to say here that despite his many helpful insights[44] Jones's recapitulation of Farrer's original but likewise undeveloped observation concerning the parallels between II Cor. 2:16b and the call of Moses, as well as his view of II Cor. 3:4f. as a reference to Paul's call, nevertheless remain unsubstantiated. This is especially true in view of the fact that elsewhere Paul portrays his call *not* in terms of the call of Moses, but in reliance on the call of the prophets, especially that of Jeremiah and/or the Isaianic "Servant of YHWH."[45] Hence, the central weakness of Jones's argument is that he jumps from the "implied comparison with the call of Moses"[46] found in 2:16b and 3:4f. to the history of the

---

41. Ibid., 40f.

42. "Second Moses," 226.

43. Where relevant, his position regarding II Cor. 3:1-3 will be taken up below, while his exegesis of 3:6–4:7 will be analyzed in my forthcoming study of II Cor. 3:4–4:6.

44. See especially his helpful interpretation of I Cor. 3:5-16 against the backdrop of the OT and wisdom traditions in "Second Moses," 220-224 and his view of the function of Paul's "letter of recommendation" in 3:1-3 (see below, chapter five).

45. See below, chapter four, p. 139 n. 108.

46. Jones, "Second Moses," 225.

tradition of the expectation of a "second Moses," *rather than analyzing the tradition of Moses' call itself and its development in the OT and non-canonical Jewish literature.* For only after this has been done can the assertion that Paul is alluding to and reflecting upon the Mosaic(-prophetic) call tradition in II Cor. 2:16b gain its necessary support. Hence, although it is also my contention that the solution to the unsolved problem concerning II Cor. 2:16b outlined above is, as Farrer observed, to be found in Paul's allusion to the LXX version of Ex. 4:10, Paul's question and the structure of his argument will become clear only when we view them within the context of the biblical and extra-biblical traditions concerning the "call" and "sufficiency" of Moses, rather than transposing II Cor. 2:16b into the, if not unrelated, then certainly more distant, context of the "second Moses" expectation.[47]

For our present purposes, however, it is sufficient simply to allow this contention to remain frozen as a "working hypothesis" to be substantiated later. For, as Jones has also pointed out (see above), the comparison between Paul and Moses alluded to in 2:16b is then picked up and further developed in 3:4–4:6. Thus the *implicit* significance of Paul's initial allusion to the call and sufficiency of Moses in 2:16b can only adequately be understood when viewed in the light of this continuing argument. It seems best, therefore, to postpone an investigation of the *traditionsgeschichtlich* background to II Cor. 2:16b until it can be combined with a detailed exegesis of 3:4–4:6.

The point to be made now is simply that II Cor. 2:16b is a rhetorical question that is intended to be answered positively and that, in doing so, it introduces Paul's *explicit* support for the assertion of sufficiency in 2:17. To examine how Paul chooses to argue *explicitly* for his sufficiency is thus the next step in our study.

---

47. See *The Apostle Paul: A Second Moses,* 351, where Jones himself admits that "II Cor. 3:4f. is the only place in Paul's writing where a second Moses conceptual framework arises to reasonable explicitness." And, of course, it could be questioned, even here, whether the apostle of the "new covenant" in fulfillment of Jer. 31:31ff. is to be seen as the second Moses of Jewish tradition.

Chapter Four

The Apologetic Function of Paul's Ministry of Suffering in the Corinthian Correspondence (II Cor. 2:17)

Paul's introduction of the sufficiency motif in 2:16b[1] and its resumption and resolution in 3:5f., together with the obvious transition in 3:7ff., make it clear that 2:16b–3:6 form the next unit of thought in Paul's ongoing apologetic for his apostolic ministry. Within 2:16b–3:6 itself, Paul's argument is further composed, however, of two distinct but closely interrelated themes:

1. Paul's question ("And who is sufficient for these things?") and his response to it in 2:17 and 3:4-6 and
2. Paul's relationship to the church at Corinth in 3:1-3.

That 3:1-3 is intended to be distinguished from Paul's first answer to the question of 2:16b is indicated in two ways. First, Paul's discussion of the Corinthians as a "letter" is introduced and occasioned by its own question in 3:1. Second, the subject matter of 3:1-3 is no longer the question of Paul's sufficiency for the apostolic ministry per se, but rather the relationship between Paul and the church in Corinth *as it relates to the question of Paul's sufficiency.* For as we shall see in chapter five, 3:1-3 is actually intended to provide further evidence in support of Paul's assertion that he is indeed sufficient to be Christ's apostle, which is first introduced as an unexpressed assumption in response to the question of 2:16b and then defended in 2:17, while at

---

1. So too, e.g., Windisch, Lietzmann, and Bultmann. See above, pp. 88ff.

98

the same time responding to the criticism implied in Paul's rhetorical question of 3:1.

A. THE PROBLEM PRESENTED BY II COR. 2:17

As we have seen above, the "for" of verse 17 necessitates that we posit an implied positive answer (i.e., "*I* am" or, in keeping with the apostolic plural, "*we* are") to Paul's question in 2:16b. Verse 17 gives support to Paul's assertion that he is, in fact, sufficient for the apostolic ministry of suffering which he has outlined in 2:14-16a. It is at this point, however, that we encounter difficulties. For the majority of commentators,[2] regardless of whether or not they agree that v. 17 presupposes a positive answer to the question of 2:16b, have nevertheless taken verse 17 to be a declaration of the genuine nature of Paul's gospel.[3] That is to say, verse 17 is understood to mean that, unlike the "many," Paul does not "water down" or "adulterate" the word of God, but instead preaches the pure and unadulterated gospel, i.e., he speaks "from purity" (2:17b). As Provence summarizes it,

> Paul contrasts his preaching with that of others who dilute, and so make inoffensive and ineffective, the Word of God. His word is pure and therefore powerful enough to lead both to salvation and destruction. . . . Thus Paul's point in this verse is to support his qualification to be a minister whose ministry leads both to salvation and destruction. His "pure" preaching contrasts with the diluted preaching of others. The "watered down" gospel of the "many" was neither offensive enough to lead to destruction nor powerful enough to lead to salvation (cf. I Cor. 1:18). Paul's gospel was such a word, however, since it was a pure gospel from God.[4]

2. See, e.g., the commentaries of Meyer, Heinrici, Hodge, H. C. G. Moule, Plummer, Windisch, Barrett, Tasker, and Héring on II Cor. 2:17.

3. It is interesting to note in this regard that this interpretation can be used to support either a negative or a positive answer to the question of 2:16b. Cf., e.g., Barrett, *Second Corinthians*, 103, for the former and Provence, "Who is Sufficient?" 58f., for the latter.

4. Provence, "Who is Sufficient?" 58f.

But if verse 17 refers to the "purity" of Paul's gospel, it becomes difficult to see how this assertion offers additional evidence for Paul's assertion of sufficiency. According to this view of verse 17, Paul's unexpressed assertion that he is sufficient for the apostolic ministry would be grounded only in the fact that he then *claims* to be the one preaching the pure gospel, with the actual support of Paul's assertion of sufficiency not being adduced until 3:2f., when Paul points out that the Corinthians themselves are his letter of recommendation.

Yet the fact that Paul's argument in 3:2f. is undoubtedly also meant to support Paul's claim to sufficiency should not blind us to the fact that Paul's *first* argument in favor of his sufficiency is *already* given in 2:17 ("for"!). And the attempt to take *kapēleuontes* in 2:17 to mean "water down," "corrupt," or "adulterate," etc., renders Paul's argument logically abstruse, since to move from an assertion of one's personal adequacy for a task to the quality of the task itself is a confusion of categories. In other words, it is not immediately clear how the purity of Paul's preaching could be used to support his own personal adequacy as an apostle. Thus, for example, Provence must insert an additional link in Paul's argument in order to facilitate the connection between 2:17 and 2:16b, namely, that the gospel of Paul's opponents, in contrast to Paul's gospel, was not effective, neither positively nor negatively. This link, however, is not only foreign to the text, but also does not correspond to the fact that Paul's opponents seem to have been enjoying tremendous success with their gospel, at least in Corinth, which was precisely the problem (cf. II Cor. 11:3f.). Finally, rather than supporting Paul's claim to be sufficient for the apostolic ministry in some way (assuming for the moment that a more suitable missing link could be found), an emphasis on the purity of his gospel in 2:17 would merely add to Paul's problems. For although Paul's gospel itself was under attack in Corinth at this time (see II Cor. 11:4), the *main* issue in Corinth when II Corinthians was written was whether or not Paul was even sufficient for the gospel he did preach, since his suffering and weakness seemed to call that gospel into question.[5]

---

5. See above, pp. 63f., and the discussion of the problem in Corinth by Beker, *Paul the Apostle,* 295-300, who emphasizes that in II Corinthians the issue is that Paul was simply weak and unimpressive and hence unfit to be a minister of the gospel of the glory of Christ. In response, "Paul attacks his opponents by focusing

Thus, for Paul to emphasize that he was the one who was preaching the pure gospel would simply raise the issue of his sufficiency for that gospel without, at the same time, positively furthering his argument. In fact, the most common interpretation of 2:17, i.e., "I am sufficient because I am the one who is preaching the pure and unadulterated gospel," only leads one to conclude that the criticism reflected in 3:1 was, in reality, warranted. Paul was simply recommending himself and doing so in a way that, at best, was logically confused. This is, of course, possible. But the difficulties with such an interpretation raise the question of whether Paul's statement in 2:17 has been adequately understood in modern research. Is it possible that 2:17 can be understood in such a way that Paul's statement in 2:17 *itself* offers some *external* evidence which, from Paul's perspective, would support his assertion that he is sufficient for the apostolic ministry? The answer to this question, as well as the key to Paul's argument as a whole, lies in a reinvestigation of the meaning of the verb *kapēleuein* in 2:17.

B. THE MEANING OF THE VERB *KAPĒLEUEIN* IN THE POLEMIC AGAINST THE SOPHISTS AND IN HELLENISTIC JUDAISM

1. The Meaning of Kapēleuein in Recent Research

The dominance in our century of the view that *kapēleuein* ought to be translated "to adulterate," "to corrupt," "to water down," "to falsify," etc., in II Corinthians 2:17 can be traced back to Hans Windisch's observation in 1924, based on the parallels listed in J. J. Wettstein's *Novum Testamentum Graecum* for II Cor. 2:17,[6] that "the expression

---

on the cruciform nature of Christian existence, in contrast to their view of it as empirically victorious and glorious." Thus, "What is at stake is the nature of the victory of Christ as it embodies itself in Paul's apostolic experience in the world" (p. 299). See below for my exegesis of II Cor. 11:4 in this regard.

6. See Wettstein II, 183. I have decided to follow the recent discussion in building my treatment around the evidence listed by Windisch rather than the sixteen pieces of evidence Wettstein listed. An examination of Wettstein's parallels

'to water down the word of God' goes back indeed to the polemic against the Sophists inaugurated by Plato."[7] For on the basis of this background, Paul's statement in II Cor. 2:17 was interpreted by Windisch to refer to those "many" who

> 1) hawk the word of God, i.e., offer it for money (cf. Acts 8:18f.), *and*
> 2) falsify it, i.e., furnish it with spurious, self-made additions (cf. 4:2, "adulterating the word of God"; Mt. 7:13).[8]

Nevertheless, in spite of this apparent *twofold* meaning of the verb, Windisch himself chose to translate it "to hawk" in his commentary since, as he concluded, "The point of view mentioned first takes precedence in consideration."[9] The most that Windisch was willing to concede concerning the second meaning was that

> the second point of view, *if Paul felt it as well,* would refer to the corruption of "another" doctrine (11:4), presumably a judaistic false doctrine. . . .[10]

But fourteen years later, when Windisch expanded his position in his 1938 article on *kapēleuein* in the *Theologisches Wörterbuch zum Neuen Testament,*[11] three significant changes took place. First, in defining the verb, Windisch now listed the two meanings "to sell or hawk deceitfully, with deception, with profiteering, with illegitimate profit" *and* "to falsify the thing or ware" as *synonymous.*[12]

Second, Windisch now incorporated the LXX into his discussion, concluding that in both Is. 1:22 and Sir. 26:29 the "retailer" *(kapēlos)* in view "stands under suspicion of being someone who falsifies the

---

makes it clear that Windisch selected the most important texts in his study. The issue is how these texts are to be interpreted.

7. Windisch, *Zweiter Korintherbrief,* 100.

8. Ibid. (emphasis added).

9. Ibid.

10. Ibid., 101 (emphasis added).

11. Windisch, καπηλεύω.

12. Windisch, καπηλεύω, in the German original, 607. In a private conversation Peter Stuhlmacher pointed out that the German "oder" (= "or") in this context does not carry the emphasis on "alternative" found in the English "or," but rather indicates that the two are synonymous and is thus here best translated "and"; hence my emphasis above.

wares, a sinner, and a deceiver."[13] Hence, in the LXX as well, "the word received an evil connotation, exactly like the 'tax-collector' *(telōnēs)*,"[14] corresponding to the "secondary meaning of the deceitful and profit-seekers" present in classical literature.[15]

Third, his investigation of Paul's own use of *kapēleuein*, especially its parallel to II Cor. 4:2, now led Windisch to conclude, in contrast to his previous, more cautious position, that the meaning "to falsify the word," although described as a "secondary meaning" *(Nebenbedeutung)*, is nevertheless clearly in view in 2:17: "[T]his secondary meaning is rejected here by many interpreters; but what follows certainly indicates that it is appropriate."[16]

As a result, Windisch's programmatic article could now be used to legitimize translating *kapēleuein* "to adulterate," "to falsify," etc. in 2:17, even though Windisch himself continued to stress that the idea of "selling" or "offering the Word of God for money," based on the polemic against the Sophists found in secular Greek literature, was the *primary* denotation of the verb. In addition, Windisch's discussion of the Septuagint's use of "retailer" *(kapēlos)*, and his allusion to Is. 1:22 in his summary statement that "in the mouth of Paul [it] also means: to falsify the word *as the 'retailer' (kapēlos) mixes the wine with water, but sells it as pure . . . ,*"[17] gave the impression that the two ideas of selling and watering down were, in reality, inextricably linked together in the same verb.

Without further investigation, therefore, it became easy for subsequent commentators to assume, on the basis of Windisch's treatment of the verb, that the Sophists and pseudo-philosophers of the ancient world had been attacked for selling their teaching under the suspicion that just as a dishonest wine dealer dilutes the wine to make a greater profit, so too the Sophists diluted their teaching in order to make it more palatable to their audiences. In this way, the two distinct meanings originally suggested by Windisch naturally melt together into a coherent whole. Consequently, Paul's statement in 2:17 could be read

13. Windisch, καπηλεύω, in the German original, 607.
14. Ibid.
15. Ibid.
16. Ibid., 608 n. 7.
17. Ibid. (emphasis added).

as implying either meaning, or both meanings, depending on the emphasis detected by the interpreter.[18] The alleged parallel between II Cor. 2:17 and 4:2, also pointed out by Windisch, simply confirmed this conclusion.[19]

It is highly significant, therefore, that also in the English-speaking world we find this exact fusion of meanings independently attested in Alfred Plummer's commentary on II Corinthians, which came to occupy the same influential role in England and America as the works of Windisch did on the continent. For although Plummer also refers to the anti-Sophist polemic as a background to II Cor. 2:17, he disregards the emphasis of "selling" altogether in his translation and simply renders this verse " 'Adulterating the Word of God' (since) 'adulterate' suggests more clearly than 'corrupt' . . . that the corruption is done for the sake of some miserable personal gain."[20] It is also significant that Plummer referred to the two occurrences of "retail dealer" in the LXX (i.e., Is. 1:22 and Sir. 26:29) as the basis for his interpretation. Plummer even ventures to suggest that "St. Paul may have had Is. 1:22 in his mind in using *kapēleuontes*."[21]

Consequently, whether one turned to Windisch or Plummer, the impression could not be avoided that the verb *kapēleuein* carried an emphasis on "adulterating" or "falsifying" the object of one's trade. Under their influence, the only exegetical decision was whether this idea should be considered to be secondary (à la Windisch) or primary (à la Plummer) in II Cor. 2:17. In recent decades, largely on the basis of the use of *kapēlos* ("retailer") in the LXX and the alleged parallel between II Cor. 2:17 and 4:2, it has been Plummer's emphasis and

18. See, e.g., Héring, *Second Corinthians*, 19; Barrett, *Second Corinthians*, 103; Tasker, *Second Corinthians*, 58.

19. This received its classic formulation in Trench, *Synonyms*, 228ff. Trench argued against those who tried to assert that *kapēleuō* and *doloō* ("to adulterate") were identical, in order to maintain that the former actually included everything implied in the latter and more! For in his view, because *kapēleuein* was also related specifically to the wine trade, it combined the aspect of mixing and falsifying denoted by *doloō* (p. 228) with the idea of selling this diluted product for a dishonest profit. He thus followed Bentley in understanding 2:17 to refer to those "corrupters of the Word of God *for filthy lucre*" (Trench, p. 230).

20. Plummer, *Second Corinthians*, 73.

21. Ibid.

translation which have won the day. Thus, for example, M. Rissi wrote in 1969,

> What *kapēleuein* means here, *can only be explained on the basis of the context of the entire train of thought.* It is not so much about "profit-seeking hawking" of the gospel, because the theme of avarice plays *no role in the context,* but rather about the falsifying of the word of God (cf. 4:2: "adulterating the word of God"). Perhaps Paul is thinking of a word from the *Old Testament,* which he applies to proclamation: 'your retailers are mixing the wine with water' (Is. 1:22).[22]

Or as T. Provence recently concluded, "it appears that Paul had the idea of adulteration primarily in mind."[23] Moreover, like Rissi, Provence bases his conclusion on Windisch's suggestion that 2:17 is parallel to 4:2 (see above), which he then maintains is "confirmed by further reference to the LXX reading of Isaiah 1:22."[24] Unlike Rissi, however, Provence goes on to argue that this interpretation "receives still further confirmation" from its contrast to "sincerity" in 2:17b, since

> "sincerity" here is a sincerity which derives from purity. Since Paul is contrasting his motives with those of the *kapēleuontes,* the image of the purity of his preaching contrasts nicely with the image of their polluting the word of God.[25]

Thus both Rissi and Provence argue, in accord with Plummer, that the context of 2:17, together with the OT parallel from Isaiah, demand that Windisch's "secondary meaning" be regarded as the *primary* and determinative meaning of 2:17.[26]

Our first task, therefore, is to reexamine, in turn, each of the three pieces of evidence usually adduced to support the supposition that *kapēleuein,* either primarily or secondarily, means "to water down" or

---

22. Rissi, *Studien,* 18f. (emphasis added). The predominance of this view is reflected in the fact that Rissi need not even refer to the opposing positions of, for example, Schlatter, Lietzmann, and Bultmann; see below.

23. Provence, "Who Is Sufficient," 59.

24. Ibid.

25. Ibid. For his interpretation of *eilikrineia* as "a sincerity which derives from purity," Provence refers to Büchsel, εἰλικρινής, 397.

26. Though neither Rissi nor Provence refers to Plummer.

"to adulterate" in II Cor. 2:17. These three pieces of evidence are (1) the anti-Sophist polemic in the Greek classics and Hellenistic Judaism, (2) the LXX usage of "retailer" in Is. 1:22 and Sir. 26:29, and (3) the context of II Cor. 2:17 itself, especially the meaning of "sincerity" *(eilikrineia)* on the one hand, and the parallel to II Cor. 4:2 on the other hand.

2. A Reexamination of the Relevant Evidence

In contrast to the impression gained from recent research, the central issue in determining the meaning of II Cor. 2:17 is not whether the idea of "falsifying," "adulterating," or "watering down," etc., ought to be regarded as the primary or secondary meaning of *kapēleuein,* as if both the ideas of "selling" and "adulterating" were always signified by the verb. Rather, the question is whether the pejorative idea of "falsifying" ought to be included as part of the wider semantic field of the verb at all. As we have seen, the first reason given for doing so is the assumption that the use of *eilikrineia* ("sincerity") in the polemic against the Sophists, inaugurated by Plato, implied that those who sold their wisdom also fell to the temptation of compromising their message by accommodating it to the likes and dislikes of their audiences. But a closer look at this polemic reveals that the issue, in reality, was quite different.[27]

a. Plato and Isocrates

Plato's problem with the Sophists was not that their practice of accepting money for their teaching compromised their message, but rather that the presupposition for their very existence, i.e., that they were the "wise ones" (and hence the name *sophistai*) whose wisdom *(sophia)* and virtue *(aretē)* could be taught to others, was fundamentally false.[28] Moreover,

---

27. This is not to deny that the temptation among rhetoricians and Sophists to accommodate their message existed in the ancient world, since it clearly did. For Paul's era, cf. Dill's chapter on "The Philosophic Missionary" in *Roman Society,* 334-383. The issue for us, however, is whether this is the critique implied in *kapēleuein* as initiated by Plato (Socrates).

28. Dodds, *Plato: Gorgias,* 7, refers to the Sophist "claim to be able to teach

in addition to this basic philosophical disagreement concerning the nature of knowledge,[29] Plato argued that the Sophist's claim to be the wise teacher was also called into question by the content of what the Sophists themselves taught. Thus, in *Theaetetus* 161C and E, Socrates is said to object to the great Sophist Protagoras's claim to teach wisdom on the basis of Protagoras's own cardinal doctrine that "man is the measure of all things," since, for Protagoras, perception was said to be equated with knowledge.[30] For in Plato's (Socrates') view, this radical empiricism implied, in effect, that no one could teach or examine another person since each person, by definition, must always be right (cf. *Theaetetus* 152C)! Hence, for Plato, Protagoras's claim to be wise and able to impart wisdom to others was not only philosophically impossible, but was also contradicted by his own most fundamental principle. As Plato put it,

> Why in the world, my friend, was Protagoras wise, so that he could rightly be thought worthy to be the teacher of other men and to be well paid and why were we ignorant creatures and obliged to go to school to him, if each person is the measure of his own wisdom?[31]

Thus, that Protagoras was the first philosopher to demand a regular fee for his teaching (cf. *Prot.* 349A), in and of itself, was not the problem. Nor was it that the Sophists' teaching was correspondingly "watered down." The problem, quite simply, was that they claimed to be able to teach what could not be taught in the first place, i.e., wisdom and virtue.[32] Therefore, when we read in the texts from Plato listed by Windisch that "the Sophist is really a sort of merchant or dealer *(kapēlos)* in provisions

---

aretē (cf. Plato, *Meno* 459C6-460A4)" as "perhaps their most distinctive common feature." For Plato's description of the Sophists as those who teach virtue, cf. *Gorgias* 519E; *Prot.* 349A; *Meno* 95B. This, of course, was to be contrasted with Socrates' view of himself as merely a "midwife," whose task it was to elicit the knowledge already latent within each person by a dialectical method of teaching; cf. Plato, *Theaetetus* 148E-151D, 157C, and 161AB. For Socrates' main point that knowledge cannot be taught, cf. Finley, *Ancient Greeks*, 109.

29. For an outline of Plato's critique of the Sophists' theory of knowledge, cf. Gauss, *Handkommentar* III/1, 31-34.

30. Cf. *Theaetetus* 151E-152C for this classic definition and its implications.

31. *Theaetetus* 161DE.

32. For a good discussion of this problem and the meaning of *aretē* itself (i.e., as "luck," "prosperity," etc., rather than "virtue"), cf. Nestle, *Platon*, 53f.

on which a soul is nourished," that the Sophists are "hawking *(kapēleountes)* [their doctrines] about to any odd purchaser who desires them, commend[ing] everything that they sell,"[33] or that the Sophist is "a retailer" in "articles of knowledge for the soul,"[34] we must be careful not to read into these statements more than is intended or to place the accent on the wrong element. Because of the negative connotations which we naturally associate with "selling" or "hawking" something in such a context, it is easy to read these two descriptions as a condemnation of the Sophist because he receives money for teaching per se. This is even more natural, given Plato's critique of the Sophists. But as W. Nestle has pointed out, we must keep in mind that it was common practice for doctors, artists, and poets to charge a fee for their instruction and that even the philosopher Zeno, himself a Socratic, accepted payment for his lectures.[35] The practice of accepting money for one's teaching was not, in and of itself, morally reprehensible.

Indeed, the statement from *Protagoras* 313CD quoted above is a response to Hippocrates' ignorance concerning the nature of the knowledge he will gain from Protagoras and is intended, within its context, simply to make clear to Hippocrates that Protagoras is claiming to be able to make one a "Sophist," or at least to be able to educate one in the Sophist tradition (cf. 311B-312B). It is not intended to criticize Protagoras for selling his teaching as such. Moreover, in contrast to the impression given in recent literature, when Socrates then goes on to warn Hippocrates that he must be careful "that the Sophist in commending his wares does not deceive us, as both merchant and dealer do in the case of our bodily food" (*Prot.* 313D), the nature of the deception in view, which is common to both the "dealer" and the "Sophist," is not that they falsify their goods, but rather that they commend *all* of their wares indiscriminately, regardless of the fact that both the dealer and the Sophist are not able to distinguish between those things which are good or bad for the body and soul respectively (cf. *Prot.* 313DE). Hence, somewhat surprisingly, Socrates can conclude by advising his young friend that

33. *Prot.* 313CD.
34. *Sophist* 231D.
35. Cf. Nestle, *Platon,* 9 with n. 3 for the relevant literature.

if you are well informed as to what is good or bad among these wares, it will be safe for you to buy doctrines from Protagoras or from anyone else you please; but if not, take care, my dear fellow, that you do not risk your greatest treasure on a toss of the dice. For I tell you, there is far more serious risk in the purchase of doctrines than in that of eatables. (*Prot.* 313E-314A)

In a similar way, Plato's sixfold description of the Sophist in *Sophist* 231DE (cf. the entire discussion from 223D on, of which the list in 231DE is merely the summary) is also intended to emphasize that the Sophist, in contrast to the statesman and the philosopher (cf. *Soph.* 217A), is, by definition, the one dedicated to trading in the knowledge conveyed by words and disputation, in contrast to the other class of "art-merchants," who deal in the kind of knowledge which is conveyed materially (i.e., in painting, sculpture, etc.; cf. 224C, E). Hence, although Plato also distinguishes between those who engage in the "exchanging" of goods which they have not made themselves *within a city,* which he calls "retailing," and those who exchange goods *from city to city* by selling and buying, which he calls "merchandising" (*Soph.* 223D),[36] the Sophist can nevertheless be described as either a "merchant" or a "retailer," or even a "seller of his own productions." The decisive characteristic of the Sophist is simply the fact that he belongs to the class of those who are "merchandising in knowledge" (see *Soph.* 224E).[37]

But here as well, the Sophist practice of selling his teaching

---

36. Although Plato's basic distinction between the retailer and retail selling (*kapēlos/kapēleuein*) and the wholesaler and wholesale trade (*emporos/emporeuomai*) holds up, the categories were by no means so well defined as they are in modern commerce. In fact, in the fourth and fifth centuries BCE the two terms could even be used interchangeably to denote "trader" / "trade" in a general, generic sense. Cf. Plato, *Republic* 260CD, 525D; Aristotle, *Politics* I.8.1256a-1258a, 1258b; Finkelstein, "Ἔμπορος," 323f., 327, 329, 332. What is important to keep in mind is that for Plato the essential nature of retail dealing was its practice of trading/selling for the sake of gain or profit; cf. *Laws,* VIII.847D. That this is also the case for Paul's day is clear from Pliny the Elder, *Natural History* 18.225.

37. *Soph.* 224E: "that part of acquisitive art which proceeds by exchange and by sale, whether as mere retail trade *(kapēlikon)* or the sale of one's own productions, no matter which, so long as it is of the class of merchandising in knowledge, you will always, apparently, call Sophistry."

receives its negative connotation in Plato as a hunt after "rich and promising youths" (223B; cf. 231D) only because of its accompanying claim to provide an education in wisdom and virtue (223A). For to Plato, the Sophist's only accomplishment is his ability to appear wise about everything, as a result of his mastery of the art of disputation, without actually conveying knowledge or wisdom about anything (235A). It is this ability to appear wise that attracts the young and the rich (cf. *Soph.* 232B-233C) and wins for the Sophists the negative reputation of being

> nothing else, apparently, than the money-making class of the disputatious, argumentative, controversial, pugnacious, combative, acquisitive art. . . .

It must again be emphasized, however, that for all its negative nuances, the point of Plato's critique in his extended discussion in *Soph.* 223D-235A is not that the Sophists "water down" their message, nor indeed that they even sell it, but instead, that they claim to sell, and appear to sell as a result of their rhetorical skills, what they do not have, do not understand well enough to be able to identify, and cannot produce, namely, the wisdom needed to nourish the soul.[38] For it must be kept in mind that the basis of Plato's criticism of the Sophists was not that they sold their wares, but that their wares, if properly understood, could not be sold. In other words, it was Plato's philosophical conviction that knowledge and wisdom could not be taught that made the practice of accepting money for teaching them reprehensible, not the fact they were being sold per se.[39] For Plato, Sophistry was a sham, and its teachers were entertainers (see *Soph.* 235A). What they sold was worthless.

That the practice of accepting money for one's instruction, in and

---

38. As Gauss, *Handkommentar* III/1, 192, puts it, they fall prey to what Plato called the second grade of "ignorance" or the "double ignorance," namely, "when someone, who does not know something, nevertheless imagines himself to know it." Cf. *Soph.* 229C.

39. As evidenced by the fact that according to Diogenes, even a student of Socrates himself, Aristippus (ca. 435-350 BCE), could charge fees for his teaching; cf. Diogenes Laertius 2.65, 72. Diogenes goes on to tell us that Aristippus sent money from his earnings to his teacher as well, though this bothered Socrates.

of itself, did not in the fourth century BCE necessarily imply either a negative judgment concerning the teaching being sold, nor a criticism of the motives of the one selling it can be further illustrated by the writings of Plato's contemporary Isocrates (436-388 BCE), who was not only influenced by Socrates, but also by the Sophist Gorgias.[40] For in Isocrates' own critique of the Sophists, those teachers who devote themselves to "disputation" manifest the perversity of their proposals not in that they offer them for money, but rather in the fact that they do not charge enough for their services, i.e., they fail to charge what their teaching would be genuinely worth if their claims were valid.

> Although they set themselves up as masters and dispensers of goods so precious, they are not ashamed of asking for them a price of three or four minae! Why, if they were to sell any other commodity for so trifling a fraction of its worth they would not deny their folly; nevertheless, although they set so insignificant a price on the whole stock of virtue and happiness, they pretend to wisdom and assume the right to instruct the rest of the world. (*Against the Sophists* 4)[41]

Conversely, in *Antidosis* 225-226 and 240-241, Isocrates can point to the fact that his pupils go to great lengths to come to him, paying him for his instruction, and that parents gladly pay him for teaching their sons, as evidence of the integrity of the education he offered. It is significant, moreover, that when Isocrates in *Antidosis* 197ff. explicitly takes up the criticisms usually leveled against the Sophists, there is no mention whatsoever of the fact that they charge a fee for their instruction. What is to be criticized is the duplicity of those Sophists who "speak contemptuously of wealth as 'filthy lucre,' claiming not to want money," while at the same time holding "their hands out for a trifling gain" (*Against the Sophists* 4).

Thus, in Plato's day, the mere fact that one charged a fee for teaching could be either positive or negative, depending on the attending circumstances. Furthermore, that one did so never implied that one's message had been accommodated or watered down according to the interests of the audience. Instead, rather than casting doubt on one's

40. Cf. Norlin, *Isocrates* I, xi-xviii.
41. Cf. also Plato, *Apology* 20B for the same critique.

message, to sell one's instruction implied that what one had to teach was valuable enough to warrant its purchase. To sell one's teaching was, in effect, to make a *positive* claim concerning the worth of one's message. Socrates himself is said to take Protagoras's demand for a fee as evidence of his confidence in his own abilities (cf. Plato, *Prot.* 348E). Conversely, Protagoras boasts that he gives "full value for the fee that [he] charge[s]—nay, so much more than full, that the learner himself admits it" (*Prot.* 328B). In fact, Protagoras is said to have only charged what people thought his teaching was worth, while his students were required to pay what he asked only if they were satisfied with what they had learned (cf. *Prot.* 328B). In Diodorus Siculus XII.53.2 we have a first-century BCE positive evaluation of the fact that Gorgias was paid. Diodorus reports that Gorgias "so far excelled all other men in the instruction offered by the Sophists that he received from his pupils a fee of one hundred minas."

This, then, is the underlying presupposition behind the anti-Sophist polemic of both Plato and Isocrates. For in selling their teaching, the Sophists were implicitly claiming a value for that which had none.

The only other occurrence of the word-group *kapēlos/kapēleuein* in the corpus of Plato's writings of significance for our study[42] is found in Book XI of Plato's *Laws*, which, as his last work, is dated between 357 and 347 BCE.[43] Here Plato takes up business dealings of all sorts, devoting a large section to a discussion of commercial honesty (cf. *Laws* XI.915D-920C), within which there is an extended treatment of the nature and limitations of retail business (XI.918A-919C). At first glance, this discussion seems to support those who wish to translate II Cor. 2:17 "water down," "adulterate," etc., since Plato's reflections concerning retail business take place immediately after his discussion of the practice of adulterating goods (cf. 916D-918A). For in Plato's words, "Following close upon the practices of adulteration follow practices of retail trading *(kapēleias)*" (XI.918A).

But a careful reading of Plato's treatment of this theme shows that

---

42. Based on an investigation of the 25 occurrences of the word-group listed by Ast, *Lexicon Platonicum* II, 139-140.

43. So Bury, *Plato* IX, vii.

these two ideas are closely linked together not because retail trading necessarily implies an adulteration of one's goods, but because both the practice of adulteration and the corruption of retail business lead to a similar sort of commercial injustice and are motivated by the same impulse of human greed. Hence, the lawgiver must deal with both areas in a similar manner (cf. XI.920B). Plato's treatment of the nature of retail business itself nowhere associates selling with the corrupting or adulterating of goods. Rather, Plato's burden is to offer an apologetic for the positive and necessary purpose of retail business, i.e., "to provide all men with full satisfaction for their needs," in spite of the fact that it "is reputed to be a thing not noble nor even respectable" (XI.928C). For in Plato's view, the problem with retail trade does not lie in its practice of selling something for a profit, for which it has even been ordained (cf. XI.918B), but in the greed of those who do the selling.[44] In his words,

> when they desire, they desire without limit, and when they can make moderate gains, they prefer to gain insatiably, and it is because of this that all the classes concerned with retail trade, commerce, and inn-keeping are disparaged and subject to violent abuse. (XI.918D)

Conversely, if someone compelled

> the best men everywhere for a certain period to keep inns or to peddle *(kapēleuein)* or to carry on any such trade,—or even to compel women by some necessity of fate to take part in such a mode of life,—then we should learn how that each of these callings is friendly and desirable; and if all these callings were carried on according to a rule free from corruption, they would be honoured with the honour which one pays to a mother or a nurse. (XI.918E)

44. The importance of Plato's position becomes clear when we compare it with Aristotle's largely negative discussion of the origin and nature of retail trade in *Politica* I.8.1256ª41-I.9.1257. For although he too seems to admit that retail trade is necessary for the state (cf. *Pol.* IV.4.1920ᵇ40-1291ª5), it nevertheless remains, in and of itself, something negative, since its aim, in his view, is to make a profit at the expense of others on the one hand (cf. *Pol.* 1258ᵇ1-2), and since it deals only in money, which for Aristotle is an "unnatural" basis for self-sufficiency, on the other hand. His position is ambiguous, however, since in *Pol.* 1258ª14-18 he seems to grant that retail business is unnecessary altogether. Cf. Finley, "Aristotle," esp. pp. 42-44.

An investigation of Plato's use of the verb "to engage in retail trade" (*kapēleuein*) thus yields a surprising result. Even if Windisch is correct in asserting that Paul's use of this verb in II Cor. 2:17 "goes back indeed to the polemic against the Sophists inaugurated by Plato,"[45] his corollary that *kapēleuein* also carries the "secondary meaning" of "adulterating" or "falsifying" the object of one's trade cannot be substantiated on the basis of Plato's writings, not to mention the attempt to consider this its primary meaning. Nowhere in Plato's discussion does the idea of retail selling for the purpose of making a profit *(kapēleuein)*, either in its concrete sense, or in its transferred sense as applied to the Sophists, denote, or even connote, the idea of falsifying or adulterating the object being sold. Rather, if that which is sold is itself of no value, then to sell it becomes reprehensible. But even more surprising is the fact that Plato nowhere disparages the Sophist practice of charging a fee for their teaching in and of itself, while on the other hand he can even defend the practice of retailing, though he recognizes that the greed of those engaged in such an occupation can easily lead to its corruption. As a result, it must be carefully regulated (see *Laws* IX.919C-929C).[46]

It is this realization that provides the key to Plato's use of "retailer"/ "to engage in retail trade" in his critique of the Sophists. For given Plato's realization that those engaged in market-trade often fall prey to their greed and are therefore tempted to take advantage of people's need in order to make an undue profit (cf. *Laws* 918E), it served Plato's purpose well to use this often pejorative *technical terminology*[47] to describe those philosophers whose message he wished to call into question. It should be emphasized that Plato did not use this motif,

45. Windisch, *Zweiter Korintherbrief*, 100.

46. Though it is nowhere explicitly stated, one cannot help but wonder, therefore, whether, even for Plato, if one's motives were pure and if virtue could be taught, if there would then be any reason that one could not sell it, as Plato himself assumes in the case of doctors, poets, artists, language teachers, music teachers, and sports instructors (cf. *Prot.* 311BC; 312AB).

47. Again, it is important to keep in mind that the word-group *kapēlos/kapēleuein* is a technical designation referring to the type of business carried on in the market. As Finley, "Aristotle," 42, summarizes it: "Greek usage was not wholly consistent in selecting among the various words for 'trader,' but *kapēlos* usually denoted the petty trader, the huckster, in the market place," i.e., it refers specifically to "trade for the sake of gain" or "commercial trade."

associated with the problem of greed in *Laws* 918DE, to criticize the Sophists for being greedy, but simply to cast doubt on their teaching in general. For as we have seen, the function of *kapēlos/kapēleuein* in Plato's critique of the Sophists is not to impugn their motives, but to cast doubt upon the value of their teaching. As such, the importance of recognizing the negative nuances associated with market-trade in Plato's day is *not* that it now provides a key to the *content* of a critique in which this motif is employed, but that it signals to us *that* a critique is intended.[48] In Plato's case, the negative connotations associated with the trader/retail dealer in his day[49] provided him with a linguistic vehicle by which he could cast doubt on the legitimacy of a particular circle of Sophists who sold their teaching, *without necessarily condemning the practice of charging a fee for one's teaching in and of itself.* In the same way, he could speak of the negative reputation of those engaged in retail trade (see *Laws* 918C-E, 919C), while at the same time defending its legitimacy (*Laws* 918E). But since for Socrates virtue and wisdom could not be taught to begin with, he refused to accept payment for his "teaching" as a matter of principle.

b. Sirach, Josephus, and Philo

The widespread nature of this negative nuance associated with *kapēlos/ kapēleuein* is evidenced by its attestation in the second-century BCE Jewish world of Jesus ben Sirach. For the statement in Sir. 26:29,

---

48. Contra Hock, *Social Context*, 52f., who writes that

the practice of charging fees, as popular as it was, was criticized by others, most notably by Socrates. Widely known for not charging fees, Socrates, particularly in the Platonic writings, compared Sophists to traders and merchants *(kapēloi)*, the comparison being made to impute to Sophists the motives of deceit and avarice.

Hock (p. 95 n. 23) lists in support of this statement *Men.* 92a; *Euthyd.* 277B (as evidence for the motive of deceit); and Xenophon, *Mem.* 1.2.7 (as evidence for the motive of greed). I was unable to find a use of *kapēlos* in either of the first two references, while in the last Socrates refuses to accept money, not because of the negative connotations associated with doing so, but because doing so would "enslave" him, i.e., he would then be forced to converse with whoever paid him.

49. For other clear examples of such negative views of marketplace trade from this period, cf. Herodotus I.152-3; Xenophon, *Cyropaedia* 1.2.3; and possibly Aeschylus, *Fragments* 322, though the fragment is too small to be sure.

> Hardly shall the merchant keep himself from wrongdoing,
> and a huckster *(kapēlos)* will not be acquitted of sin

is surely built on the premise expressed in 27:1-3 that

> many have sinned for the sake of gain;
> and he that seeketh to multiply (gain) turneth away his eye.
> A nail sticketh fast between the joinings of stones,
> and sin will thrust itself in between buyer and seller.
> My son, if thou hold not diligently to the fear of the Lord,
> thy house will soon be overthrown.

Hence, for Sirach as well, although it was not sinful to engage in retail trade in and of itself (there is no admonition to leave this sort of work altogether),[50] it undoubtedly carried with it an undeniable note of suspicion and caution.

Moreover, the writings of Philo and Josephus illustrate that this same negative connotation was still current among Hellenistic Jews of Paul's day, and that it could be employed in a variety of ways. In *De Gigantibus* 39, Philo supports his admonition not to seek wealth or glory, which "infects philosophy with the baseness of mere opinion," by referring to the practice of those philosophers who sell their teaching in the market. Equally important for our study, however, is that Philo can assume that his judgment concerning these philosophers is common ground between him and his readers, thus presupposing an opinion which must have been widespread. In his words,

> For manifest surely and clear is the disgrace of those who say that they are wise, yet barter their wisdom for what they can get, as men say is the way of the pedlars who hawk their goods in the market. And sometimes the price is just a trifling gain. . . .

Thus, although, like Isocrates, Philo's critique of those who barter their wisdom seems to focus on the fact that they cheapen it by selling it for

---

50. It is therefore misleading to relate Sir. 26:29 to the condemnations of traders in Zech. 14:21 and Zeph. 1:11, as Windisch, καπηλεύω *(TDNT)*, 603 n. 2, does, inasmuch as these latter passages are not general denunciations of those engaged in trade, but rather, as Windisch himself points out, a specific judgment against foreign traders who were selling on the Sabbath. Cf. Neh. 10:31; 13:16-22.

so little,[51] and not on the fact that it is sold per se, it is nevertheless clear that he assumes that his readers would agree with him that for a philosopher to be compared to a peddler is no compliment. This is confirmed by his statement in *Vita Mosis* II.212, where Philo asserts that true wisdom

> must not be that of the systems hatched by the word-catchers and Sophists who sell their tenets and arguments like any bit of merchandise in the market, men who forever pit philosophy against philosophy without a blush. . . .

Here as well, the fact that the Sophists are associated with the retail practice of the marketplace obviously casts a shadow of suspicion on the quality of their wisdom. But once again, the problem in view is not the practice of selling, but rather, in this case, that the Sophists manifest the disunity of their teaching by competitively pitting one philosophy against another, in contrast to the unity of the true wisdom represented by Philo. Nevertheless, the marketplace continues to carry the negative connotation necessary to call the Sophists into question.

In yet a third context, Josephus expands the prohibition in Lev. 21:7, which for the sake of purity forbade a priest to marry a harlot, by adding to it those women who "gain their livelihood by hawking *(ek kapēleias)* or innkeeping" (*Ant.* III.276). In doing so, Josephus seems to be influenced by the targumic practice of translating the Hebrew *zwnh* ("harlot") with *pwndqyt'* (from the Greek *pandokeuein*, "to keep an inn"), perhaps due to the ill-fame of inns in the ancient world.[52] It is significant, therefore, that "retail trade" is drawn into this negative association—an indication that it too must have carried a similar negative connotation, though the precise nature of this connotation remains unclear.[53]

51. Philo describes their practice with *epeuōnizōn,* which is best translated as "selling cheap"; cf. Colson and Whitaker, *Philo* II, 486, §123 and *De cher.* 123.

52. So Thackeray, *Josephus* IV, 241, note. He refers to the targumic rendering of Josh. 2:1; Jud. 11:1; I Kgs. 3:16 as examples. Jastrow, *Dictionary,* 1144, lists in addition the Targum to Ezek. 23:44 and translates the word "keeper of a public house, harlot."

53. Cf. also *c. Ap.* I.61 where Josephus uses *kapēleia* together with *emporia* ("inter-city commerce") without any negative overtones. It is possible that Josephus is using *kapēleia* here to mean "inn-keeping" or "tavernkeeping," as in Xenophon, *Anabasis* 1.2.24; Plutarch, *Isis and Osiris* 369; Dio Cassius, *Roman History* 62.14.2;

Hence, although the nature of the negative connotation associated with the marketplace and those engaged in its trade could vary from the "cheapness" associated with bartering, to its competitive nature, to the morally "shady" character of its milieu, it is nevertheless evident that to be compared with the "retailers" meant to suffer guilt by association.[54] Indeed, the significance of the usage of this motif by Philo and Josephus lies in the fact that the marketplace can now be seen to represent a *variety* of negative attributes depending on the context in which it is employed.[55] In other words, the semantic field encompassed by this word-group and its synonyms has obviously been widened with time to include a broad spectrum of related negative connotations and qualities.[56]

But there is still no evidence for the supposition that the verb *kapēleuein* ("to sell as a retailer") itself can mean "adulterate," "water

---

65.10.3. Cf. also Rostovtzeff, *Hellenistic World* III, 162 n. 196, who points out that "the meaning of the term *kapēlos* in Ptolemaic Egypt appears to be, not retail trader in general, but dealer in certain foodstuffs and caterer, keeper of an inn, of a tavern, or of a wineshop. . . ."

54. We must be careful, however, not to assume that this was always the case. Thus, for example, when Liddell-Scott list Demosthenes, *Against Aristogeiton* 25.46 as an example of a metaphorical use of *kapēlos* to mean a "dealer in petty roguery" (*Greek-English Lexicon*, 876), we should not assume that *kapēlos* itself carries this negative connotation. In the context it simply refers to Aristogeiton's practice of dealing in wickedness. This same thing is true of their references to Dio Cassius, *Roman History* 60.17.8 and Herodotus III.89. In both cases the negative judgment falls not on retail trading, but on the fact that those in view were selling what should not have been sold. Finally, Liddell-Scott also list Dionysius of Halicarnassus, *Roman Antiquities* IX.25.2 to support the meaning of "cheating, knavish" for *kapēlos*. But all we learn from this reference is that "no Roman citizen was permitted to earn a livelihood as a tradesman or artisan."

55. Cf., e.g., Aeschylus, *Seven against Thebes* 545 (531 in Verrall's enumeration), where *kapēleuein* can even represent the idea of acting in a small and insignificant manner, based no doubt on the fact that most retail trading in the ancient world was done on a very small scale. For in describing the fifth chief to come up against Thebes, the poet writes, "once arrived he will do no petty cozening in the trade (*ou kapēleusein*) of war, but something worthy of the long journey he hath travelled."

56. This same negative connotation concerning merchants is also found later among the rabbis; cf. b. Erubin 55a and b. Kidd. 82a; though Pirke Aboth II.2 illustrates the positive value attached to the practice of those rabbis who supported themselves with an occupation.

down," or "falsify," etc. The variety of negative connotations which now surround this verb have not changed its basic meaning, but are all related to the general practice of selling as it was carried on by the lower-class retail traders in the market. With this in mind, we can now turn our attention to the last, and perhaps most important, uses of *kapēleuein* for our study, namely, its use by the second-century writer Lucian in his essay *Hermotimus* 59 on the one hand, and in Is. 1:22 on the other hand. For here we encounter what appears to be the strongest evidence for the idea that the verb could also signify the idea of "watering down" something, as a wine dealer dilutes his wine. As such, these two passages become the non-Pauline proof texts most often cited in support of the idea that Paul is accusing his opponents of adulterating the gospel in II Cor. 2:17.[57]

c. Lucian, Philostratus, and Isaiah

In turning to the voluminous works of Lucian (ca. 125-180 CE), the first thing to note is that the verb *kapēleuein* itself nowhere occurs in his writings, although the two related nouns, "retailer" *(kapēlos)* and "bazaar" *(kapēleion),* occur three and two times respectively.[58] Thus, in *The Wisdom of Nigrinus* 25, in a description of the disgust Nigrinus felt over those "self-styled philosophers" of his day who frequented the dinner parties of the rich, Lucian comments that not only did Nigrinus think this ridiculous, but he also

> made special mention of people who cultivate philosophy for hire and put virtue on sale over a counter, as it were: indeed, he called the lecture-rooms of these men factories and bazaars *(kapēleia).*

But, as we saw in the case of Isocrates and Philo, here too this negative reference to the practice of selling one's own lectures is not grounded in the fact that to do so is itself reprehensible, but in the fact that by

57. Cf. for example, besides the commentaries already listed above (see nn. 18, 20, 22), the standard New Testament lexicon of Bauer (1957[1], 404; 1979[2], 403), where we read, "Because of the tricks of small tradesmen (Dio Chrys. 14 [31], 37f.; Lucian, *Hermot.* 59 . . . Is. 1:22 . . .) the word comes to mean almost *adulterate* (so Vulg., Syr., Goth.)."

58. According to Iacobitz, *Lucianus,* 551-552.

doing so these philosophers contradict their own teaching, thus becoming hypocrites.[59] As Lucian puts it, "one who intends to teach contempt for wealth should first of all show that he is himself above gain."[60] Hence, Nigrinus gave "instructions without recompense to all who desired it . . ." (*Nigr.* 26).

Moreover, Lucian's essay *On Salaried Posts in Great Houses* makes it clear that earning a living or receiving a salary for teaching philosophy is not, as such, morally wrong. For here one of his basic criticisms of those who attached themselves to the households of the rich was not that they were seeking money for their teaching, but that they sold their teaching (and, in effect, themselves) for a trifling of what it was worth. Hence, although it often appeared to be otherwise from the outside, Lucian can maintain, albeit with a great deal of irony, that those philosophers who became the resident intellectuals for rich patrons had settled for an existence which was financially no better than poverty (cf. *Salaried Posts* 4, 5, 20-22, 30, 38-39).

In his later essay, *Apology for the "Salaried Posts in Great Houses,"* Lucian goes on to defend the practice of being paid as a philosopher, as well as to respond to those who would criticize him for now being paid himself as a government employee. He does so by reminding them that previously he had commanded "the highest fees for the public practice of rhetoric" and that his "fees were as high as those of any professor"— for which he was never criticized (*Apology* 15).

Finally, in *A Professor of Public Speaking* 9, Lucian regards the fact that the teachers of the old and arduous school of rhetoric demanded large sums of money for their education as a *positive* indication of its value, in contrast to the short and easy education in oratorical methods which was becoming increasingly popular in his own day and which might have been characterized by its free teaching.[61] As a result, we must be careful not to create a general maxim out of what in *The Wisdom of Nigrinus* 25 was intended merely as a criticism of a specific instance of hypocrisy.

59. For this same point, cf. Lucian, *Menippus* 5.
60. On the centrality of the theme of hypocrisy in Lucian's writings, which he applies to almost all of the professions alike except historians, cf. Anderson, "Lucian," 66f. He calls Lucian's various uses of the critique of hypocrisy "the main achievement of Lucian's satirical output."
61. Cf. the introduction to the essay by Harmon, *Lucian* IV, 133.

This same caution must be expressed concerning the statement in the *Life of Apollonius* (I.13) by Philostratus (born 170 CE). Here we read that Apollonius attempted to "wean" his rival Sophist Euphrates "of his love of filthy lucre and his huckstering his wisdom *(tēn sophian kapēleuein)*." But here, too, this disparaging comment owes its origin to Apollonius's own extremely ascetic life-style and not to a widespread and popular condemnation of selling one's instruction (cf. *Life,* I.13-14). In fact, as Philostratus's own biographical treatise *The Lives of the Sophists* shows, Sophists of his day enjoyed tremendous popularity and amassed huge fortunes from their teaching (cf. *Lives,* 527, 566). Indeed, the presence of a leading Sophist often brought great benefits to a city (cf. *Lives,* 530-533).[62]

Consequently, the same ambiguous attitude toward selling one's teaching that we encountered almost five centuries earlier in Plato and Isocrates continues to be attested in the writings of Lucian and Philostratus. Furthermore, when Lucian and Philostratus wish to criticize certain circles of philosophers for selling their teaching, though they themselves assume and even defend the right of philosophers to be paid, they too draw on the marketplace/selling analogy to do so.[63]

This becomes even clearer in Lucian's important statement in *Hermotimus* 59, where we find the assertion that wine and philosophy have one thing in common, namely, "that philosophers sell their lessons as wine merchants *(kapēloi)* their wares—most of them adulterating and cheating and giving false measure." This statement seems to be the ideal prooftext for the usual understanding of II Cor. 2:17 because of the use of *kapēlos* to mean "wine merchant" and because of the link between the wine merchant and the practice of adulterating

---

62. For a recent discussion of this theme, cf. Bowie, "Importance of Sophists," who argues that the primary factor in the rise of the Sophists to positions of wealth and power was not their professional status and abilities, but their aristocratic family backgrounds (cf. p. 53).

63. This corresponds to the negative view of the marketplace current among the Roman upper class in general. Cf. the entry *kapēlos* in MacMullen's "Lexicon of Snobbery," in his *Roman Social Relations,* 139. Of the seven sources listed, however, only Cicero, *De off.* I.150 predates the second century CE—and there is a question just how representative Cicero's view actually was. Cf. below, pp. 137f.

one's wares *(doloō)*, which seems to support the decision to read II Cor. 2:17 in the light of 4:2.

But the use of *kapēlos* to refer specifically to those who sell wine in *Herm.* 59 does not signify a new technical use of the word, but refers back to *Herm.* 58, where the retailer in view had already been explicitly defined as one of those retailers, good and bad, who deal in wine. This is confirmed by the fact that in *Herm.* 61 *kapēlos* is again used, in a different context, to refer to those merchants who deal in grain, while in *Pseudologista* 9 and *Nigrinus* 25 on the one hand, and in *How to Write History* 16 on the other hand, *kapēleion* and *kapēlos*, without further specification, maintain their general and neutral sense of "bazaar" and "peddler" respectively.[64]

Thus, *Herm.* 59 also refers to a *particular* criticism of philosophers, i.e., that they water down their teaching, which can only be associated with "retailers" in this context because the dealers in view have already been identified specifically as wine merchants. Moreover, even though this identification has been made, the related idea of "watering down" or "adulterating" is still not implied in the ideas of "retailer" or "bazaar," but is only expressed by the *additional* assertion in the context concerning those in the wine trade (and not all, but "most of them") who "water down" *(doloō)* their wine. In a word, it is *doloō* and not *kapēleuo* which signifies this idea.[65]

---

64. This confirms for the second century CE what Finkelstein, "Ἔμπορος," 334, observed for the fourth and fifth centuries BCE, namely, that *kapēlos* cannot be linked exclusively to the wine trade, since "all the evidence clearly indicates that this commercial terminology took in every aspect of trade." This is against the position expressed by Trench, *Synonyms*, 228f.

65. Again, one must be careful not to read too much into *kapēlos*. For example, Hock, *Social Context*, 95 n. 24, lists Lucian's references in *Nig.* 25 and *Herm.* 59 as evidence for his assertion that this noun is applied to "greedy philosophers," although we have seen that the idea of greed is not in view in either context, though it is associated with *kapēleuein* in Philostratus, *Life* I.13, also listed by Hock. But even in *Life* I.13 this idea is not carried in the verb *kapēleuein* but is expressed by an additional assertion. So it is not at all certain that *kapēleuein* itself could imply this nuance. Hock also refers to Philostratus, *Lives of the Sophists* 526 as evidence for the idea that Sophists were labeled *"kapēloi"* when they were thought to be deceitful or avaricious (cf. pp. 53, 95 n. 24). But I am unable to find any mention of *kapēloi* in this text. In fact, the Sophists in view in this context, Dionysius and Lullianus, are both treated very favorably.

In the same way, in Is. 1:22 (LXX), "Your silver is worthless, thy wine merchants *(kapēloi)* mix the wine with water," *kapēlos* receives its specific connotation "wine dealer" only because of the explicit reference to wine in the sentence. Furthermore, as in Lucian's statement in *Herm.* 59, here too the idea of "watering down" or "adulteration" is not signified by *kapēlos*, but by the predicate "they are mixing" *(misgousi*, from *mignumi,* "to mix"). In addition, it is important to note that the point of Is. 1:22, as part of Isaiah's condemnation of Judah and Jerusalem (cf. vv. 1ff.), is to illustrate the idea expressed in v. 21 that the faithful city of Zion, which once was full of judgment, has now become a harlot, i.e., that that which *once* was good, is now corrupt. Hence, the merchants in view, like the silver, only carry negative connotations because they are now explicitly said to have been corrupted, not because, as we saw in Sir. 26:29, they are retailers (of wine) and therefore inherently suspect.

d. Conclusion

Our investigation of the use of *kapēlos/kapēleuein* in the polemic against the Sophists and its attestation in Hellenistic Judaism thus leads to two important conclusions. First, to my knowledge, there is no evidence that this word-group ever directly signified the idea of "watering down," "adulterating," or "falsifying" or that these ideas were ever present as part of the wider semantic field of the verb.[66] When the idea of "adulterating," etc., is present in association with the verb "to sell as a retailer," it is not signified by the verb itself, but by an *additional* verbal statement (i.e., "to water down" [*doloō*] in Lucian, *Herm.* 59, "to adulterate" [*kibdēleuein*] in Plato, and "to mix" [*mignumi*] in Is. 1:22) *and* by a *contrast* with the ideal practice, exemplified in those with whom the ones "selling" their wares/teaching are compared (e.g., Socrates, Isocrates, Moses [!] in Philo, *Vita Mosis* II.212, Nigrinus, Lucian, and Appollonius).

66. Cf. also Moulton/Milligan, *Vocabulary,* 321, who list no evidence of it ever meaning "to adulterate" and even state that "this verb is confined in Biblical Greek to 2 Cor. 2:17, where the meaning 'deal in for purposes of gain' rather than 'adulterate' may be illustrated from BGU IV.1024vii23. . . ."

The parallel to Paul's usage is clear. Unless Paul is deviating from normal semantic usage, for which there is no indication in the context, II Cor. 2:17 ought to be rendered "selling the Word of God as a retail dealer sells his wares in the market."[67] The attempt to read "to sell as a retailer" in 2:17 as a direct synonym of "to water down" or "to adulterate" in 4:2 finds no lexical support in the evidence available to us. This is not to deny that 2:17 and 4:2 are related or even parallel. It is simply to suggest that these two statements, though parallel in function, nevertheless represent two *distinct* assertions, i.e., Paul wishes to deny that he is selling (2:17) *or* watering down (4:2) God's word.

Second, on the basis of the literary evidence available it is clear that this market motif, when used in a transferred sense in reference to the practice of selling one's teaching, always carries an additional *negative nuance*, although the precise nature of this negative connotation is by no means uniform, but can vary given the particular nature of the critique intended by the author. Hence, in II Cor. 2:17 Paul is intending to *criticize* the "majority" rather than simply indicating that they are earning their living from the gospel. This is confirmed by the comparative structure of 2:17 itself, in which Paul presents *himself as the representative of the ideal practice.*

This conclusion concerning the negative metaphorical use of the marketplace imagery finds an important confirmation in *Didache* XII.5, where the Church is warned about those who wish to live off the Church's generosity without working, i.e., one who is simply "making traffic of Christ" *(christemporos)*. Once again, however, this warning ought not to be taken as a prohibition against earning one's living from the gospel per se. For as *Didache* XIII.1-6 makes clear, genuine local prophets *are* to be supported by the firstfruit offering of the Church, while prophets who are traveling may receive two days' lodging and food to last for the next day's journey (cf. XI.5f.). Thus, here as well, the practice of earning one's living from the gospel is viewed positively, while those who are fraudulent in claiming this privilege can be appropriately described in marketplace imagery.

The impression left by the evidence available to us, therefore, is that the practice of selling in the market was suspicious enough in the

---

67. So too Wendland, *An die Korinther,* 177.

ancient world to enable this idea and its synonyms to be used in a pejorative sense without the nature of that suspicion being so well defined that the verb *kapēleuein* itself came to imply a standard criticism. It thus provided an ideal vehicle for those who wished to call someone into question who was earning their living from teaching without calling into question the practice of being paid for teaching itself, since it cast doubt upon the integrity of their being paid and/or their teaching, while at the same time leaving room for the individual author to supply the content of that criticism.

Hence, the question before us, once it becomes clear that II Cor. 2:17 cannot be translated "to water down" or "adulterate," as found not only in the Vulgate,[68] but also in the majority of modern commentaries, is twofold. First, what is the nature of Paul's criticism of those in view, implied by his use of this marketplace imagery and the comparative structure of 2:17; and second, how does this criticism support his own claim to be sufficient for the apostolic office? The answers to these questions can only be determined on the basis of II Cor. 2:17 itself and its place within the Corinthian correspondence.

C. THE THEME OF II COR. 2:17 AND ITS PLACE WITHIN THE CORINTHIAN CORRESPONDENCE

Once it becomes evident that II Cor. 2:17 refers to the practice of selling in the marketplace, Paul's decision to employ this motif to support his claim to be sufficient for the apostolic ministry, albeit in a negative way, indicates that the issue in view is again Paul's refusal to seek his financial support from the Corinthian church. Paul's insistence that he not be classed with those who are "selling the Word of God" is no doubt intended to remind the Corinthians of his prior discussion in I Cor. 9, where Paul had explained in detail the reasons for his refusal to earn his living from the gospel.[69]

---

68. *Non enim sumus sicut plurimi adulterantes verbum Dei.*

69. See Munck, *Paul*, 181, who recognized that 2:17 referred to the fact that Paul is not a peddler of God's word and hence concluded that "we see, therefore,

At the same time, however, Paul's use of the marketplace motif to describe those with whom he compares himself also points forward to II Cor. 11 and 12. The negative connotations which certainly surround "selling the word of God" in this context anticipate the intensely polemical nature of Paul's later discussion of this theme as part of his apology for his apostolic ministry in chapters 10–13. As a result, not only the meaning of II Cor. 2:17 itself, but also the organic relationship in our present context between Paul's view of his suffering, his claim to sufficiency, and his refusal to accept financial support from the Corinthians will only become clear in the light of Paul's prior discussion of these themes in I Cor. 9 and their resumption in II Cor. 11:7-21 and 12:12-19.[70]

1. I Cor. 9

a. The Function of I Cor. 9 within Paul's Argument in I Cor. 8–10

The first observation to be made concerning I Cor. 9, as well as the first point of significance for our study, is that Paul's discussion of his apostolic life-style of self-support in I Cor. 9 is not accorded an independent status. Instead, rather than being discussed for its own sake, Paul's self-support is brought up in chapter 9 within and as an integral part of his larger discussion of the problem in Corinth concerning meat offered to idols, which extends from 8:1 through 11:1.[71] For as the close parallels between Paul's admonitions to the Corinthians in 8:9; 10:24, 32 and his own practice as outlined in 9:12, 18-22; 10:33

---

that the question of Paul's economic independence is an old problem for the Corinthians. . . ." But as we shall see below, although II Cor. 2:17 does refer back to I Cor. 9, the issue of Paul's decision to support himself was an intensification of the "old problem."

70. The issue here is whether 2:17 relates to the polemic against the teaching of Paul's opponents in chs. 10–13 (e.g., 10:5f.; 11:4)—i.e., if 2:17 is taken to be a contrast to those who "water down" the gospel—or to his discussion of his decision to support himself in 11:7-15 and 12:12-19. Those commentators who render *kapēleuein* "adulterate," etc., naturally do not see these important parallels.

71. For the opposite position, cf., e.g., Conzelmann, *Erster Korintherbrief*, 187.

make clear, Paul's decision not to take advantage of his apostolic right to financial support was intended to provide an illustration of the ethical principle of love-controlled freedom (cf. 8:1) articulated by Paul as the solution to the Corinthians' problem.[72] Especially important are the parallels between 8:9 and 9:12 and between 10:32 and 9:20-22a:

8:9	Watch lest this right of yours become a stumbling block to the weak	9:12	we did not use this right in order that we might not give any hindrance to the gospel of Christ
10:32 (cf. 10:24)	Become without offense to the Jews	9:20-22a	and we became to the Jews as a Jew to those under the Law as under the Law
	to the Gentiles		to those apart from the Law as apart from the Law
	to the Church of God		to the weak, weak (summarized in 9:19, 22b)

In a word, those Corinthians who were "strong" in knowledge[73] and hence felt free to eat such meat were to join Paul in "becoming a slave" (9:19) to the weaknesses of others in order that, by not placing

---

72. Hock, *Social Context*, 60f., appropriately refers to this as the "paradigmatic function" of ch. 9, which he summarizes by saying that

> just as Paul had not exercised his right to be supported (cf. 9:6) in order not to hinder the gospel in any way (v. 12), so the Corinthians were encouraged to waive their right to eat meat offered to idols in order not to offend any weaker brother (see esp. 8:9).

See also Lüdemann, *Paulus* II, 110. However, neither Hock nor Lüdemann stresses the relationship between chapters 9 and 10.

73. For the content of this "knowledge," cf. the credal statement in 8:6 and the implications Paul draws from it in 8:4f. and 7.

undue obstacles in the way of the gospel, as many people as possible might be saved (cf. 8:9, 11, 13; 9:12, 19-22; 10:29, 32). For in Paul's opinion, "the love which edifies" (8:1) does not insist upon its own rights, but is willing "to do all things for the sake of the gospel" (9:23),[74] whether this means giving up the right to earn one's living from the gospel in Paul's case, or refusing to exercise one's right to eat meat offered to idols in the case of the Corinthians. Hence, Paul can point to his own apostolic life-style as the paradigmatic example of the embodiment of this ethic of love since it is orientated to the spreading of the gospel. As a result of this orientation, it is also determined by the weakness of others. As Paul summarizes it in 9:22: "I have become all things to all men, that I may by all means save some."[75]

But it is important to realize that Paul intended his apostolic life-style not only to illustrate the ethic Paul proposed, but also to serve as an authoritative standard for his churches. This is evidenced in I Corinthians not only by the parallels indicated above, but also by the reoccurrence of the "imitate me" motif in 10:32–11:1. For given his authority as the father of the Corinthian church,[76] and his conviction that his life as an apostle conformed to the life of the crucified Christ,[77]

74. For the importance of this Pauline principle for other aspects of Church life, cf. I Cor. 14:3-5, 12, 17, 19, 26; Rom. 14:9; 15:2. It is significant, therefore, that in II Cor. 10:8 and 13:10 Paul interprets his own apostolic authority as having been given to him by God for the purpose of building up the Church, and that he defends his boasting in chs. 10–13—which is not an apology—by asserting that, in reality, he has been speaking "for your upbuilding" (II Cor. 12:19). We will return to the function and significance of this motif within Paul's defense below.

75. Although it is beyond the scope of our present study, it is important to note that Paul's argument in I Cor. 8:1–11:1 is strikingly similar to the argument in II Thess. 3:6-15, where Paul's work and practice of self-support are pointed to as a "model" for the church to follow (3:7, 9b) and of the "tradition" which the Thessalonians had received (3:6f.). It seems that Paul's practice of working to support himself constituted an important part of his regular catechetical instruction (see 3:10).

76. Cf. I Cor. 3:10; 4:14-16 (where Paul's authority as the father of the Corinthian church also leads to the command, "Become imitators of me"); 9:2; II Cor. 10:14; 11:2.

77. So too Dautzenberg, "Verzicht," 224, who concludes that Paul's refusal to be paid and the "difficult work that resulted from it" is to be understood "as part of the special relationship of the apostle to the suffering of Christ."

Paul could thus conclude his discussion of the important ethical principle outlined in chapters 8–10 with the admonition:

> Give no offense either to Jews or to Greeks or to the Church of God; *just as I also* please all men in all things, not seeking my own profit, but the profit of the many, that they may be saved. Be imitators of me, *just as I also* am of Christ. (10:32–11:1, NASB, emphasis added)[78]

The significance of these observations concerning the function of I Cor. 9 for determining the larger context of the passage lies in the light they shed on the status of Paul's apostolic authority when I Corinthians was written. The very fact that Paul can enlist his practice of preaching the gospel free of charge to support his larger hortatory purpose in chapters 8–10 indicates that when the letter was written[79] Paul's apostolic life-style of self-support was still being held in high esteem among the Corinthians themselves.[80] In other words, rather than being seen as in conflict with Paul's apostolic authority, his refusal to accept financial support from his church was still being taken as an appropriate expression of Paul's standing and authority as an apostle. For if this had not been the case, Paul's larger argument in chapters 8–10, based as it is on his own example (cf. esp. 11:1), would have collapsed.

This is not to suggest that Paul intended the unusual character of

---

78. Again, see the similar way in which Paul's example to the Thessalonians functions to support the strong commands given in II Thess. 3:6 and 12, which there too are related to the authority of Christ himself.

79. As in the case of II Thessalonians. See, e.g., Bruce, *Thessalonians*, xxvii, who concludes from the evidence that Paul's relations to the Thessalonian and Macedonian churches "were outstandingly happy." If II Thessalonians is deutero-Pauline (which I doubt), this impression is simply strengthened, since one hardly writes in the name of someone whose authority is disputed.

80. Contra Dautzenberg, "Verzicht," 213, who argues that ch. 9 is a response to criticism from the Corinthians. The idea that in I Cor. 9 Paul must defend himself before the Corinthians is, of course, very widespread in recent literature. To give just one representative position, cf. C. Wolff, *Erster Korintherbrief* II, 19, who then goes on to relate this controversy to the fact that Paul worked with his hands to support himself, which "for the Greeks was unworthy of a free citizen . . . to begin with," so that "one would have used this as an argument to call Paul's apostleship into question (cf. also 15:1-11)." But it is by no means clear how representative this negative view of craftsmen in antiquity actually was, since it seems to be confined to the extremely small upper class. See below, p. 137, and Sir. 38:24-34.

his decision to support himself to be taken for granted by the Corinthians. Paul's contrast between his own practice and that of "the rest of the apostles, and the brothers of the Lord, and Cephas" (9:5), together with the theological and practical significance for his own ministry which Paul attaches to this practice in 9:12 and 9:15-22, not to mention its "paradigmatic function" for the Corinthians, all indicate the vital importance of this aspect of his apostolic ministry—both for himself and for his church. But all this does suggest that here too we encounter evidence that at the writing of I Corinthians Paul's authority as an apostle was still basically accepted in Corinth.

Thus, Paul expected the rhetorical questions of I Cor. 9:1 to be answered affirmatively and without hesitation.[81] He could also count on the fact that his statement in 9:2 would be accepted as adequately representing the state of affairs in Corinth at the time the letter was received: even if Paul's apostleship was being called into question *elsewhere*, Paul could be sure that his apostolic authority was basically still intact in Corinth. For as we saw above in our discussion of I Cor. 4, the problems in Corinth at the time of the writing of I Corinthians were not essentially problems between Paul and his church, but rather problems of strife within the church. The crucial point, therefore, is to see that, on the one hand, Paul *distinguishes* in 9:2 between how the Corinthians will react and how the "others" respond to his claim to be an apostle, while, on the other hand, the subject matter of 9:4ff. and 9:1 are *not* identical. In 9:1f. the question concerns *whether or not* Paul is an apostle, while in 9:4ff. the question concerns the rights of those who *are* apostles.[82]

---

81. Although commentators emphasize that these rhetorical questions function to support Paul's apostolic authority, it is not often pointed out that Paul raises these questions precisely *because* he knows how they will be answered, not because he must argue for his legitimacy. Cf. Schlatter, *An die Korinther,* 270; Lietzmann, *An die Korinther,* 39; Barrett, *First Corinthians,* 200f.; Conzelmann, *Erster Korintherbrief,* 187ff.; C. Wolff, *Erster Korintherbrief* II, 20, who points out that Paul expects a positive answer, but goes on to conclude, "But Paul is conscious of the fact that his apostleship is being doubted by the Corinthians and therefore refers to the decisive characteristic of an apostle . . ."; and Lüdemann, *Paulus* II, 79 and 108f., who identifies the themes of 9:4ff. with Paul's rhetorical questions in 9:1.

82. Contra Lüdemann, *Paulus* II, 108f., and most commentators, who fail to make this distinction.

This means, however, that Paul's "defense" in I Cor. 9:3ff. actually served a *double* function. For the Corinthians who accepted the authority of Paul's apostleship and the propriety of Paul's practice of self-support, Paul's arguments in support of the right of earning one's living from the gospel in I Cor. 9 served as the background necessary to demonstrate that Paul's own decision not to exercise this right was the perfect illustration of the ethical principle of love Paul advocated.[83] This explains why Paul must argue so extensively for the legitimacy of this right in 9:7-14 even though it was not itself a point of contention between Paul and his church.

In contrast, the many commentators who see I Cor. 9:4-14 as a defense of Paul's apostolic authority against those who criticized Paul for *not* being paid must explain why Paul argues so extensively for this right, when, if he was being attacked for not being paid, it would merely add to his problems! The point of Paul's argument in 9:4-14 is rather that apostles, as such, have this right (not Paul alone), and that, *as a result,* Paul shares it more than anyone else in the case of the Corinthians, since, as the one who founded the church in Corinth, he is specifically *their* apostle (cf. 9:1f., 12). Thus, Paul's entire argument rests on the fact that the validity of Paul's apostleship is assumed. Paul's burden is not to argue for the legitimacy of his apostleship, but to show that this apostleship, *by definition,* meant that he had the right to be paid for his ministry.

For the "others" (cf. 9:2) who were questioning Paul's apostleship, Paul's argument served to demonstrate that even though Paul did not make use of his apostolic rights to financial support, he nevertheless included himself within the category of those who possessed this right (cf. 9:4-6). His reason for doing so was the existence of the Corinthian church itself (cf. 9:2b, 12a)—sure evidence that he too performed the work characteristic of an apostle (cf. 9:11, 14).

The weight of Paul's "apology" thus rests on his relationship to

83. As H. F. von Campenhausen, *Die Begrundung kirchlicher Entscheidungen beim Apostel Paulus* (1957), 11 n. 15, observed, Paul's purpose in 9:4-14 was to "set forth his well-known decision not to accept support from his congregation in a new, explicitly 'pedagogical' interpretation" (quoted in Dungan, *Sayings of Jesus,* 13), though von Campenhausen saw this to be the sole purpose of Paul's argument (see Dungan, p. 13).

the Corinthian church, not on his argument for the right to be paid. Hence, Paul's "apology" in I Cor. 9 provided the Corinthians with a powerful *a fortiori* inducement to obey Paul's injunctions in 8–11:1 (i.e., "if our apostle, to whom we owe our very lives as Christians [cf. 9:11], has given up his 'rights,' how much more ought we to give up ours!"). But it also provided his supporters with the ammunition they needed to defend their apostle from those who might use his practice of self-support to attack his authority (cf. II Cor. 5:12 for this same purpose). For we should not underestimate the fact that in I Cor. 9:2 the contrast is not between various groups within the church, but between the Corinthians as a whole and the "others" who question Paul's authority.

Thus, Paul's mode of argumentation in I Cor. 8–11:1 is parallel to and based upon the same presuppositions as his previous argument in 3:1–4:16 (see above, pp. 59ff.). For as we have seen above, Paul supported his prior plea that the Corinthians not become arrogant in their relationships with one another, as reflected in the party-strife currently existing in Corinth (cf. 3:3, 18, 21; 4:6f.), by pointing to the theological significance of his own apostolic suffering (cf. 4:6, 14). In 8:1–11:1, Paul's response to this same underlying problem of arrogance (cf. 8:1), now manifested in the indiscriminate eating of meat offered to idols, is likewise supported by an aspect of his own apostolic experience, i.e., his decision to offer the gospel without charge, which we will see in a moment is also part of his suffering as an apostle. Thus, in both instances, Paul's exhortations to the Corinthians can be based upon and illustrated by his own apostolic way of life. And in both instances, Paul is able to do so because his experience as an apostle is still accepted as an appropriate expression of his apostolic authority, which itself remains common ground between Paul and the Corinthians.[84] It is not surprising,

---

84. This is also the conclusion of Dunn in "Responsible Congregation," 230f.:

At all events it is clear enough that at least a significant section of the church in Corinth, presumably those converted during Paul's initial visit and so the founding members of the church, were ready to acknowledge Paul's authority as apostle (I Cor. 9:1-2). And the reference of the various issues to him, which provided the occasions for I Corinthians, provides sufficient proof that Paul's authority with respect to the Corinthian church was widely recognized by the Corinthian believers.

therefore, that Paul can conclude *both* of these arguments with the same admonition: "Imitate me" (cf. 4:16; 11:1).

b. The Structure of Paul's Argument in I Cor. 9

The second point of significance to be drawn from I Cor. 9 for our study derives from the structure of Paul's argument itself. A closer investigation of the reasons Paul adduces for his decision not to avail himself of his apostolic right to financial support reveals that Paul's refusal to earn his living from the gospel is intended to be seen as a sign of his *love* for the Corinthians,[85] as evidenced by his voluntary decision to *suffer* for them. In 9:12, the fact that Paul refuses to exercise his right to be supported by the Corinthians (cf. 9:11) means, by contrast, that he "endures all things." In the light of what Paul has just said in 4:12, where the fact that Paul "labors, working with his own hands" is listed as part of his "catalog of suffering,"[86] it is natural to understand the "all things" of 9:12 to refer primarily to those hardships and sufferings which resulted from Paul supporting himself.[87]

This is confirmed by what we know about the actual experience of the itinerant, small-scale hand-worker or artisan in the ancient world. For as Hock has recently pointed out, many of the difficult

---

85. See Dautzenberg, "Verzicht," 222-224, where he also stresses that from Paul's perspective his refusal to be paid was a sign of his love for the church.

86. That Paul works to support himself in his preaching of the gospel is also listed in his other catalogs of suffering in II Cor. 6:1-10 (v. 5) and II Cor. 11:23-33 (vv. 23 and 27).

87. In addition, as Dautzenberg, "Verzicht," 224, has once again insightfully pointed out, that Paul includes his work as part of those experiences which comprise his "being condemned to death" in I Cor. 4:9ff. is not at all strange given Paul's anthropology. In his words,

> The close linking of suffering and constant work into a common perspective is possible precisely within the horizon of the Jewish view of humanity: in both spheres one is concerned with the effort of . . . life, i.e., with the denial of the enjoyment and happiness of life and therefore, from the Jewish and Semitic point of view, with the nearness of death.

(This conclusion is based on his major work, *Sein Leben Bewahren* [1966], pp. 114-123.)

sufferings and hardships listed by Paul in I Cor. 4:11-13 were the common lot of the traveling craftsmen of Paul's day.[88] Hence, Paul's statement in 9:12 that his lack of support by the Corinthians necessitated that he "endure" the many hardships associated with trying to support oneself by working with one's hands would not have struck Paul's readers as strange. But that he would do so *voluntarily*, when he, more than anyone else, possessed the "right" or "authority" to be supported by the Corinthians (cf. 9:11-12a), would have been striking indeed. As such, the adversative relationship between Paul's right to support on the one hand (9:12a), and his decision to suffer instead of exercising this right on the other hand (9:12b), provides a powerful foundation for Paul's overall argument in 8:1–11:1.

But, as indicated by the purpose clause in 9:12d itself, it also raises the question of Paul's personal purpose or motive for embracing such suffering. In Paul's words, he "endures all things," "in order that we might not give any hindrance to the gospel of Christ." The parallels between this statement and Paul's prior statements in 8:9 and 13 ("stumbling block" / "cause to stumble" / "hindrance") make it clear that by "hindrance" in 9:12d Paul is referring to those things, which, although legitimate in and of themselves, would nevertheless hinder the progress of the gospel and therefore ought to be avoided "because of the gospel" (9:23a). In the Corinthians' case, this meant not eating meat which had been offered to idols in the presence of those Christians whose consciences were still "weak" (8:10-12), and in front of those unbelievers for whom idol worship was still a reality (10:27-28).[89] In Paul's case, this meant, among other things, offering the gospel "free of charge" (cf. 9:18).

It cannot be emphasized too strongly, however, that Paul's conscious decision to adapt himself to the weakness of others for the sake of the gospel was not merely a matter of pragmatic mission strategy, though it aimed to facilitate the spread of the gospel (cf.

88. Hock, *Social Context*, 35-37, 60, 78 n. 17, 84 n. 94, and cf. p. 28 in reference to II Cor. 11:27.

89. Conversely, it must also be emphasized that the position of the "weak" did not involve, from Paul's perspective, "sin," and thus could be tolerated, in contrast to the problems cited in I Cor. 5:1-5; 6:15-20; and 11:17-22. Cf. Schrage, *Ethik*, 186.

9:19-22).[90] Instead, as we have already pointed out above, Paul's decision to support himself, like his admonitions to the "strong" in Corinth, is grounded in the fact that to do so is to walk in the way that surpasses all other ways (12:31), namely, that of Christian "love" (cf. 8:1).

It is not simply a coincidence, therefore, that the contrast between knowledge/arrogance and love, with which Paul opens his discussion of the issue of meat offered to idols in 8:1, is also found in Paul's definition of love in 13:2 and 4; or that Paul uses the same formulation to describe love in 13:7 that he uses to describe his own practice of self-support in 9:12: love "endures all things." For Paul intends his own example of self-support to be seen as an embodiment of that same Christian principle of love which he is admonishing the Corinthians to follow. It thus becomes crucial for understanding Paul's apostolic self-conception, as well as for understanding his ethical admonitions in general, to realize that Paul saw his own decision to "become all things to all men" (9:22) to be an extension of the basic ethical principle, "Let no one seek his own (good), but that of his neighbor" (10:24). For inasmuch as this mode of behavior was to be equated with love (cf. 13:4f., "Love does not seek its own"), it was the only behavior appropriate to the gospel itself.

Hence, for Paul, the way to avoid causing a hindrance to the gospel was to embody that gospel by following the ethic of love, as illustrated by his own refusal to exercise his right to support from the Corinthians. In other words, 9:12, 19 (and its explication in 9:20-21), and 22 all interpret one another. Paul's decision to support himself (i.e., to endure all things) is an *outworking* of his desire to "make himself a slave to all," or "to become all things to all men"; while his purpose in doing

90. Despite the many insights that Theissen brings to this text, I remain unconvinced concerning his central thesis that I Cor. 9 reflects a conflict between the two basic types of missionary practice, the "wandering charismatic" and the "community organizers," rooted in the Palestinian "Jesus movement" and the Hellenistic Gentile mission respectively. See his "Legitimation," 202, 211, 213. Theissen's thesis cannot do justice to Paul's positive argument for his right to be paid in 9:4-14, which Theissen can only describe as "curious," given his supposition that Paul is being criticized in Corinth for his practice. In short, Theissen seems to fall prey to the temptation to read opposition into Paul's argument where it does not exist.

so, i.e., that he might not place a hindrance in the way of the gospel, is an expression of his goal "to win the more," or "to save some," or as Paul summarizes it in 9:23a, to do all things "because of the gospel":

9:12	but we endure all things	in order that we might not give any hindrance to the gospel of Christ
9:19	I enslaved myself to all	in order that I might win the more
9:22	I became all things to all men	in order that I might save some

The adversative relationship which exists between Paul's decision, expressed in the ground clauses of 9:12, 19, and 22, and his "apostolic" "rights," referred to in verses 4, 5, 12a, and 19a, indicates that these purpose clauses are to be taken as an expression of Paul's love for the Corinthians.[91]

Thus, although I agree with Hock that I Cor. 9:19 must be interpreted in the light of the preceding verses, I am not convinced that the main point of his article is correct, namely, that "I enslaved myself" ought to be viewed exclusively in the light of what precedes.[92] That is to say, for Hock, 9:19 refers specifically to the fact that Paul worked with his hands in a trade and thus reflects "the snobbish and scornful attitude so typical of upper class Greeks and Romans."[93] In Hock's view, in speaking of "enslaving himself," Paul is thus referring to the fact that his trade made him appear "slavish," since "by

---

91. That Paul intended the Corinthians to understand his refusal to accept support to be an expression of his love for them is further confirmed by the parallel structure of Paul's argument in I Thess. 2:7-9. Here Paul's decision to support himself is also the visible sign or outworking of his love for his church (2:7c), since it was his love which motivated his willingness to do so (2:8a, c). And here too, Paul is able to argue that his suffering (cf. 2:2 with 2:8b and 9) is a sign of his love for the Thessalonians only because the hardships involved in supporting himself were endured *in spite of the fact* that, as an apostle of Christ, Paul had every right to be supported by them (2:7a). Hence, Paul's hardships were suffered as a result of his voluntary decision not to demand support for his preaching. Thus his working day and night can only be taken as an expression of Paul's love for his church.

92. Hock, "Tentmaking," 558.

93. Ibid., 562.

entering the workshop he had brought about a considerable loss of status. . . ."[94] In his later study, *The Social Context of Paul's Ministry: Tentmaking and Apostleship,* Hock then goes on to argue that "free" in 9:19 refers to the fact that Paul "was economically dependent on no one. . . ."[95] Hence, Hock interprets 9:19 to mean: "He could be economically independent only by plying a slavish trade. . . ."[96]

The main problem with Hock's view is that Paul explicitly says that he has made himself a slave "to all." From the context it seems clear, therefore, that what Paul has in mind is his decision to become "under the Law," "apart from the Law," and "weak" for the sake of the gospel (vv. 20-22), in which the "all" of v. 19 is further defined. Furthermore, it must be asked whether Paul's argument would be served by demeaning the very work in which the majority of the Corinthians themselves were probably engaged,[97] especially when this would only intensify the conflicts between the various social levels which already existed in Corinth.[98] Moreover, although in Paul's day artisans and small traders were often high in income, but low in occupational prestige,[99] Paul's own very positive admonitions concerning working with one's hands in I Thess. 4:11f. (see too II Thess. 3:10-12 and Eph. 4:28) would seem to belie Hock's emphasis on Paul's "snobbish" attitude. In addition, M. Rostovtzeff has pointed out that in the Roman and Hellenistic periods, retail traders were, in fact, one step below the upper class, together with teachers, doctors, etc., and formed the "backbone of municipal life."[100] To be a member of this working class (not *lower* class) need not, therefore, necessarily carry negative connotations.

It has also been questioned how representative this "snobbish" attitude of the upper class towards the working class actually was.[101] Hence, as MacMullen stresses, when we read statements such as that found in Cicero, *De off.* I.150, which demean those engaged in the trades and retail dealing, we must bear in mind that this is the judgment of the small, rich minority and that it was

94. Ibid., 559f. See the evidence listed by Hock for this view. His key text is Cicero, *De off.* I.150.

95. Hock, *Social Context,* 61.

96. Ibid.

97. See Meeks, *Urban Christians,* 51-73, who argues convincingly that "the 'typical' Christian . . . , the one who most often signals his presence in the letters by one or another small clue, is a free artisan or small trader" (p. 73).

98. This has been pointed out in the various works of Theissen. See now his collection, *The Social Setting of Pauline Christianity: Essays on Corinth,* tr. John H. Schütz, 1982.

99. What is technically called "high status inconsistency (low status crystallization)"; see Meeks, *Urban Christians,* 73 (cf. 61, 65).

100. Rostovtzeff, *Roman Empire* I, 190.

101. See MacMullen, *Roman Social Relations,* 88-91.

based on the conviction that poverty was vile, dishonorable, and ugly, and that only the rich could afford to be honest,[102] a presupposition certainly foreign to Paul. Finally, the "snobbish" attitude Hock attributes to Paul also seems to be out of place in the light of the positive Jewish view of labor reflected in Aboth 2:2. Hock objects that this source is late, but it is no more remote than the writings of Cicero.

It seems best, therefore, to see Paul's decision to support himself as an application of his more basic principle of becoming a slave "to (the consciences) of all" and to interpret his "freedom" in terms of the "rights" in view in chapters 8–10 (cf. 8:9/10:29).[103]

c. The Nature of Paul's Boast in I Cor. 9:15-18

This brings us to our third and final point concerning Paul's argument in I Cor. 9, namely, the nature of Paul's "boast" as outlined in verses 15-18. For inasmuch as Paul's decision not to earn his living from the gospel is to be taken, from the perspective of the Corinthians, as an indication and demonstration of Paul's love for them, it also becomes, from Paul's perspective, an aspect of his apostolic ministry about which he can "boast" and for which he will be recompensed.[104]

This becomes clear from the structure of Paul's argument in verses 15-18. In 9:15a, Paul wants to eliminate the possibility that the Corinthians might take his extended defense of the legitimacy of being

---

102. MacMullen, *Roman Social Relations,* 115-117, 199- 200 nn. 90, 91, esp. his reference to the attitude of the slave Trimalchio, the custom of advertising one's occupation on one's tombstone, and the quotation from Petronius, *Satyricon* 29. See too Liebeschuetz, *Antioch,* 52f., who refers to Libanius's very positive view of shopkeepers. For the view that Cicero's judgment was representative, see, besides Hock, Finley, *Ancient Economy,* 45-54, 60, 122.

103. Meeks, *Urban Christians,* 61, also accepts Hock's view that Paul's manner of talking about his work resembles that found among the higher social levels, but he expresses himself very cautiously in simply concluding that Paul's decision to do menial work was thus "something worthy of comment." He does not refer to I Cor. 9:19 at all. If Paul did share an upper-class attitude toward work, this would naturally make his working even more striking to the Corinthians, but there does not seem to be a basis for concluding that Paul refers to his work as such as "slavish."

104. The connection between Paul's argument concerning his ministry to the Corinthians in the rest of ch. 9 and his own reward as an apostle in vv. 15-18 becomes clear once the former is recognized to be the basis for the latter.

paid as an apostle in 9:6-14 to be a hidden plea that he too now be paid by the Corinthians for the preaching of the gospel. For as the anacoluthon in 9:15b makes clear, there is nothing more important to Paul, even his very life, than the fact that he offers the gospel free of charge. The reason for the almost inconceivable weight which Paul thus attaches to his practice of self-support lies in his understanding of this practice as his "boast," which would be "nullified" or "invalidated" should someone pay him for his ministry.[105] Hence, Paul would rather die than lose this "boast," because, as verses 16 and 17 point out, the fact that Paul preaches per se cannot, in Paul's case, be a ground for boasting in and of itself (9:16a).

The reason for this surprising, and by no means self-evident, statement lies in Paul's self-conception as an apostle,[106] which in our context is expressed in terms of the "necessity" or "constraint" laid upon Paul to preach (9:16b).[107] As is often pointed out, in speaking of the "constraint" laid upon him Paul is portraying his own apostolic experience of preaching the gospel in terms of the experience of those OT prophets who felt compelled to deliver the divine message entrusted to them, regardless of their own desire, or lack of desire, to do so.[108] As W. Grundmann put it, "In this office Paul has the same

105. For the meaning of *kenoō* ("nullify" or "invalidate") in I Cor. 1:17; 9:15; II Cor. 9:3; Rom. 4:14, cf. Oepke, κενός, 661f.

106. On I Cor. 9:16 as a statement reflecting Paul's call and/or self-conception, cf. Stuhlmacher, *Paulinisches Evangelium* I, 87, 246; Beker, *Paul the Apostle,* 7; Eichholz, *Theologie des Paulus,* 39f.; Munck, *Paul,* 22, 40f.; and Conzelmann, *Erster Korintherbrief,* 194 with n. 6.

107. For the meaning of *ananke* as "necessity" or "constraint" elsewhere in Paul, cf. Rom. 13:5; I Cor. 7:37; II Cor. 9:7; Philem. 14; and in the rest of the NT, Mt. 18:7; Lk. 14:18; Heb. 7:12; 7:27; 9:16; 9:23; Jude 3. Cf. also II Macc. 6:7; 15:2; III Macc. 4:9; 5:6. In the LXX it is usually used, however, of the constraint laid upon one due to suffering or distress and thus comes to mean simply "distress" or "tribulation," etc. See I Kgs. 22:2; Job 5:19; 15:24; Pss. 24(25):17; 106(107):6, 13; Jer. 9:15, etc. This meaning is also found in Paul (I Cor. 7:26; II Cor. 6:4; 12:10; I Thess. 3:7) and in Luke 21:23.

108. The classic example of this is Jeremiah's lament in Jer. 20:9; but see also Jer. 4:19; Is. 21:3; Amos 3:8; Micah 3:8, and the "hand of God" motif in Is. 8:11; 10:10; 28:2; Jer. 15:17; Ezek. 3:14, 24; 37:1, which, as Heschel, *Prophets,* 444, points out, "is the name the prophet used to describe the urgency, pressure, and compulsion by which he is stunned and overwhelmed. . . ." For Heschel's excellent

experience as the prophets; he is under a divine constraint which he cannot escape."[109] The "necessity" Paul refers to in 9:16 is not to be equated, therefore, with the inescapable "necessity" of an impersonal fate,[110] but is rather the "necessity" or "constraint" which results from the call of God itself.[111] The statement in I Cor. 9:16 thus reflects Paul's understanding of his "conversion-call" in which, according to Gal. 1:15f., the revelation of God's Son was inextricably linked with Paul's call to *preach* Christ among the Gentiles (cf. Gal. 1:16b).

Hence, Paul understood his call to preach the gospel to be part and parcel of his "conversion" to Christ.[112] In other words, Paul was not first called to follow Christ and then made an apostle; rather, Paul was called to follow Christ *as an apostle*.[113] Paul's identity as a follower of Christ was thus *identical* with his self-conception as an apostle. This explains why, in our context, Paul is able to move directly from a discussion of his own apostolic practice in I Cor. 9:19-23 to a discussion of the

---

summary of the prophetic compulsion, see p. 444. That this idea was also present elsewhere in the early Church is shown by the parallel idea in Acts 4:20.

109. Grundmann, ἀναγκάζω, 346. For a good summary of this constraint as it relates to Paul's call in general, see Kim, *Origin*, 65f.

110. Contra, e.g., Hock, "Tentmaking," 59, who suggests that the center of Paul's argument in 9:16-18 is "the philosophical problem of fate and free will."

111. The most important contribution and main point of Käsemann's study of I Cor. 9:15-18 is his emphasis on the centrality of this "necessity" motif for Paul's argument and his corresponding polemic against all attempts to interpret it as merely some sort of ethical "duty to one's vocation" or psychological compulsion deriving from Paul's gratitude to God; see "Variation," 232-234.

112. As already stressed by Nock (*St. Paul*, 69), who argued that Paul's "vocation and conversion were identical." The classic treatment of this point is now that of Stendahl, "Call." Although I agree with Stendahl's emphasis that Paul's Damascus road experience did not mean that Paul changed religions, it nevertheless seems better to retain the language of conversion in the light of the drastic change which took place in Paul's thinking and life as a result of the revelation of Christ which he experienced. I have thus chosen to describe it as a twofold, though inseparable experience, and have opted for the clumsy terminology of "conversion-call."

113. My change in terminology from talking about Paul's call to preach the gospel to his apostleship is intentional and meant to reflect the fact that for Paul the two were, in fact, synonymous. So too Käsemann, "Legitimität," 31; Stuhlmacher, *Paulinisches Evangelium*, 68f.; "Ende des Gesetzes," 25f. n. 26; Hofius, " 'Gott hat unter uns,' " 17 with n. 66; Kim, *Origin*, 57-59.

necessity of enduring in faith in 9:24–10:13. In addition, it also explains why Paul cannot boast in the fact that he preaches the gospel per se. For the compulsion he feels to preach is identical with the compulsion or necessity which brought him to faith in Christ and vice versa.

Consequently, since his call to preach cannot be separated from his call to Christ, any boasting which might be associated with the fact that Paul preaches is eliminated on the basis of the principle of grace established in I Cor. 1:26-31: God has chosen his people in spite of their distinctives, in order that "no flesh might boast before God" (v. 29). The adversative relationship which stands at the heart of Paul's statement about himself in 15:8-10 demonstrates, moreover, that Paul viewed his own call in terms of precisely this same grace, i.e., the grace which eliminates boasting.

Finally, the identity between Paul's conversion and his call also explains Paul's somewhat surprising ability to support his assertion that he is under constraint to preach the gospel by pointing out that eschatological judgment awaits him if he fails to carry out his mandate (cf. 9:16c). For in the light of this identification, not to preach would be to deny Christ himself, the result of which is to be "anathema" (cf. 16:22).

In 9:17 Paul then goes on to support his main point in verse 16, i.e., that his preaching per se provides no ground for boasting, by establishing a contrast between "voluntary" / "involuntary,"[114] on the one hand, and "reward" / "stewardship," on the other hand.[115] Paul's call to preach is now defined as that "stewardship" entrusted to him by God,[116]

---

114. For the meaning of *hekōn* and *akōn* as "voluntary" and "against one's will and intention" respectively, cf. Hauck, ἑκών, 469-470.

115. Based on the punctuation given in Nestle-Aland, *Novum Testamentum Graece*, 1979[26], and taking the two conditional statements of v. 17 as unreal and real respectively.

Reumann's attempt in "Οἰκονομία-Terms," 159, to interpret I Cor. 9:17b and 18a as one statement, so that "but if involuntarily, I have been entrusted with a stewardship" becomes the protasis of a conditional sentence, with "what then is my reward?" as its apodosis, although possible grammatically, fails to be convincing for two reasons. First, he must interpret 9:16a: "For if I preach the gospel *on the basis of remuneration that the others have,* then there is no ground for glorifying me." But this addition to the protasis (which I have italicized) is neither necessary nor implied in the context.

Second and even more telling, however, is that Reumann's interpretation which in the light of I Cor. 4:1 certainly refers to the fact that Paul has been entrusted with the "mysteries of God" (i.e., Paul considers himself to be "a steward of the mysteries of God").[117] Thus, since this stewardship is received "involuntarily," Paul's faithfulness in carrying it out

---

demands that we understand Paul to be contradicting himself in 9:17-18. For in Reumann's reconstruction, the conditional statement in 9:17a is construed as the "actual case," rather than an unreal condition—i.e., Paul does *not* preach "voluntarily." But inasmuch as 9:17b is also "a statement of the actual situation," Paul is therefore asserting that he preaches voluntarily and involuntarily at the same time! In Reumann's words,

> Thus Paul sees himself as a free man, working voluntarily, with apostolic authority. But he cannot help stating also, in absolute humility, that his very apostolic office involves the sort of compulsion and necessity that is laid on a "steward," one who fills the steward's role in a Greek household—an office usually held by a slave.

But such an interpretation not only renders Paul's thought highly confusing, it also ignores the explicit statement in 9:15, which defines Paul's boast as his voluntary decision not to be supported, thus destroying the antithetical parallelism which seems to be clearly established in the text.

Reumann's view seems to be motivated by his desire to deny that Paul could be speaking of a reward in the real sense of the term. As he asserts, ". . . strictly speaking there is in 17 and the following verses no reference to a future reward. The only reward he mentions is one now in the present, involving a ground for boasting." But in the light of I Cor. 3:8ff. the opposite seems to be the case. Cf. also Barrett, *First Corinthians*, 209f., who also tries to read vv. 17 and 18 as one statement because he cannot see a "good reason" why "reward" and "stewardship" should be construed as alternatives, i.e., he poses the question, "Why, if I am entrusted with an office, should I not be rewarded for carrying it out?" (p. 210). But once the status of the steward as slave is given its due weight in the passage, this objection falls away.

116. For the idea of a "stewardship" being entrusted to someone by God, cf. Is. 22:21 LXX; and for the idea of "a stewardship" being entrusted with a message to be delivered, cf. Esther 8:9 LXX. Reumann, "*Oikonomia* = 'Covenant,' " 282, based on his extensive study of this terminology in his doctoral thesis, interprets I Cor. 9:17 and Col. 1:25 to refer to Paul's "commission" or "stewardship" or the "divine office granted to him in God's program." He refers to Lk. 16:2-4 as a good example of the usual classical sense of the office of the steward (p. 282 n. 1).

117. Cf. Paul's parallel statements in Gal. 2:7 and Phil. 1:16, from which it becomes clear that the "mysteries of God" refer to the gospel itself. Moreover, as Reumann, "Οἰκονομία-Terms," 161, points out, following Bornkamm and R. Brown (see p. 161 n. 1 for references), these "mysteries" are to be interpreted against the background of the *swd/rz* in the OT, i.e., they are God's revealed secrets as made known to his servants the prophets. This becomes especially clear in Eph. 3:1-12, esp. vv. 2f.

cannot be a ground for boasting since the corresponding slavery-status of stewards places their obedience in the realm of that "forced labor" for which there is no "reward." In contrast, Paul can refer to the fact that he offers the gospel free of charge as his reward since, by definition, the voluntary nature of this act means that it is a work for which Paul expects to be recompensed, i.e., to receive a reward in the eschaton. As a result, it seems impossible to avoid the conclusion that in I Cor. 9:15-18 Paul makes an ontological distinction between his preaching per se, in which he cannot boast (i.e., no reward is expected for it), and his preaching free of charge, for which he will be recompensed and in which, therefore, he does boast.[118] Paul thus establishes two categories of conduct which may be represented in the following chart:

Preaching per se	**Preaching free of charge**
result of "constraint"	no "constraint" to do so
done "involuntarily"	done "voluntarily"
"woe" expected if not done	"reward" expected if done
classified as a "stewardship"	classified as a "boast"

Rather than expressing a Pauline paradox,[119] or even a joke,[120] Paul's summary statement in I Cor. 9:18 is therefore best interpreted

118. Part of the problem in reading this text is that we are so conditioned by the negative connotations associated with the idea of boasting elsewhere in Paul's letters (cf. Rom. 3:27; I Cor. 1:29; 3:21; 4:7; 5:6; 13:4; II Cor. 11:16, 18) that it becomes almost impossible to recognize that "boasting" as such is *not* a negative moral category for Paul. Rather, the issue for Paul is what one boasts in, not whether one boasts or not. Paul can therefore speak positively of his own boast and even encourage his readers to boast in him as well (cf. Rom. 15:17f.; I Cor. 15:31, cf. 15:10; II Cor. 1:14; 7:14; 8:24; 9:2f.; 10:8, 13; 11:10; 12:5f.; I Thess. 2:19; Phil. 2:16; II Cor. 5:12; Phil. 1:26). For other positive uses of the idea of "boasting" in something, cf. Rom. 4:2; 5:2, 3, 11. It is debatable whether the boast of the Jews referred to in Rom. 2:17, 23 ought to be seen as negative or positive.

119. I.e., that Paul's "wage" existed in the fact that he has no wage, so Käsemann, "Variation," 228; Conzelmann, *Erster Korintherbrief,* 195.

120. So Dungan, *Sayings of Jesus,* 23, who sees Paul's argument in I Cor. 9:16-18 as a joke based on a pun. In his opinion, Paul turns "jocular" at this point, "facetiously asking, 'What are the wages of someone who is not entitled to any?' he answers, 'Why, to do the work for free!' " He then goes on to lament that Paul's joke "has largely been wasted on centuries of sober-sided Christian exegetes," myself included.

as a restatement of verse 15, with Paul's question in verse 18a taken to refer to that for which he expects to be "paid" in the last judgment. Moreover, Paul's criterion cited in 3:14 that only the work which "remains" will receive a reward explains why Paul can be confident (in 9:15ff.) that his commitment to preach the gospel without charge will be recompensed. For as we have seen above, Paul's decision to support himself is, in essence, an expression of his *love,* which, according to 13:13, is the greatest of the three essential Christian qualities that "remain" (cf. 13:13). Rather than not having anything in common with one another as Käsemann maintained,[121] Paul's refusal to be supported by the Corinthians was itself an expression of his love, which, because it would *remain* through the fire of God's judgment, would be recompensed. As such, Paul could boast in it.

Paul's boast in I Cor. 9:15c thus brings us back to the first two points concerning I Cor. 9 of significance for our study of II Cor. 2:17. As we have seen, Paul's commitment to support himself as portrayed in I Cor. 9 is to be understood as an expression of his *love* for the Corinthian church. This commitment of self-support derives its significance for Paul's larger argument from the generally, if not universally, accepted *authority* of the apostle itself. As such, Paul's practice of preaching the gospel free of charge can still be looked to not only as an appropriate outworking of his apostolic calling, which provides an authoritative example of the ethic of love worthy of emulation, but also as an essential part of Paul's own *boast* as an apostle, precisely because it is an outworking of that love. Moreover, the foundation upon which these three interrelated motifs are built and the force which molds them into an organic unity is Paul's self-conception as one to whom God has entrusted his "mysteries." As God's "steward," Paul is consequently constrained by that gospel to preach throughout the Gentile world. For Paul's apostolic *authority* resides in his call to preach the gospel; his *love* is defined as whatever serves to further its advance; and his *boast*

---

121. Käsemann, "Variation," 228. This objection derives, however, from the common assumption that that which is done for a reward cannot at the same time be an act of love. On the inappropriateness of this assumption for understanding NT ethics, cf. Piper, *'Love your enemies,'* 166, and his convincing discussion of the role of rewards in the teaching of Jesus in Luke's Gospel on pp. 162-170, and in general on pp. 60f.

is that he has given up his rights as an apostle in order not to place a hindrance in its way. With this in mind, the startling nature of Paul's treatment of these same themes in II Corinthians becomes readily apparent.

2. II Cor. 11:7-15

Paul's reintroduction of the theme of his commitment to preach the gospel without charge in II Cor. 11:7-11 is framed within two comparisons.[122] In 11:5f. Paul asserts that he considers himself not to be inferior in any way to the "super apostles," while in 11:12-15 he refuses to allow the "false apostles" of 11:13a to be compared to himself. Thus, in the first case, the comparison is directed from Paul to the "super apostles" and is *positive* in nature, while in the second case the comparison is *negative* in nature, being directed from the "false apostles" to Paul. Moreover, each of the two comparisons functions to provide a ground or support for Paul's statements in 11:1-4 and 11:7-11 respectively, while at the same time providing a transition to the next unit of thought. Paul's positive comparison in 11:5f. is intended to support his concern that in accepting "another Jesus," "different spirit," and "different gospel" from those who have come into Corinth—different from that which they had received from Paul (cf. 11:4)—the Corinthians have, in fact, been tricked by Satan into abandoning the truth (cf. 11:3). For the unexpressed thought between verses 4 and 5 is the implied mistaken rejection of the authority and legitimacy of Paul's own ministry and gospel inherent in the Corinthians' willingness to accept the intruders (e.g.,

---

122. Malherbe, "Antisthenes," 168, 172, has argued that Paul refers to his life-style of self-support already in II Cor. 10:1 (following Hock in taking 10:1 as a reference to Paul's "voluntary self-humiliation" as a result of supporting himself with manual labor) so that the issue in 10:1-6 is not that of an "intellectual confrontation," but rather a matter of Paul's conduct. Malherbe therefore concludes concerning 10:1-6, as I will also below concerning 11:7ff. and 12:12ff., that Paul's "humble life, in which God's power is manifested, is the armament with which he attacks his opponents. Thus he calls on his readers, not to listen to him, but to look at what is right in front of their eyes (10:7)" (p. 172). As a result, Malherbe also suggests that the closest parallel to II Cor. 10:3-6 is II Cor. 2:14-16 (p. 166 n. 131).

"And in so doing you have mistakenly rejected my authority and gospel, for . . .").[123]

Paul asserts that he is equal to the "super apostles" in order to make clear to the Corinthians that in rejecting Paul's gospel they have abandoned the basic apostolic gospel common to both Paul and the Church, which is represented by and built upon the original "pillar apostles." As such, Paul's positive comparison in 11:5 recalls his prior statements in I Cor. 15:1-11. There Paul identified the gospel which he preached and the Corinthians received (note the parallels between I Cor. 15:1 and II Cor. 11:4) with the tradition Paul himself had received (cf. I Cor. 15:3), both from Jerusalem and from the churches in Damascus and Antioch, as the tradition *common* to all the apostles (cf. Gal. 1:18f.; 2:2, 6-9). This explains why Paul can make the surprising statement in I Cor. 15:11 that it is of little significance whether the Corinthians originally heard the gospel from Paul or from one of the other "apostles" listed in 15:3-7, since they all represent the same message.

That this is the backdrop to Paul's comparison in II Cor. 11:5 becomes evident in 11:6, when Paul makes explicit that his "knowledge," here referring to the gospel,[124] is in no way deficient, being on

---

123. Windisch, *Zweiter Korintherbrief*, 329, also recognized the need for such an "intermediate thought" and supplied " 'thus, please allow my appearance to please you also.' " But this attempt finds no support in 11:1-4 and becomes, in reality, the introduction to an independent section in Paul's argument since, for Windisch, 11:5-15 is a "digression" in Paul's thought. It is improbable, however, that Paul's introductory thesis statement itself would remain unexpressed. It seems more appropriate to treat 11:5-15 as an integral part of Paul's ongoing argument and to anchor this unexpressed assertion as closely as possible to its context. Bultmann's attempt, *Zweiter Korintherbrief*, 205, to supply this missing thought is therefore more helpful: " 'endure me as well as you bear them!' " Nevertheless, this too does not adequately explain the actual force of v. 5 as a support for Paul's concern in 11:4. This is also the weakness in the attempts of those like Barrett, *Second Corinthians*, 277f.; "Paul's Opponents," 243; Lietzmann, *An die Korinther*, 146, who suggest that v. 5 actually relates back to Paul's statement in vv. 1 or 3. For the most natural reading is to take it as a support for what immediately precedes.

124. The close connection between "knowledge" in II Cor. 2:14 and "the Word of God" in 2:17 makes this identification probable, as well as Paul's definition of this knowledge in II Cor. 4:6 as "the knowledge of the glory of God in the face of Christ." Of course, "knowledge" in the Corinthian correspondence can have a much broader denotation and can be both positive and negative in connotation; cf. I Cor. 1:5; 8:1, 7, 10, 11; 12:8; 13:2, 8; 14:6; II Cor. 6:6; 8:7; 10:5.

a par with the gospel delivered by the "pillar apostles" themselves, even if his delivery of that gospel was not couched in sophisticated rhetoric (cf. I Cor. 2:1, 4; II Cor. 1:12). Thus, to stray from *Paul's* gospel is to stray from the gospel of the "pillar apostles," and hence from the gospel of the Church as a whole. By implication, therefore, Paul's comparison isolates his opponents, represented in II Cor. 11:4 by the impersonal "the one who comes," from the position and prestige of the "super apostles," thus denying them any possibility of claiming to be the true representatives of the genuine apostolic tradition and authority.

Perhaps the most fundamental exegetical decision to be made concerning Paul's argument in II Cor. 11–12 is whether the "super apostles" of 11:5 and 12:11 are to be identified with the "false apostles" (= deceitful workers = servants of Satan) in 11:13-15, who as Paul's opponents have recently arrived in Corinth and are represented collectively as "the one who comes" in 11:4; or whether the two designations represent two distinct groups, with the "false apostles" being closely related to and even claiming to represent, in some fashion, the "super apostles," but nevertheless remaining a distinguishable entity. In this latter position, which I share, the "super apostles" belong to the same circle of apostles as the "pillar apostles" of Gal. 2:9, though they need not be coterminous with it, and are associated, above all, with the "mother church" in Jerusalem. The two basic positions have already been set out in detail by E. Käsemann, who argued that the two designations represented two distinct fronts,[125] and R. Bultmann, who attempted to respond to Käsemann's view.[126]

The major supporter of Käsemann's basic position has been C. K. Barrett,[127] although he disagrees with Käsemann's description of Paul's opponents in Corinth as "pneumatics."[128] In Barrett's view, the opponents are Jewish Christian Judaizers from Palestine who claimed the pillar apostles as their source of legitimacy, so that the situation behind II Corinthians essentially parallels that behind Galatians, except that in Corinth the Judaizing gospel has been mixed with certain Hellenistic elements (which Barrett calls the process of "Corinthianization") not found in the " 'pure' Judaizing" at work in Gala-

125. Käsemann, "Legitimität," esp. 38f., 41-43, 45-49.
126. In *Exegetische Probleme*, esp. 20-30.
127. Cf. Barrett, "ΨΕΥΔΑΠΟΣΤΟΛΟΙ"; "Christianity at Corinth"; *Second Corinthians*, 30-35; and his last major article on the subject, "Paul's Opponents."
128. Cf. Käsemann, "Legitimität," 37f.

tia.[129] Although I find the arguments of Käsemann and Barrett compelling, especially the observation that Paul would hardly compare himself positively to those in 11:5f. whom he then later describes as "servants of Satan" in 11:14f., their view remains the minority position.

For a recent attempt to bring the two basic positions together, see the essay by M. E. Thrall, "Super-Apostles, Servants of Christ, and Servants of Satan." She argues that although the term "super apostles" refers to the Jerusalem apostles, it is nevertheless used by Paul to refer to the missionaries now in Corinth because he thinks it possible that some of the Jerusalem apostles might be included among them.[130] Paul thus oscillates in his discussion, speaking alternately to the false apostles and the super apostles, since he is not sure whether both are present in Corinth or not.[131] But Thrall's attempts to explain Paul's sudden switch in subject matter from the one to the other in 11:12 and 11:18-23 remain unconvincing to me, as well as her attempt to argue that Paul could describe the servants of Christ in 11:23 as servants of Satan in 11:13-15 because of the twofold role of Peter in the Synoptic tradition.[132] Paul's point in 11:13-15 is not that true apostles can sometimes act in a way that is not appropriate to the gospel, but that the false apostles are deceitful in disguising themselves as true apostles of Christ. Is it probable that Paul would say this about Peter or James? Instead, the term "super apostles" itself seems best explained as Paul's attempt to emphasize that these apostles were called before him (I Cor. 15:5ff.) and enjoyed undisputed recognition and authority (Gal. 2:6).[133]

The point to be emphasized, therefore, is that in the light of Paul's prior statements in I Cor. 15:3ff., the fact that Paul's opponents preach a "different gospel" than the one Paul preached also means that they no longer belong to the common apostolic tradition, regardless of their purported claim to be "apostles" themselves, or to represent the pillar apostles. From Paul's perspective, they are "pseudo-apostles" and "deceitful workers" who "disguise themselves as apostles of Christ" and as "ministers of righteousness" (11:13, 15). Hence, given Paul's identification of his own gospel with the common apostolic tradition in II Cor. 11:1-6 and his ability to characterize his opponents' teaching

129. Barrett, "Paul's Opponents," 251.
130. Thrall, "Super-Apostles," 42, 46, 48.
131. Ibid., 48, 50.
132. Ibid., 52-54.
133. As suggested to me by Peter Stuhlmacher in a private conversation.

as a "different gospel," it seems implausible simply to maintain, as G. Theissen does, that "his opponents were hardly the 'false apostles, deceitful workers and servants of Satan' (II Cor. 11:13)" that Paul accuses them to be, but that they were "normal, early Christian missionaries, who held themselves more to the rules for wandering charismatics than Paul did."[134] For regardless of whether one agrees with Theissen's reconstruction of the two types of missionary practices among the early Christians and their origins, there must have been substantial differences in doctrine between Paul and his opponents as well.

This brings us to Paul's insistence in 11:12 that these "false apostles" are not to be classed together with him in their "boast" (cf. 11:12b),[135] which is Paul's rationale for his continuing decision not to accept financial support from the Corinthians (cf. 11:9). But in order to see how Paul's negative comparison in 11:12 actually accomplishes this purpose, it will first be necessary to trace the logic of Paul's argument in II Cor. 11:6b-11 in the light of our prior discussion of this same theme in I Cor. 9.

The first observation to be made in this regard is that Paul's argument in II Cor. 11:6b-11, which leads to the negative comparison of verse 12, is intended to perform the same function as the positive comparison established in verse 5, namely, to support the validity of Paul's gospel. For in verse 6b Paul goes on to assert that he himself has demonstrated or revealed *to the Corinthians,* in an all-inclusive man-

---

134. Theissen, "Legitimation," 221.

135. Following Zmijewski, *Stil,* 146 with n. 273, and the majority of commentators in taking the second purpose clause of 11:12b as dependent on *tōn thelontōn aphormēn* ("of those desiring a platform") and thus representing the desire of Paul's opponents, though I would emphasize that this is given from Paul's perspective. It appears that Paul interpreted at least part of the motivation behind his opponents' criticism of his practice to be their desire to eliminate the obstacle to their own demand for support created by Paul's decision to support himself. Thus, Paul is determined to maintain his practice for the same reason that his opponents would like him to change it, i.e., because it is *different* from the norm. For an opposing view, cf. Hock, *Social Context,* 100 n. 118, who argues that II Cor. 11 is a reversal of I Cor. 9 in that Paul now wants his opponents to conform to his practice. But Paul's purpose in II Cor. 11 seems to be to expose his opponents' true identity as servants of Satan, not to reform their behavior.

ner, the genuine nature of his knowledge (of Christ). That is, in verse 6b Paul argues that not only his harmony with the common traditions of the Church, but also the nature of his own ministry, provides evidence that his knowledge (= gospel) is, in fact, the true and authoritative one. Paul's support for this assertion is then introduced in verse 7 with a rhetorical question introduced with "or," which, in order to bring out its logical function in the argument, must be transported into a negative indicative statement introduced with a grounding conjunction: "*because* I did not sin in humbling myself in order that you might be exalted, in that I preached the gospel of Christ to you without charge."[136]

Construed in this manner, Paul's rhetorical question in verse 7 supplies the first support for his assertion in verse 6b that his own ministry has made the genuine nature of his gospel evident by indicating that Paul's ministry in Corinth was aimed at benefiting the *Corinthians*, i.e., its purpose was that *they* be exalted. The second half of the question reminds the Corinthians of the *way* in which this purpose was accomplished, namely, by Paul's decision to support himself during his ministry in Corinth. Verses 8 and 9 then explain how this was possible, given the shaky financial circumstances which often surrounded the itinerant craftsman in Paul's day and the assumption that as the ministry grew in scope Paul's ability to work might have been diminished, though not abrogated.[137]

The main point of verses 8 and 9 is to assert further, however, that Paul's goal in supporting himself was, and continues to be (cf. v. 9b), to keep from being a "burden" to the Corinthians. Thus, on the one hand, the expected negative answer to the rhetorical question in verse

---

136. For other examples of this same use of a rhetorical question introduced with "or" in Paul, see Rom. 2:4; 3:29; 6:3; 9:21; 11:2, 35 (from Job 41:3); I Cor. 1:13c; 6:2, 9, 16 (depending on the variant chosen), 19; 9:6, 8, 10; 11:22; 14:36; II Cor. 1:17; 3:1; 6:15; 13:5.

137. Cf. too Meeks, *Urban Christians*, 66, who points out that Paul's refusal of support from the Corinthians was not absolute. On the precarious situation of the artisan in ancient society, cf. Hock, *Social Context*, 35, 37-42, 65, and 93 n. 2, who argues that 11:9 refers to the fact that the Macedonian aid was intended only to compensate for the needs Paul could not meet with his own work and not to replace his need to work itself (cf. p. 93 n. 2).

7 is supported both by Paul's reference to his purpose in doing so stated *within* the question (i.e., "in order that you might be exalted") and by his further emphasis in verse 9 on the fact that in doing so he has never been, nor will ever become, a burden to the church in Corinth.

On the other hand, verses 7-9 also combine to support Paul's prior assertion in verse 6b that the nature of his ministry itself serves as evidence of the genuine nature of his gospel. They do so by pointing out to the Corinthians that there is no ground *in his behavior* for the accusation of his opponents that Paul was using the ministry of the gospel to serve his own ends (cf. 12:16-18).[138] Quite the contrary, *as his decision to support himself demonstrates,* Paul humbled himself in order that the Corinthians might be exalted. Moreover, from Paul's perspective, the fact that he has never become a burden to the Corinthians by relying on them to support him provides *concrete evidence* that his motives in preaching the gospel were not duplicitous.

Finally, we know from Paul's prior argument in I Cor. 8–10 that Paul viewed his decision to preach the gospel free of charge to be an expression of that very gospel itself (cf. especially the concrete example in 8:13 of the principle stated in 9:19-22 and its summary in 10:33). Hence, Paul can point to the fact that he preached the gospel free of charge, i.e., he can point to an essential aspect of his humiliation and *suffering,* as evidence not only of his sincerity and single-mindedness, but also of the genuine nature of his gospel. For Paul presupposes that a genuine gospel produces a genuine apostolic life-style. And in addition to the passages from I Corinthians just referred to, Paul's statement in II Cor. 11:7a that he humbled *himself* in order that the *Corinthians* might be exalted also recalls Paul's prior principle in I Cor. 10:24 that one should not seek his own good, but the good of his or her neighbor.

That Paul is building his argument in II Cor. 11 on the foundation he has already laid in I Cor. 9 is then further confirmed in 11:10, which is simply a reiteration of what he has already argued for in more detail

---

138. This is the common view of these verses. For regardless of how one understands the identity of Paul's opponents or their theology, it seems apparent that they accused Paul of somehow using his ministry in general, and most probably the collection in particular, to defraud the Corinthians.

in 9:15-18, i.e., that this decision to preach free of charge in Corinth is an essential part of his "boast" and thus will not be (allowed to be) stifled (cf. the passive construction in v. 10). This statement thus picks up Paul's prior allusion in verse 7 to the criticism he is suffering in Corinth based on his decision to refuse their support. In doing so, it forms a transition to his conclusion in verses 11-15. For the fact that in verse 7 Paul chooses to describe his refusal to accept, or indeed, demand support from the Corinthians as a possible "sin" reflects one of the accusations raised against Paul in the polemical situation in which he now found himself.[139] Although the precise nature of the sin Paul was accused of committing remains unclear,[140] it appears, in the light of 11:11 and 12:16-18, that Paul's practice was being construed as a manifestation that he did not love the Corinthians, but was engaged, instead, in working out an elaborate scheme to defraud them. At any rate, Paul responds by reminding the church in Corinth that what his opponents label "sin" is, in reality, an essential part of the very boast for which he fully expects to be *rewarded* by God in the eschatological judgment (cf. II Cor. 11:10; I Cor. 9:16-18, and the discussion of this latter text above). Their criticism is Paul's boast!

Having said this, verse 11a then poses the question raised by Paul's statement in verse 10, namely, Paul's actual purpose in deciding to preach the gospel free of charge. The first answer to this question, given in verse 11b, is the answer now being given by Paul's opponents or the Corinthians themselves: Paul refuses the Corinthians' support because he does not love them. But against the backdrop of Paul's prior detailed exposition of the nature of his "boast" and the reason for its reward in I Cor. 8–10, Paul can now simply dismiss this suggestion with a

---

139. So too Friedrich, "Gegner," 188, who also concludes that 11:7 is not ironical, as most commentators argue, but comes from the reproach of Paul's opponents.

140. Given that from Plato's day on the act of selling one's teaching was often viewed as implying a positive claim concerning the worth of one's message (see above), that Paul refused to do so could have been presented by his opponents as cheapening the value of the gospel (i.e., sinning against the gospel), or as an indication that he was ashamed of what he did preach (cf. Rom. 1:16f.), since he knew it to be inferior to the true gospel of his opposition (i.e., sinning against the Corinthians by preaching a false gospel). This latter possibility seems more probable.

reference to the divine sanction ("God knows") which accompanies his decision. Paul's decision has already been shown to be an expression of his love for the church, which, as such, carries God's approval (cf. I Cor. 13:12f. and my discussion above).

The new element in Paul's argument in II Cor. 11 is his own answer to the question of 11a in verses 12-15. According to verse 12, Paul refused and continues to refuse to accept support from the Corinthians in order to establish a canon by which the true and false apostles may be distinguished from one another. Or in the words of the text, Paul refuses to be supported by the Corinthians, which is his "boast," in order that there will be no possibility for the "false apostles" to compare their missionary practice, centered no doubt in a demand for support as their "boast," favorably with Paul's. The need for such a "canon of true apostolicity" is then grounded in the deceptive nature of those who have disguised themselves as apostles of Christ but are, in reality, "ministers of Satan" (cf. 11:13-15).

In establishing this negative comparison, Paul once again turns his opponents' criticism on its head. Paul makes *his* behavior the criterion of *their* actions, rather than attempting to follow his opponents' attempt to establish their behavior as the criterion for his practice. Moreover, as we have just seen in Paul's statements in verse 11, the decisive issue in determining who is, in fact, the true apostle is the question of motive, i.e., whether Paul's missionary practice (and, by implication, his gospel) or that of his opponents (with their "different gospel") is the one being motivated by love.

Paul's argument is clear. It is his practice which ought to function as the true canon of authenticity since it results solely from his *voluntary* decision to give up his legitimate rights as an apostle (cf. I Cor. 9:12, 17). Such a decision can only be interpreted as an expression of love for the church. In contrast, it is his opponents' insistence on their rights which reflects an attempt to take advantage of the Corinthians (cf. 11:20). Thus, Paul's accusation in 11:20 that his opponents are "enslaving" the Corinthians is intended to be read in stark contrast to his own decision to become the "slave of all," as expressed in I Cor. 9:19, and to his commitment to preach as the Corinthians' slave, stated in II Cor. 4:5. The question raised by Paul's response to his opponents' criticism in 11:7-11, therefore, is whether it is likely that Paul's refusal to burden the Corinthians is an expression of a deceitful motive, or whether it is more probable that his opponents' demand to be supported reflects an attempt to use the Corinthians deceitfully. In addition, Paul maintains that this outward behavior not only expresses a corresponding inner motive, but that it also reflects the veracity or falsehood of the gospel with which it is bound. Hence, not only the determination of the "true apostle," but also the preservation of the "true gospel" hangs in the balance. As a result, the decision the Corinthians are now faced with in reading II Cor. 11:7ff. is whether Paul is to be the "canon of authenticity" by which his opponents are to be evaluated, or whether his opponents' claim to be the canon against which Paul is to be measured is, in fact, justified.

3. II Cor. 12:12-19

Paul's final discussion of the theme of his monetary self-support in II Cor. 12:12-19 is once again introduced with a positive comparison of his own apostolate with that of the "super apostles" (compare 12:11 with 11:5). This time, however, the fact that Paul is recalling his prior discussion in I Cor. 15:1-11 becomes explicit in his adversative conditional qualification "even if I am nothing" (12:11d). For, rather than being an ironical allusion to the criticism by his opponents,[141] this statement is best interpreted as Paul's own positive reference to his prior assertions in I Cor. 15:8f. Moreover, here too it is Paul's own activity in Corinth which is adduced as evidence for the legitimacy of

---

141. As is usually done; see Barrett, *Second Corinthians*, 320, although Barrett also points out the parallel to I Cor. 15:8f.; Windisch, *Zweiter Korintherbrief*, 396, who takes it to refer to Paul's weakness in parallel to II Cor. 11:6; Bultmann, *Zweiter Korintherbrief*, 233, who withholds judgment concerning the two alternatives; and Prümm, *Diakonia Pneumatos* I, 678f. and II/2, 107f., who sees this as another example of Paul's ironical comparison of his own ability and status with that of his opponents. In contrast, my view is informed by my prior decision that the "super apostles" are to be equated with the pillar apostles of Gal. 2 and I Cor. 15, so that there is no need to view this qualification in 12:11 as ironical. It is, rather, an expression of Paul's understanding of his call as the "last of the apostles," he who had previously persecuted the Church and was therefore unfit to be an apostle apart from the grace of God.

this comparison: the "signs of an apostle" which accompanied Paul's ministry in Corinth indicate that his apostleship is in no way inferior to that of the "super apostles" (compare 12:12 with 11:6b). And finally, the issue in 12:12-19 is once again whether Paul's practice of preaching the gospel free of charge is a positive or negative indication of his motives in Corinth (compare 12:15 with 11:11). For the opponents, it was an indication that Paul considered the Corinthians "inferior" to his other churches, since elsewhere he had been supported for his ministry (cf. 12:13). For Paul, it was a concrete indication of his fatherly love for the Corinthians, since it was his desire not to "burden" them which motivated his actions (cf. 12:13-16).

Thus, as part of the same "role reversal" which we saw in chapter 11, Paul again turns his *opponents'* criticism into his own badge of honor by insisting that it is his own apostolic practice which, in fact, demonstrates what it means to love the Corinthians; indeed, it indicates that he was the one who loved the Corinthians *"more"* (cf. 12:15b). In the light of *Paul's behavior* it is his opponents who are exposed as those who are seeking what the Corinthians have, rather than the Corinthians themselves (12:14). The point of Paul's argument in 12:12-19 is seen most clearly therefore in the summary statement of verse 16. For from Paul's perspective, it seems absurd to maintain that he was somehow trying to deceive the Corinthians financially, when he himself refused their support. His adversative statement in 12:16b is an ironical reaction to the idea that his very refusal to take money from the Corinthians was itself part of Paul's plan to deceive them. Verses 17 and 18 then extend Paul's self-defense to his co-workers in order to emphasize the unity of their actions and, hence, of their motives as well.[142]

---

142. Against those who have argued that Paul was using the good reputation of Titus to bolster his own image and authority (e.g., Plummer and Georgi). Cf. Oostendorp, *Another Jesus*, 77 n. 4, for the relevant literature and the key argument against this view. In a word, Titus belongs to the sphere of Paul's authority and not vice versa. As Hughes, *Second Corinthians*, 466, puts it,

there is no question of Paul's trying to "spread" the responsibility in the matter of this collection. On the contrary, he stands squarely on his own feet. It was at *his* instigation that Titus had gone to Corinth, and it was he again who was responsible for sending "the brother" with him. The character of Titus and "the brother" in their conduct of affairs in Corinth reflected on the character of Paul who had sent them.

The most significant aspect of Paul's argument in 12:12-19 for our study, however, is Paul's own interpretation of the *nature* and *purpose* of his argument in 12:19. For having presented what appears to be a defense of his apostolic ministry before the scrutiny of the Corinthians in 12:12-18, Paul then concludes this section, and perhaps 10:1–12:18 as a whole, by making the startling assertion that, in reality, he has not been engaged in an apology before the Corinthians at all! Instead, Paul is speaking "before God in Christ" (12:19a). Furthermore, Paul's purpose in doing so has not been to support *himself,* but to strengthen the *Corinthians* (12:19b).

The key to understanding the first of these two statements is its parallel to Paul's prior declaration in 11:11 ("God knows") and the accompanying underlying assumption, explicitly expressed in I Cor. 4:4f., that since only God can reveal the motives of the heart, it is God alone who is fit to examine or evaluate Paul's ministry (cf. Rom. 14:10-12). Thus, from Paul's perspective, it is senseless and unnecessary to defend oneself before others, when one's only judge is the Lord. Paul's "defense," therefore, is "before God," not "before them."[143] Paul does not deny that he has been engaged in an apology, but only that the Corinthians are his judges.[144] As such, Paul's statement that he speaks "before God in Christ" is intended to prohibit the Corinthians from drawing the conclusion that the validity of Paul's ministry, though demonstrated before the Corinthians, is somehow dependent upon the Corinthians' approval.

Paul's second statement in 12:19 is then intended, yet again, to use his opponents' own criticisms against them, which we have seen to be Paul's purpose throughout 11:7ff. and 12:12ff. Rather than defending

---

143. This understanding of 12:19 stands in contrast to that of those such as Prümm, *Diakonia Pneumatos* I, 694f., who sees Paul's denial as merely an attempt to avoid the terminology of "apology" since this is too easily associated with "self-glorification" and "boasting in the flesh." See, e.g., Barrett, *Second Corinthians,* 328, and Windisch, *Zweiter Korintherbrief,* 406. But cf. Bultmann, *Zweiter Korintherbrief,* 239, and Hughes, *Second Corinthians,* 470, who also point to I Cor. 4:3f. as the unexpressed background to 12:19.

144. Again, cf. Hughes, *Second Corinthians,* 469 n. 156, who correctly emphasizes that *humin* ("to you") in 12:19 is "emphatic by position" and translates the question, "Have you been thinking all along that I have been defending myself before you?" So too Bultmann, *Zweiter Korintherbrief,* 239.

himself against the attacks of his opponents, Paul has been laying out his case before God in order to give the Corinthians the opportunity, *as bystanders,* to be strengthened in their faithfulness to Paul. Given the identification between Paul and his message, this is, at the same time, an opportunity to recommit themselves to the true gospel. As a result, Paul's statement that "all things are for your edification" is, in reality, an implied *warning* to the Corinthians, since Paul is already confident of God's judgment concerning his apostolic ministry (cf. 1:12; 10:7, 18; 11:11, 31). Hence, contrary to the supposition of the Corinthians, Paul is not the one who is presently on trial before them; the Corinthians are on trial before Paul! This explains why Paul can switch so suddenly from his own "defense" to his concern for the Corinthians in 12:21–13:10. For as he puts it in 13:6f., his hope is that the Corinthians will not make the mistake of thinking that he has failed the test and thus reject him, since, in reality, they are the ones who must test *themselves* to see if they are still in the faith (13:5). The test, of course, is whether or not they reject Paul and his gospel.

4. Conclusion

The essential difference between Paul's discussion of his decision to support himself in I Cor. 9 and its counterpart in II Cor. 11 and 12 is the transformation in context which has taken place between the two discussions. In I Cor. 9 Paul's apostolic authority is still basically intact in Corinth, although certainly already being challenged elsewhere (cf. 9:1f.). In II Corinthians Paul's apostolic authority is no longer common ground between Paul and his church. But it is also important to see the decisive influence of Paul's opponents on his epistolary purpose in II Cor. 11 and 12. Whereas in I Cor. 9 Paul can use his distinctiveness over against the "pillar" or "super apostles" in a *positive* way as the very foundation of his argument in chapters 8 and 10 (i.e., that he has *voluntarily* given up his *common* right to financial support, which he shares with Peter, the brothers of the Lord, and the rest of the apostles, for the sake of the gospel), in II Cor. 11 and 12 it is this distinctiveness itself which now calls Paul's apostleship into question. The comparison between Paul and the "super apostles" which inaugurates both II Cor. 11:7ff. (cf. 11:5) and 12:12ff. (cf. 12:11) indicates that the "false apostles" were no doubt using this common apostolic right to financial support as the basis not only for their own demands for such support, but also for criticizing Paul. Paul is thus forced to respond in such a way that his opponents' claim to be the true representatives of the original apostolic tradition, as embodied in the pillar apostles, is defused, while at the same time affirming his own continuity with these apostles, since they too represent the common and true apostolic tradition.

Paul accomplishes this in two ways. First, he reminds the Corinthians that his *difference* from the pillar apostles, i.e., that he preached the gospel without seeking support from the Corinthians, is his "boast." Paul's preaching free of charge is part of his voluntary response to the stewardship entrusted to him by God, and not a negative reflection of the quality of his gospel or ministry (cf. 11:5; 12:11), an expression of his disdain for the Corinthians (cf. 12:13), an integral part of an elaborate plan to defraud them (see 12:16-18), or in some other way a "sin" (11:7). Hence, although his practice regarding his financial support differed from the normal practice of the "super apostles," this difference is nevertheless an outworking of their common gospel. This is the reason Paul emphasizes in 11:10 that his "boast" will not be stopped "in the regions of Achaia." For in doing so he stresses that his practice of self-support is not intended to be a critique of the super apostles, whose sphere of ministry lies outside of Achaia. Rather, the specific circumstances at hand in Corinth made this practice necessary in order to facilitate the spread of the gospel (cf. I Cor. 9:12, 23).[145] Paul's qualification in 11:10b enables him to

---

145. Unfortunately, we do not know what those circumstances were. The common assumption that Paul refused such support in order to distance himself from the wandering Cynic philosophers of his day who also preached openly in the markets and on the streets of the ancient cities has already been seriously questioned by Nock in *Conversion*, 191-192. Nock's point was that this comparison suggested by modern scholars was irrelevant, inasmuch as Paul's locus of activity was the synagogue and home and not the open-air market. For this same point, see now Stowers, "Social Status," who argues convincingly that such public speaking required a kind of social status, reputation, and recognized social role not possessed by Paul and that, from the NT accounts themselves, it is clear that the synagogue, workshop, and, most importantly, the private home provided the contexts for Paul's

avoid a direct confrontation with Jerusalem, while at the same time underscoring that his decision to support himself means not only that he loves the Corinthians, but that he loves them "more" than his opponents (cf. 12:15).

Second, Paul interprets his corresponding refusal to "burden" the Corinthians financially (cf. 11:9; 12:13f., 16) as the necessary result and outward expression of his love for the Corinthians in preaching the gospel. By doing so he insinuates that the outward similarity of his opponents' practice with the practice of the "super apostles" actually masks the fact that it is they who are attempting to take advantage of and deceive the Corinthians. By responding in this way, Paul is able to "turn the tables" on his critics. Rather than calling his legitimacy as an apostle into question, his apostolic practice now becomes the "canon of authenticity" for the true apostolic practice in Corinth (cf. 11:12), as well as the "test of genuine faith" for the Corinthians themselves (cf. 13:2-7).

Finally, Paul's response is made possible and supported by his underlying conviction that God alone is his judge, together with his corresponding confidence that he enjoys this divine approval (cf. II Cor. 13:6f.). Both this conviction and this confidence are expressed in Paul's declaration that he speaks "before God in Christ" (12:19). He stands before God's judgment in the confidence that comes from being "in Christ" (cf. 10:7). In turn, this conviction and confidence are themselves built upon Paul's understanding of his call to be an apostle as the one upon whom the prophetic compulsion has been laid to preach the gospel to the Gentiles (I Cor. 9:16). Hence, Paul's discussion of his decision to support himself in II Cor. 11 and 12 once again reveals that Paul understood his authority as an apostle to reside in his *call* to preach, which resulted in a *concrete display of love* for the Corinthians in which he could *boast* as that for which he would one day be rewarded and to which he could point as *evidence* for the authenticity of his call itself.

---

preaching and teaching (cf. p. 81). Stowers thus concludes, apparently independent of Nock's earlier emphasis, that "the widespread picture of Paul the public orator, sophist or street-corner preacher is a false one" (p. 81). Thus, the reason for Paul's refusal of financial support remains unknown.

Paul's "apology" in II Cor. 11 and 12 thus picks up and is built solidly upon the same themes which we saw to be at the heart of Paul's prior discussion in I Cor. 9. Having come this far, and with this in mind, we are now in a position to understand the meaning of Paul's statement in II Cor. 2:17 and its function within Paul's argument in 2:14–3:3.

D. THE MEANING OF II COR. 2:17 AND ITS FUNCTION WITHIN PAUL'S ARGUMENT IN 2:14–3:3

In the light of our previous investigations it now becomes clear that Paul's negative comparison in II Cor. 2:17a performs a twofold function. On the one hand, Paul's use of the verb *kapēleuein* in 2:17 to describe the practice of "the majority" or "the many"[146] is intended to call the genuineness of their ministry into question by depicting it in terms of the retail dealer who sells his wares in the market. Although the precise nature of the negative nuance associated with market trade in Paul's day was not uniform, so that the use of this verb alone cannot be used as the key to the *content* of Paul's critique in 2:17,[147] the

---

146. On the use of *polloi* as a noun with the article to mean "the majority" or "the most," cf. Jeremias, πολλοί, 540. He refers to this as the "exclusive" meaning: i.e., "many, but not all" and points to Mt. 24:12 as the other example of its use in the NT. For the "inclusive" meaning, i.e., "the totality which embraces many individuals," see Rom. 5:15b; 5:19; 12:5; I Cor. 10:17, 33; Mk. 9:26 (pp. 541, 543).

147. The tendency among those commentators who do argue that *kapēleuein* refers to selling in the marketplace is to read too much into Paul's use of this imagery. Cf., e.g., Bultmann, *Zweiter Korintherbrief*, 72f.; Georgi, *Gegner*, 226f.; Friesen, *Glory*, 29; Hughes, *Second Corinthians*, 38; Hock, *Social Context*, 63. A good recent example of this tendency is McDonald, "Paul and the Preaching Ministry," 42f., who rightly emphasizes that the verb here means "to make a trade of the word of God," but goes on to take this to mean "to reduce preaching to a worldly occupation and so denude it of its 'ultimate' or eschatological concern." Paul's point thus becomes that "no ordinary preaching, with ordinary human motivation, is sufficient here: no mere professional performance, nor well-turned rhetoric, nor evangelistic sideline. . . ." But the verb alone cannot bear this load; it was used metaphorically to represent a variety of different criticisms, not only concerning the motives of those involved, but also concerning the quality of the message sold as well. Moreover, as already indicated above, I am skeptical of Hock's suggestion that

imagery nevertheless does cast serious doubt on the integrity of those so described. But the significant point is that this technical, transferred use of *kapēleuein* also allowed Paul to call into question the practice of those he refers to as "the majority," *without calling into question the apostolic right of being paid for one's preaching in and of itself.* The well-established tradition of using the marketplace metaphor in this way, which we have seen attested from Plato and Isocrates to Lucian, Philostratus, and the *Didache*, as well as the general note of caution and negative connotations associated with retail trade in general in Sirach, Philo, and Josephus, provided Paul with a widespread linguistic convention which was admirably suited to his needs. Thus, in adopting this polemical, metaphorical use of the verb "to sell as a retailer," Paul was able to criticize the practice of the majority without contradicting or rescinding his previous argument in I Cor. 9:7-14 for the basic legitimacy of making one's living from the gospel.

On the other hand, Paul's introduction of the "hawking"-motif is also intended to support the legitimacy of his own apostolic ministry. In fact, Paul's *primary* concern in 2:17 is not to criticize his opponents. Paul's criticism of the "majority" as those who "sell the word of God as a retail dealer sells his wares in the market" is not presented for its own sake, but instead forms the counterpart to Paul's negative comparison. Paul's primary purpose in criticizing his opponents, therefore, is to make a positive assertion concerning the nature of his own ministry, here presented as the ideal, and in so doing to offer *evidence* for his sufficiency as an apostle. 2:17 is itself Paul's first support for the unexpressed answer to 2:16b and not an interruption or parenthesis in Paul's thought.[148] The implications of this comparison and the nature of the evidence Paul adduces from it are then made explicit in 2:17b. Hence, in order to ascertain the actual meaning of Paul's statement in 2:17, the identity of the "majority" and the nature of Paul's criticism signaled by his use of "to sell as a retailer" must first be clarified.

Paul's use of *kapēleuein* "further underscores Paul's snobbish attitude toward work" ("Tentmaking," 562 n. 43).

148. This point will be developed below. For examples of the view that Paul's evidence for his sufficiency is first given in 3:1-6, cf. Bultmann, *Zweiter Korintherbrief,* 73; Lambrecht, "Structure and Line of Thought," 366.

1. The Identity of the "Majority" and the Point of Paul's Criticism

Paul's decision to contrast himself *negatively* to those he simply identifies as the "majority" or the "many" in II Cor. 2:17, together with the nature of the critique itself, indicate that Paul is not referring to the circle of apostles listed in I Cor. 9:5 or their counterpart, the "super apostles," in II Cor. 11:5 and 12:11. Rather, Paul is contrasting himself to those who have recently arrived in Corinth and are now questioning his authority and sufficiency as an apostle, i.e., the "false apostles" of II Cor. 12:13-15.[149] For as we have seen, in both I Cor. 9 and II Cor. 11–12 Paul explicitly compares himself *positively* to the "other apostles," etc., and "super apostles," respectively, while at the same time *distancing himself* from the "false apostles."

Moreover, we have also seen that Paul's criticism of his opponents in II Cor. 11 and 12 revolved around their motives, i.e., that their insistence on being supported in Corinth did not derive from a love for the Corinthians, but from a desire to take advantage of them (see II Cor. 11:20). In contrast, in I Cor. 9 Paul does not directly criticize either the legitimacy of "living from the gospel" as such, or the fact that the other apostles were availing themselves of this right. Indeed, Paul himself advances a detailed argument to support both its legitimacy and its implementation in 9:7-14. The idea that the common apostolic practice of living from the gospel actually derived from a deceitful desire to take advantage of the Church is thus foreign to Paul's discussion in both I and II Corinthians. Hence, not only the negative comparison established in 2:17, but also the clearly negative imagery associated with the verb *kapēleuein* when used in a transferred sense, necessitate that we identify the "majority" with Paul's opponents currently in Corinth, in distinction to the "pillar apostles" in view in I Cor. 9; II Cor. 11:5; and 12:11.

It is not necessary at this point, however, to advance a theory

---

149. See Georgi, *Gegner,* 219-220, for his list of the eight elements in common between II Cor. 10–13 and 2:14–7:4, which support the supposition that the identity of Paul's opponents in these two sections is the same. Georgi, however, identifies these opponents with the "super apostles" of chs. 11 and 12 (see pp. 39, 48).

concerning the precise identity of Paul's opponents in order to understand Paul's statement in 2:17 or his larger argument in 2:14–3:6. It is enough merely to keep in mind that the structure of Paul's argument in II Cor. 11 and 12 (see above) indicates that Paul's opponents were building their case for the legitimacy of their own apostolic authority and ministry on the similarity between their practice and that of the "pillar apostles." This is confirmed by the fact that Paul's use of the marketplace imagery in 2:17 accomplishes the same dual purpose we saw to be at work in Paul's argument in chapters 11 and 12, namely, to cut off his opponents from the common apostolic tradition, despite their *seemingly similar practice,* and in so doing reassert his own unity with this tradition, in spite of his *obviously different practice.* For the point of Paul's criticism, as reflected in this imagery, is not that being paid for one's preaching is, in and of itself, morally wrong or inherently inferior to Paul's practice of supporting himself.[150] In fact, not only does Paul himself argue for its legitimacy in I Cor. 9, but we have also seen that, within the development of the *kapēloi*-motif from Plato on, the very act of selling one's teaching per se was often interpreted in the ancient world as a positive claim concerning the value of the message being sold.

Rather, as the argument in II Cor. 11 and 12 makes clear, his description of his opponents as those who are selling the word of God like a retailer in the market is intended to raise the question of their *integrity* in doing so, i.e., the question of their *motives*[151] and hence

150. Contra the basic position represented, for example, by Windisch, *Zweiter Korintherbrief,* 101, who, because of his identification of the "false apostles" with the "super apostles," must conclude that in II Cor. 2:17 Paul is forced by the critique of his opponents to disdain a custom that is sanctioned by the Lord and otherwise highly thought of by Paul himself. See too Hock, *Social Context,* 49-59, 63, who argues that Paul's criticism is based on the fact that, of the four possible means of support available to the philosopher of his day, Paul considered working the most suitable and honorable. Hock thus casts Paul's view in the light of that found in the Cynic epistle of Ps-Socrates, *ep.* 1.1-2, in which we read, "I generally do not regard it right to make money from philosophy, and that goes for me especially, since I have taken up philosophy on account of the command of God" (taken from Hock, 49). But in I Cor. 9 Paul argues that one *should generally* be paid for preaching if one is called by God to be an apostle and that his practice is the *exception* which is *not* necessitated by his call.

151. At this point Paul's use of the marketplace motif parallels its most classic formulation as first seen in Plato's presentation of Socrates' critique of the Sophists.

of their practice as well. What is conveyed in 11:13-15 with the prefix "pseudo-," the adjective "deceitful," the verb "to disguise," and the comparison to Satan's strategy is thus also represented by Paul's choice of the marketplace metaphor in 2:17. Like *dishonest* merchants in the market, Paul's opponents are attempting to deceive the Corinthians, or, in terms of the metaphor itself, their ministry is best described as a "shady business." For although Paul's opponents have assumed an outward appearance of legitimacy by following the common apostolic custom regarding financial support represented by the "pillar apostles," this appearance is a "sham." Their purpose is simply to take advantage of the Corinthians. Paul's use of *kapēloi* in 2:17 therefore raises a general suspicion concerning the motives of his opponents, although the specific nature of this suspicion is left undefined.

But even in raising this general suspicion Paul has already accomplished his goal of distinguishing their practice from the true and genuine apostolic practice outlined in I Cor. 9 and exemplified by the "pillar apostles." For Paul's opponents could have used his own strong arguments from I Cor. 9 for the legitimacy of seeking one's living from the gospel to call Paul's own apostolic claim into question. Thus, although it is not his primary purpose in II Cor. 2:17, Paul's description of his critics as retail merchants dealing in the word of God is designed to defuse this potentially explosive criticism without denying the legitimacy of seeking one's living from the gospel in and of itself.

Paul's statement in II Cor. 2:17 therefore occupies a mediating position between his prior argument in I Cor. 9 and his direct criticism

---

In addition to my study above, see Hock, *Social Context*, 53 (cf. also p. 95 nn. 23 and 24), who comments that

> Socrates, particularly in the Platonic writings, compared Sophists to traders and merchants *(kapēloi)*, the comparison being made to impute to Sophists the motives of deceit and avarice. This criticism of Sophists became traditional, but was also extended to philosophers too, if they charged fees or otherwise were perceived as suspect.

Hock points to Plato, *Apol.* 19D-E; 31B-C; 33A-B; *Prot.* 313C-D; *Men.* 92A; Xenophon, *Mem.* I.2.6-7, 61; 6.1-5, 11-14; *Apol.* 16.26; Diogenes Laertius 2.27; and Plato, *Euthyd.* 277B. But this parallel by no means indicates dependence.

of his opponents in II Cor. 11 and 12. On the one hand, Paul's use of the metaphor of selling in the marketplace refers back to and is built upon his contrasting practice of supporting himself as outlined in I Cor. 9. On the other hand, it also assumes and anticipates Paul's criticism of his opponents in II Cor. 11 and 12. This becomes even more clear in the light of the primary meaning of Paul's statement in 2:17, to which we now turn our attention.

2. The Meaning and Significance of II Cor. 2:17

The point of Paul's negative comparison in 2:17 is made explicit by the two "but as"-constructions *(all' hos)*, the second of which complements the first by further defining the nature of Paul's speaking "from sincerity," and by two prepositional phrases:

> but as from sincerity, but as from God before God in Christ we are speaking.

The second "but as"-clause and the prepositional phrases which follow do not introduce an additional contrast between Paul's ministry and the practice of the many described in 2:17a. Instead, they serve to indicate the larger context within which Paul's own practice of speaking "from sincerity" is to be understood. For the second "but as"-construction is repeated without an intervening coordinating conjunction and/or new verbal idea. The impression thus given by the syntax of 2:17 is that after having specified the nature of the contrast between himself and his opponents, Paul then decided to expand this contrast by placing it within the context of his apostolic self-understanding as the one who speaks "from God before God in Christ." Therefore, although the second construction and the prepositional phrases which follow modify the verb "we are speaking," they nevertheless also support Paul's assertion that he speaks "from sincerity" by emphasizing the *source* of Paul's preaching and the *motivation* behind his proclamation.

But the precise meaning and significance of this densely formulated affirmation, which in and of itself remains opaque due to its brevity, only becomes transparent in the light of Paul's negative comparison in 2:17a, upon which it is based, together with Paul's other discussions of this and related themes throughout his letters.[152]

Paul's assertion that he speaks "from sincerity" is stated in contrast to the "many," whose *motives* (and hence activities) in preaching the gospel are suspected to be deceitful. This indicates that Paul's point in 2:17 is to stress that his own proclamation is *sincere*, being based on *pure* intentions.[153] Such an interpretation is in distinction to that of those who, due to their prior decision that *kapēleuein* means "to water down" or "adulterate," have consequently taken 2:17b to refer to the purity of Paul's message rather than his motives. But it is also confirmed by the fact that the phrase "as from sincerity" is clearly adverbial, functioning to modify the verb "we speak," rather than adjectival in dependence on the unexpressed object of the verb, i.e., "the word of God."

Moreover, that Paul's positive statement in 2:17b does not refer to the quality of his message per se is also supported by the other two occurrences of "sincerity" *(eilikrineia)* in the Corinthian correspondence. For in I Cor. 5:8 "sincerity" and "truth" are the two qualities which ought to characterize the Corinthians' *behavior.* This can be seen not only by their contrast to "sin" and "wickedness" in I Cor. 5:8 itself, but also by the larger context as a whole, in which the issue in view is the association of the Corinthians with those guilty of immorality of all sorts (cf. 5:1-5; 9:1-13). It is also significant to note that although

152. Friesen, *Glory*, 29f., is a good representative of the common approach to this difficult passage. For like Friesen, commentators have usually been content simply to interpret this text in a general way as a reference to the fact that Paul's sincerity is witnessed to by his refusal to accept money, the divine origin of his message, and from the fact that Christ is the center from which Paul spoke. Although this interpretation is certainly correct, it stops short of explaining how Paul's argument in 2:17 actually works both to support the legitimacy of his own apostleship and to offer a defense against his opponents' claims.

153. The noun *eilikrineia* ("sincerity") occurs only three times in the NT, all within the Corinthian correspondence. For a discussion of the other two references (I Cor. 5:8 and II Cor. 1:12), see below. The corresponding adjective, "sincere," occurs in Phil. 1:10 and II Pet. 3:1. For the basic meaning of the noun, "moral purity," cf. Büchsel, εἰλικρινής, 397-398. Cf. Philo's use of the adjective in *De post.* 134; *De ebr.* 101; *De som.* II.20, 74; *De spec. leg.* I.99; *De Ab.* 129., etc. Of special interest is Philo's statement in *De vit. Mos.* II.40 that the translators of the LXX are to be considered prophets and priests "whose sincerity and singleness of thought has enabled them to go hand in hand with the priest of spirits, the spirit of Moses."

"truth" and "sincerity" in this context are themselves inner qualities or attitudes, Paul is nevertheless able to pit these inward dispositions *directly* against the immoral conduct of those from whom the Corinthians are to separate themselves (compare I Cor. 5:8 with 5:11). Paul's mode of expression in I Cor. 5:8ff. consequently reveals the same unexpressed presupposition we saw at work in his argument in II Cor. 11:5ff. and 12:11ff., namely, the assumption that one's outward behavior is a direct expression of one's inner motives or disposition. For it is this identification which enables Paul to move freely from the one category to the other, as he does in I Cor. 5:8ff., or even to speak of "obeying" or "not obeying" the truth in Gal. 5:7 and Rom. 2:8 respectively.

Moreover, it is Paul's understanding of humanity's plight which explains why in II Cor. 1:12 he describes his own behavior, both in the world and toward the Corinthians, as being carried out "in . . . the sincerity of God," which he then further clarifies as being done "not in fleshly wisdom but *in the grace of God.*" In view of humanity's bankrupt nature, the sincerity which is the source or means of Paul's behavior can only be a divine sincerity, i.e., a sincerity which belongs to God or which finds its origin in God.[154]

Hence, since the sincerity which characterizes Paul's behavior originates in God, his conduct can also be described as taking place "in the grace of God," rather than "in fleshly wisdom." Furthermore,

---

154. Taking the genitive "of God" as a *genitivus auctoris.* See Eckstein, *Syneidesis,* 194. He points to the commentaries of Schlatter and Grosheide as also representing this view (cf. p. 194 n. 71). Eckstein himself opts for a *genitivus obiectivus,* interpreting Paul's meaning to be that he "demonstrates then his sincerity 'before God,'" thus taking Paul's statement as a description of the nature of his conduct, rather than in parallel to "in the grace of God" (cf. pp. 197f.). As such, its function corresponds to Paul's statement in II Cor. 12:19 that he speaks "before God in Christ" (p. 194). But as I have argued, the two conceptions, though related, are distinct, as the change in prepositions itself from "from" (*ek*) to "before" (*katenanti*) in 2:17 indicates. Surprisingly, Eckstein does not bring 2:17 into his discussion at all. Moreover, the similar structure throughout II Cor. 1:12 indicates that Paul is attempting to make *one* point, not two, as necessitated by Eckstein's position. It is nevertheless important to emphasize that, as the source of Paul's activity, the sincerity of God also characterizes his activity, so that in pointing to the "ground of its possibility" Paul is also expressing something about the nature of his activity itself.

the parallels between this contrast in II Cor. 1:12 and the contrast between the "wisdom of the world" and the "wisdom of God = Christ crucified" in I Cor. 1:20-24 (cf. 2:5), together with Paul's statement in II Cor. 5:16f. that he no longer knows Christ in a fleshly manner ("according to the flesh"),[155] being a "new creation," indicate that the contrast between "in fleshly wisdom" / "in the grace of God" in II Cor. 1:12 is a contrast between his standing apart from Christ and his standing as one called by Christ to be his apostle. For in I Cor. 1:26-31, the decisive factor in recognizing the divine wisdom in Christ is God's "call" or "election" (cf. vv. 26, 27, 30), with its concomitant gift of God's Spirit (2:12), through whom God reveals those things which he has freely given in Christ (cf. 2:7-12, with 2:12 recalling 1:30). Similarly, in II Cor. 5:18 Paul's new creation, with its new understanding of Christ, comes "from God, who reconciled us to himself through Christ and gave to us the ministry of reconciliation." Thus, Paul is able to assert in I Cor. 2:13 that "that which we also are speaking, we speak not in words taught by human wisdom, but in words taught by the Spirit," and in II Cor. 5:20 that God makes his plea "through us" (cf. 6:1). Paul's affirmation in II Cor. 1:12 that his conduct is "in the sincerity of God" / "in the grace of God" is at the same time, therefore, an affirmation concerning his call to be a Christian apostle.

Conversely, in II Cor. 1:12, as in I Cor. 2:1-4 and II Cor. 6:3ff., Paul can point to his mode of *behavior* as that which supports his legitimacy, since it is intended to be seen as a direct result of the activity of God, i.e., God's sincerity, within him. For although Paul's vacillation in his travel plans appears to be a mode of behavior "according to the flesh" (1:17), in reality it corresponds to God's own faithfulness in carrying out his promises in Christ (1:18-20). Paul's purpose in not going through with his aforementioned plans was "to spare" the Corinthians. Like God's actions in Christ, Paul's decision to change

---

155. Taking "according to the flesh" to modify "we know." For the various positions which have been suggested concerning this text and a good discussion of the view I accept, cf. Bruce, *Paul and Jesus*, 15-22. Bruce argues that in II Cor. 5:16 "the contrast which Paul is making is one between his former attitude to Christ . . . and his present attitude toward Christ . . ." (p. 20). Paul's past understanding of and attitude toward Christ, as well as his conception of the Messiah as such, have now been fundamentally altered by his encounter with Christ himself (cf. pp. 20-22).

his plans was carried out for their sake as an expression of his love for them. In other words, Paul did so in order that the Corinthians might be saved (cf. 1:23; 2:4; 7:9, 12). Hence, rather than being an act of duplicity or deceitfulness which calls his apostleship into question, Paul's change of plans, being an act of love carried out "in the openness and sincerity of God," becomes his "boast" (cf. I Cor. 9:14ff.!), confirmed by the "testimony of his conscience."[156]

In the light of I Cor. 5:8ff. and II Cor. 1:12, and against the background we have sketched out briefly above, Paul's assertion in II Cor. 2:17b thus also implies that his practice of self-support, as an outworking of this "sincerity," is a true expression of the elective grace of God in his life. Conversely, Paul's description of his opponents as those who sell the Word of God like peddlers in the market not only casts suspicion on their personal motives in preaching, but also calls into question, by implication, the very legitimacy of their call to be apostles, and with it the truth or validity of their gospel (cf. II Cor. 4:2).[157] For if Paul's call as a result of the grace of God creates a sincerity within him that expresses itself in a self-supporting ministry in Corinth in conjunction with his proclamation of the gospel revealed by the Spirit, then his opponents' insistence on being paid for preaching

---

156. The other example of Paul's use of his "conscience" as a witness to his own integrity is Rom. 9:1, where once again this witness is linked to Paul's (potential) activity, which would be undertaken if it could save his fellow Jews (cf. 9:2f.). For an extended discussion of both of these texts, cf. Eckstein, *Syneidesis*, 179-199.

157. Cf. too II Cor. 6:7 where Paul lists the fact that his ministry is characterized by the "word of truth" as one of the factors which commend him as a "minister of God." For a good discussion of this point, see Barrett, "ΨΕΥΔΑΠΟΣΤΟΛΟΙ," 383-389. Barrett argues for the inseparableness of genuine apostleship and right doctrine in Paul's thinking, pointing especially to Gal. 2:7f. He then goes on to relate this basic conviction to Paul's criticism of the false apostles in II Cor. 2:17; 4:2; 5:12; 10:12-16; 11:3f., 13, 26. Barrett's main point is that Paul's criticism of his opponents in these texts focuses on the fact that they are not just guilty of an innocent error in preaching, but instead, are engaged in an "intended deception," which leads to a "deliberate falsehood," for which Paul can have no tolerance (cf. pp. 383, 386, 388f.). Concerning 2:17 he rightly points out that although *kapēleuein* need not necessarily include the intent to deceive, the parallel between II Cor. 2:17 and 4:2 indicates that Paul probably also meant to emphasize that his opponents falsified the word they preached (cf. p. 384).

and their corresponding criticism of Paul's practice must result from what Paul calls in II Cor. 11:4 a "different spirit," while the content of their message is "another Jesus," i.e., a "different gospel." Paul's assertion that he is not like those who seek support from the Corinthians is thus an *evidential argument for the divine origin and nature of his apostolic ministry and gospel*, as well as an implicit criticism of his critics. For from Paul's perspective, one's outward behavior is a direct result and reflection of one's inner motives.

This evidential argument is then buttressed by the second contrast and the following two prepositional phrases in which the sincerity of Paul's proclamation is *explicitly* brought into the context of Paul's call to be an apostle (i.e., he speaks "from God")[158] and its corresponding motivation (i.e., he speaks "before God in Christ"). The significance of Paul's assertion that he speaks "from God" only becomes clear, however, once it is recognized as merely one part of the larger theme expressed by this terminology running throughout the Corinthian correspondence, namely, that God is the one source of everything that exists (cf. I Cor. 8:6; 11:12), including the Christians' redemption and existence in Christ (cf. I Cor. 1:30; II Cor. 5:18) and the Spirit which Paul has received (cf. I Cor. 2:12). In I Cor. 7:7 this fundamental and common Christian conviction expresses itself in Paul's affirmation that "each has his own gift from God," which, in turn, demands that Paul refrain from insisting that his celibate life-style become the binding norm for all believers. In the same way, although the "from God" terminology is not present in I Cor. 12, Paul's statement in 12:4-6 nevertheless betrays this same conviction. It is this conviction, then, which undergirds his insistence in 12:7ff. on the organic unity and mutual interdependence of the individual members of the body of Christ, despite the *diversity* of their gifts. As a result, this conviction also underlies the admonition to maintain the unity of the church by accepting one another, which is implicit throughout this chapter (cf. especially 12:7, 12, 14, 20f., 25).

Thus the point in I Cor. 7:7 and chapter 12 is essentially the same. The recognition that God is the giver and source of all gifts within the

158. So too Munck, *Paul*, 181, who translates *"ek theou"* in 2:17: "as commissioned by God."

Church necessitates that the validity of each person's gift(s) be recognized. Of special significance for our study, therefore, is the fact that I Cor. 12:28 makes explicit that this implied imperative refers to the gift of apostleship as well. Against this backdrop, Paul's assertion in II Cor. 2:17 that he speaks "from God" is not only a reminder to the Corinthians of the divine origin of his own calling,[159] but also an implicit *warning* to them not to usurp God's sovereignty by calling Paul's apostleship into question.[160]

Moreover, Paul's reference in II Cor. 4:5 to his commitment to become the "slave of all" and his corresponding insistence that he does not preach himself, but Christ as the "Lord," make it evident that Paul's defense of his own authority and hence legitimacy as an apostle in II Corinthians is intended to meet the twofold criterion[161] established for determining the genuine nature of spiritual gifts in I Cor. 12–13. For on the one hand, "no one speaking by the Spirit of God says, 'Jesus is accursed' and no one can say 'Jesus is Lord,' except by the Holy Spirit" (I Cor. 12:3, NASB). On the other hand, the purpose and use of the genuine gift or calling is the common good of the Church (12:7; cf. ch. 13 and 14:12), as Paul's own evaluation of the gift of tongues and his regulation for its use in the Church in I Cor. 14 makes clear.

The point of Paul's assertion in II Cor. 2:17 that he speaks "from God" is not, therefore, to "pull rank" on the Corinthians by relegating the question of his apostolic authority to the inaccessible realm of divine judgment, thus removing his ministry from the possibility of

159. For the same assertion concerning the divine origin of Paul's apostleship, see Gal. 1:1; 2:7f.; Rom. 15:15f.; and I Cor. 15:10. It is important to note, moreover, that in each case Paul's affirmation of his call carries within it an implied apologetic designed to underscore the legitimacy of his apostleship and/or gospel.

160. This implied *exhortative* function of Paul's statement in II Cor. 2:17b, which I will develop more below, brings to expression the implied apologetic force of Paul's entire discussion in II Cor. 2:14–3:6 and is a classic example of what Furnish, *Theology and Ethics,* 97, describes as Paul's "use of indicate statements in order to exhort," i.e., what he terms the "imperatival indicative" (see his discussion on pp. 97f. for other examples).

161. Similarly Dunn, "Responsible Congregation," 223-225, distinguishes three such criteria: (1) the confession "Jesus is Lord," (2) love, and (3) the test of edification or community benefit. Since the act of edification is, by definition, love (see I Cor. 13:4-7), I have combined the last two into one category.

human scrutiny and ruling out the ability of the Corinthians to evaluate his apostleship as a matter of principle. Instead, Paul's statement serves to caution the Corinthians that a rejection of his authority as an apostle would, in effect, be a rejection of God's authority itself. Both the *content of his message* (i.e., that Paul stands in continuity with the common apostolic tradition which preaches Christ as Lord) and the nature of his practice (i.e., that Paul's decision to support himself is an expression of his love for the Corinthians, being made for their good) have already demonstrated to the Corinthians the genuineness and divine origin of his gift of apostleship, i.e., that he speaks "from God." Since Paul's apostleship has already passed this necessary test by meeting the twofold criterion of authenticity established in I Cor. 12–13,[162] to reject his authority because his practice of supporting himself differed from the usual apostolic "norm" is to usurp God's sovereignty in delegating his gifts. Or in Paul's own words, it would mean committing the sin of "judging the servant of another," namely, the servant of God (Rom. 14:4).

Once again it must be emphasized, therefore, that Paul's positive declaration that he speaks "from God," like his prior assertion that he speaks "from sincerity," is supported by visible proof, i.e., by his decision to support himself in Corinth. Moreover, since Paul has shown himself to be *speaking* "from God," to reject his apostleship is to reject the true word of God with which he has been entrusted. For in affirming that he speaks "from God," Paul is affirming that his speech is the speech of God.[163]

Finally, Paul completes his densely formulated affirmation by

---

162. By this I do not mean to imply that this "test" was a prerequisite to becoming an apostle, but that the nature of Paul's apostleship was a subsequent demonstration of the legitimacy of his call, which is the only "prerequisite" Paul considered valid (cf. I Cor. 15:8-10). See Bultmann, *Zweiter Korintherbrief*, 73. But contra Bultmann, p. 78, Paul's point is that he has given the Corinthians evidence of this "call."

163. For this identification see I Cor. 14:37. Bartling, "God's Triumphant Captive," 894 n. 16, therefore goes so far as to translate Paul's statement that he speaks *ek theou*, "inspired by God," pointing to II Pet. 1:21 as the key parallel. For a similar view, cf. Windisch, *Zweiter Korintherbrief*, 101. Besides II Pet. 1:21, Windisch points to Mt. 10:20 par.; I Thess. 2:13; I Pet. 4:11a; Odes Sol. 26:10; and John 3:31 as parallels.

asserting that he speaks "before God in Christ." Fortunately, we are provided with an important insight into the meaning and function of this last aspect of Paul's statement by its repetition in II Cor. 12:19 and the parallel thought found in 4:2 and 5:9-11. In view of the former, it becomes clear that Paul's assertion that he speaks "before God in Christ" in 2:17 is also intended to prevent the Corinthians from drawing the conclusion that Paul is on trial before them, or that he is seeking their approval (see above, pp. 156ff.). Unlike 12:19, however, the "speaking" referred to in 2:17 is not *primarily* Paul's prior discussion, but rather his proclamation of the Word of God. Paul's main point, therefore, is that his proclamation of the gospel, being characterized by the sincerity which he possesses as a result of the work of God's grace in his life, is not dependent upon *their* approval for its authority and legitimacy, since Paul carries it out before the judgment of God himself. At the same time, Paul is also confident that he does enjoy God's approval inasmuch as he speaks before God "in Christ," i.e., from his position or status as a Christian (cf. 4:2; 5:11b).[164] And, although it is not the primary referent of 2:17, it seems appropriate to assume, given the polemical tone of 2:14ff., the identification of the message with its messenger which we have seen to be such an integral part of Paul's thinking in 2:14-16a, and the conclusion which Paul himself draws from 2:17 in 3:1 (see below), that Paul also intends to include his prior discussion of his own apostolic ministry of suffering (2:14-16a) as an essential part of his ministry of the Word of God which Paul preaches "before God in Christ."

Thus, having completed his affirmation concerning the nature (2:14-16a) and source (2:17b) of his apostolic ministry, Paul is quick to point out, as he also does in 3:1 and 12:19, that this affirmation ought not to be misconstrued as an attempt on Paul's part to seek his approval from the Corinthians. The fact that Paul has indeed demonstrated the legitimacy of his apostolic calling *to* the Corinthians should not be taken to mean that he also derives his authority *from* the

---

164. For the corresponding motif that there is no righteousness or ground for boasting "before God" apart from Christ, even in the "works of the law," see Rom. 3:9, 20; I Cor. 1:29; Gal. 3:11, etc. Conversely, for the one who is "in Christ," his or her praise comes "from God" (Rom. 2:29), while his or her boast is in the Lord (I Cor. 1:31; II Cor. 10:17f.; cf. Rom. 15:18).

Corinthians. God is Paul's only judge. He is the one before whom Paul speaks.[165]

This is also brought out in the close parallel to 2:17 found in 4:2, in which Paul again asserts that the purity of his motives, i.e., that he has renounced "the hidden things of shame," results in a standard of behavior which recommends him to every person's conscience "before God." Here too Paul's conduct is portrayed as a demonstration of his legitimacy to the Corinthians, though it is carried out "before God."

Finally, the parallel in thought between Paul's assertion that he speaks "before God in Christ" in 2:17 and his statement in 5:9-11 makes it clear that in the former case Paul's reference to the judgment of God also functions to express the source of Paul's *motivation* in his ministry. Rather than seeking to please the Corinthians, as if his authority and legitimacy derived from their approval, Paul's consciousness of Christ's coming judgment is the mainspring of his apostolic activity. As he puts it in 5:11, "knowing therefore the fear of the Lord, we persuade men." Hence, Paul's assertion that he speaks "before God in Christ" provides additional support for his statement that he speaks "from sincerity." For since Paul is aware that his motives and actions as an apostle will one day be revealed and judged (5:10; cf. I Cor. 3:12-14; 4:1-4; Rom. 14:10), this affirmation, like his ministry as a whole, must be able to endure the scrutiny of Christ. As a result, Paul's insistence that he is free from the judgment of the Corinthians does not mean that he is free from judgment altogether.

The meaning of Paul's statement in II Cor. 2:17 can now be *summarized* as follows. Paul's refusal to seek financial support from the Corinthians is evidence of the purity of his motives,[166] as well as of the divine legitimacy of his ministry, in contrast to that of the "majority," whose motives in preaching are clouded with the suspicion

---

165. Although it cannot be developed here, this forensic interpretation of "speaking before God in Christ" in 2:17 is also supported by the corresponding motif of standing "before God" found elsewhere within II Corinthians. See 7:9-12 and 8:16-21.

166. As such, 2:17 finds an exact parallel in 7:2, where Paul simply states what he here provides evidence for, namely, that he "wronged no one, corrupted no one, took advantage of no one," as well as making explicit the admonition which is implied in 2:17, i.e., "make room for us."

of deceit as those who are misusing the apostolic custom of living from the gospel in order to take advantage of the Corinthians. For as Paul's prior argument in I Cor. 9 makes clear, his decision to support himself in Corinth was occasioned by his call to be an apostle and was thus a direct result of the grace of God in his life. Hence, Paul's call brought with it a twofold realization: first, that his proclamation of the gospel found its source in the divine sincerity created within him by the grace of God (i.e., he speaks "from sincerity"), since he preaches the gospel as God's appointed spokesman (i.e., he speaks "from God"); second, that as God's apostle Paul's motivation was the fact that his ministry was being carried out before the appraisal and judgment of God himself (i.e., he speaks "before God in Christ").

It is for this reason that Paul's decision to support himself in Corinth can be seen as an expression of the sincerity of his love for the church and an outworking of his desire to please God (i.e., to secure a "boast," in the positive sense, before God). As such, rather than calling his sufficiency as an apostle into question, Paul's decision to support himself can be adduced by Paul as evidence that he is the one who, in reality, is sufficient for the apostolic ministry. For Paul's practice of self-support is a result of the sincerity of God within him and hence an attestation of the grace of God in his life. II Cor. 2:17 thus provides the same argument for Paul's sufficiency found in I Cor. 15:9f., namely, that Paul's sufficiency derives from the grace of God which he has received, a grace which can be seen in the fact that he labored in the work of the gospel more than all the rest of the apostles.

This interpretation of Paul's affirmation in II Cor. 2:17 is confirmed by Paul's earlier, more detailed statement in I Thess. 2:3-10, in which we encounter the same constellation of motifs present in II Cor. 2:17, but without the metaphorical clothing and densely packed formulations which make 2:17 so hard to penetrate. I Thess. 2:3-10 thus provides a running commentary on II Cor. 2:17, not only confirming our exegesis of this difficult passage, but also indicating that both the structure and content of Paul's "apology" in II Cor. 2:17 represent a common piece of Pauline catechesis, which in turn reflects that important aspect of Paul's self-understanding as an apostle which set him apart so dramatically from his opponents. The parallels between these two texts become immediately evident once the elements of the two passages are isolated and compared with one another:

II Cor. 2:17	I Thess. 2:3-10
For we are not as the majority	For we did not come . . . but we became gentle . . . (2:5, 7-10)
selling as in a market-place the Word of God	in a word of flattery . . . nor in a covering of greed . . . nor seeking glory from men (2:5f.)
but we are speaking as from sincerity	For our exhortation was not from evil, nor from uncleanness, nor in deceit (2:3)
but we are speaking as from God	but just as we have been approved by God to be entrusted with the gospel, thus we are speaking (2:4a)
we are speaking before God in Christ	(we are speaking), not as pleasing men, but God, who tests our hearts (2:4b)

Finally, that Paul's statement in II Cor. 2:17 is once again concerned fundamentally with Paul's apostolic self-conception provides an important insight into the meaning and function of his argument as it continues in 3:1-6. Thus, before turning our attention to 3:1-3, it will be helpful to conclude this chapter by summarizing the role of 2:17 within the argument of 2:14–3:3 as a whole.

3. The Place of 2:17 within the Argument of 2:14–3:3

Paul's thesis-like presentation of the revelatory function of his apostolic ministry of suffering in II Cor. 2:14-16a naturally led to the question of Paul's "sufficiency" in 2:16b for two reasons: first, because Paul's "weakness" as an apostle was the central point of contention in the dispute between Paul and his opponents in Corinth (see 4:7ff.; 6:3ff.; 10:7-10; 11:6f., 21-23; 12:9f; 13:4, 9); second, because of the life-and-death significance which Paul himself attached to his ministry in 2:15. However, Paul's answer to the question "Who is sufficient for these things?" in 2:16b, though unexpressed, is not so self-evident. For in spite of his opponents' insistence that Paul's weakness and suffering called his apostleship into question (cf. especially 10:10; 11:21), and in the face of the magnitude of the apostolic task itself, Paul nevertheless asserts that he is, in fact, sufficient for the apostolic ministry. This is the clear implication of the ground clause in 2:17a. The negative comparison in 2:17 is intended to supply the reason or ground for this bold assertion. As we have seen above, it does this by adducing Paul's commitment to support himself as *evidence* of the genuine nature of his apostolic commission, including the gospel he preached. For as Paul had argued earlier in I Cor. 9, his practice of self-support in Corinth was a visible demonstration of his love for the Corinthians in response to and in conformity with his prophetic call to preach the gospel, while the sincerity motif in 2:17 itself also attributes Paul's practice to the sovereign work of God's grace in his life (cf. I Cor. 15:9f.).

Furthermore, our investigation has also demonstrated that there is an internal, organic unity between Paul's apostolic ministry of suffering (2:14-16a), his claim to be sufficient for this ministry (2:16b), and his refusal to accept payment for it (2:17). For an essential part of his suffering or weakness as an apostle was his voluntary decision to support himself and the tribulations which accompanied this practice (cf. I Cor. 4:11f.; II Cor. 6:4f.; 11:26f.). Hence, given that the subject matter remains the same, the transition in thought from 2:14-16a to 2:17 is a natural one. Paul simply moves from a statement concerning the nature and function of his apostolic ministry of suffering in general to a specific aspect of that suffering.

The rationale for this move becomes apparent in the light of Paul's discussion in chapters 10–13. There it is evident that Paul's practice of self-support was one of the central bones of contention between Paul and his opponents in Corinth (cf. 11:7-15; 12:13-19). Against this background, the evidence for Paul's sufficiency in 2:17 also functions as an apologetic rebuttal to the criticisms of his critics. Indeed, the very form of 2:17 itself, i.e., the negative comparison, serves not only to defend Paul from those who criticized him on the basis of his practice of self-support, but also to return the volley of criticism back into the court of his opponents. For in 2:17 Paul adduces as evidence for his sufficiency to be an apostle the very weakness and suffering which his critics argued called that sufficiency into question. As a result, Paul's negative comparison defends his own sufficiency by casting suspicion on the practice and hence sufficiency of his opponents.

Paul's argument in 2:17 thus completes the train of thought introduced in 2:14 by meeting the two needs created as a result of his description of his apostolic ministry in 2:14-16a. On the one hand, it provides the evidence necessary to support his own unexpressed assertion of his sufficiency in response to the natural question of 2:16b. On the other hand, it serves to refute those who would question or deny that assertion, while at the same time casting doubt on any counter-assertion of sufficiency based on a demand for support from the Corinthians.

But having come this far in his argument, Paul realized that the evidential support for his sufficiency adduced in 2:17 could be mis-construed as merely a "self-recommendation" since it was, in the final analysis, still dependent upon Paul's own interpretation, i.e., that his practice of supporting himself was, in fact, done "from sincerity" and "from God."[167] Paul's evidence in 2:17 thus raises the question of 3:1a, which Paul then immediately extends by a second, related question in 3:1b. Hence, Paul's statement in 2:17 not only ends one discussion, it creates another, and in so doing occupies the pivotal position upon which Paul's argument in 2:14–3:3 turns. For just as Paul's assertions in 2:14-16a lead to the question of 2:16b, the answer of which is left unexpressed but then supported in 2:17, so Paul's assertion in 2:17

---

167. It is important to emphasize that the questions of 3:1 relate to what Paul has just said in 2:17, not to what he has said previously in 2:14-16a, thus jumping over this crucial intermediary statement, as Plummer, *Second Corinthians,* 76, does. For the view that 3:1 is occasioned by the fact that 2:17 could be interpreted as "self-praise" or as an inappropriate self-recommendation, see Barrett, *Second Corinthians,* 106; Windisch, *Zweiter Korintherbrief,* 102; Lietzmann, *An die Korinther,* 109f.; and, most recently, Lambrecht, "Structure and Line of Thought," 351. The most extreme statement of this relationship to my knowledge is that of Schoeps, *Paul,* 79, who takes 3:1 as a reflection of Paul's opponents' reproach that he had become mad with "overwhelming conceit" and "crazy with boasting," since Paul "appears to derive his vocation to the apostolic office from his own intrinsic strength." But we will see below that the issue involved is not Paul's pride, but the competing modes of recommendation employed by Paul and his opponents.

leads to the questions of 3:1, the answers of which are also left unexpressed but then supported in 3:2f. And in repeating the structure of 2:14-17, the support for the unanswered questions in 3:1 found in 3:2f. provides the second pillar in Paul's defense of his apostolic calling, i.e., his ministry of the Spirit.

Chapter Five

Paul's Ministry of the Spirit as Corroboratory Evidence of His Sufficiency (II Cor. 3:1-3)

In II Cor. 3:1 Paul responds to his evidential argument in 2:17 by asking two interrelated questions, which in turn lead to the affirmations of 3:2f. The key to Paul's argument in 3:1-3, as well as its place within 2:14–3:6 as a whole, thus lies in understanding the significance of these two questions and their relationship to one another.

A. THE MEANING OF II COR. 3:1

The first thing to be taken into account in determining the meaning of Paul's questions in 3:1a is that their form and function correspond to the "false conclusion," which is one of the central rhetorical features of the "diatribe," though their historical and literary context are not diatribal. Rather than being a part of an extended diatribal discourse constructed to be used in a philosophical school or in a general pedagogical situation, II Cor. 2:14–3:6 is "polemical." It is bound to the specific situation at hand in which Paul must defend the legitimacy of his apostolic ministry. As such, the use of the common diatribal device of the "false conclusion" in 3:1 is another example of the widespread use of the diatribal elements in nondiatribal literature.[1] Moreover, as Stowers has demonstrated in his

1. For an analysis of the diatribe as a style of discourse and argumentation used in the philosophical schools and an examination of the seven or eight (depend-

recent study of the diatribe, the pedagogical device of the "false conclusion" is "usually stated rhetorically and usually (implies) an objection."[2] Furthermore, "false conclusions are predominantly found as questions."[3] But most important for our purposes is that

> when objections and false conclusions appear at the beginning of a new section[4] in the diatribe they are not usually the result simply of some necessary internal logic of the preceding argumentation. Instead, they appear as the result of two factors: First, they are connected with the previous line of argument and come as a reaction to it. Second, they are the result of the author's perception of his intended audience, their needs and responses. Objections and false conclusions usually appear at a point where the author anticipates a certain understanding or reaction from his audience and wants to effect or guard against certain types of behavior or philosophical-ethical teachings. At a point where the author sees the need to effect or guard against a certain tendency an objection or false conclusion is thrown out and the discourse shifts in another direction. In the diatribe objections and false conclusions are an artificial and rhetorical replacement for the input of the students into the discussion.[5]

Stowers adds in a note to this statement: "Except, of course, on those occasions when actual objections have been recorded."[6]

II Cor. 3:1 is an example of precisely this kind of rhetorical "false conclusion," based, however, on the existence of a real objection. For as the presence of the adverb "again" in 3:1a indicates, Paul is con-

---

ing on whether Philo ought to be included) examples of this type or genre of literature from antiquity, see Stowers, *Diatribe*, 7-78. II Cor. 3:1 seems to be an example of what Stowers says are those "few texts in some of the apostle's other letters [i.e., other than Romans] where he employs the style of the diatribe, but these are isolated within the larger context of the letter where he is dealing with the specific problems of the churches, as in I and II Corinthians" (p. 179). I have taken 3:1 to be diatribal in style since, unlike II Cor. 10:10, Paul is not directly quoting his opponents, but anticipating their response (cf. Stowers' distinction on p. 179).

2. Ibid., 119. Cf. pp. 119-122, where Stowers lists the objections and false conclusions in Romans and outlines their formal characteristics.

3. Ibid., 127.

4. As here in II Cor. 3:1.

5. Stowers, *Diatribe*, 140-141.

6. Ibid., 233 n. 139.

cerned that his assertion in 2:17 will be misconstrued by his opponents and the Corinthians under their influence as another "self-recommendation." Thus anticipating his opponents' accusation, Paul himself raises this "false conclusion" at the beginning of this new section in the form of *two* rhetorical questions—in order to deny it.

That the two questions in II Cor. 3:1 both refer to the same problem of Paul's apparent "self-recommendation," rather than to two distinct objections (i.e., that Paul recommended himself *and* that he lacked letters of recommendation from others)[7] is indicated by the structure of Paul's argument in 3:1 itself. Unlike in Romans, where Paul always immediately and explicitly denies the diatribal false conclusion, usually with "May it never be!" *before* a new section or false conclusion is introduced, Paul's response to his first question in II Cor. 3:1 is not to express its denial. Instead, Paul immediately follows his first question with a second rhetorical question introduced with "or," before supplying the necessary negative answer (still lacking for 3:1a) by means of the negative particle *mē* in the question of 3:1b.[8] Thus, the two questions of II Cor. 3:1 are to be taken together as Paul's *single* response to the anticipated objection that his statement in 2:17 was merely a "self-recommendation."

Paul's initial denial of this charge in 3:1a derives, once again, from his ability in 2:17 to point to his own practice of self-support in Corinth

7. As implied by those who treat the two issues separately. See, e.g., Schlatter, *An die Korinther,* 500-503; Barrett, *Second Corinthians,* 105-107; Bultmann, *Zweiter Korintherbrief,* 74; Windisch, *Zweiter Korintherbrief,* 102f. On the other hand, Georgi, *Gegner,* 242f. (cf. p. 245), correctly sees that the letters of recommendation were "an extension of this type of self-recommendation . . ." (i.e., that referred to in 3:1a), although he nevertheless misses the precise nature of the self-recommendation which unites them. For according to Georgi, both 3:1a and b are to be taken as an expression of the opponents' demonstration of their possession of the Spirit (cf. p. 243). But although it is true in and of itself that Paul's opponents probably did point to their spiritual gifts and attainments in order to support their claims in Corinth, I will argue below that the issue in 3:1 is quite different, namely, that of the proper criterion as such.

8. Cf. Rom. 3:1, where the two questions, taken together, are then explicitly answered in 3:2. Cf. also Rom. 3:9; 6:2; 6:15; 7:7; 7:13; 9:14; 11:1; 11:11 (following Stowers' analysis, *Diatribe,* 119-122). Among recent commentaries, only that of Windisch, 103, has emphasized that the negative answer expected for the second question is also intended to refer back to the first. But even Windisch says that this negation only "applies indirectly also to the first question."

as the evidence needed to establish his claim to be sufficient for the apostolic ministry. For it became clear in chapter four that Paul's statement in 2:17, far from being an exercise in "self-recommendation," was based upon his *divine call* to be an apostle on the one hand, and upon the *nature of his ministry in Corinth* on the other hand. Paul need not recommend himself and is not recommending himself—his work as an apostle speaks for him (cf. I Cor. 15:10).[9]

But from Paul's perspective, it is precisely *because* this first accusation, i.e., that Paul is simply recommending himself, cannot be maintained that his need for letters of recommendation is also eliminated. If Paul were *not* in a position to point to such evidence, as he does in 2:17,[10] then he too would need such letters in order to provide the external witness or corroboratory evidence for his claims otherwise lacking in his own apostolic ministry. That is to say, in Paul's view, whatever their origin might have been,[11] these letters of recommenda-

9. It would take us too far afield for our present purposes to develop the closely related motif of "to demonstrate oneself" within II Corinthians as a whole (see 4:2; 5:12; 6:4; 7:11; 10:12; 10:18; 12:11). Suffice it to say that Paul's reference to his own accomplishments as his recommendation in 3:1 conforms to his use of this theme throughout the letter. To be recommended by the Lord (10:18) is to be able to point to what one has accomplished "in the Lord," as Paul does in 4:2; 6:4ff.; 12:11f., and as the Corinthians can do in 7:11; while to "recommend oneself" in the negative sense is to lay claim to something for which one has no such evidence (see 3:1; 5:12; 10:12).

10. Besides the evidence we have discussed in chapter four, see Paul's statement in II Cor. 12:11b. It seems impossible to dismiss or reinterpret the fact that Paul too buttressed his claim to authority by referring to his pneumatic accomplishments and gifts, as Bultmann, *Exegetische Probleme*, 21, and Käsemann, "Legitimität," 70f., attempt to do. For a good discussion of this point, see Holmberg, *Paul and Power* (1978), 77-79. Holmberg correctly concludes that the problem in Corinth was that "both (Paul's) power and his sickness were conspicuous and the latter tended to throw discredit on the former. . . . But he did not interpret it as a paradoxical identification of strength and weakness, as if only his weakness were visible, God's power through him being invisible" (p. 78).

11. This issue need not, and probably cannot, be decided with any degree of convincing probability on the basis of the evidence now available to us. For as Lightfoot, *Galatians*, 373, concluded over a century ago, "It is wisest to confess plainly that the facts are too scanty to supply an answer." Among those who argue that the letters came from the authorities in Jerusalem are Windisch, *Zweiter Korintherbrief*, 102f.; Käsemann, "Legitimität," 44-47; Schoeps, *Paul*, 74f., 79, 82; for the position that they came from other churches in the Hellenistic world, because

tion function as a *substitute* for the ability to boast in one's own work, i.e., for the ability to demonstrate one's own legitimacy (cf. 4:2; 6:4ff.; 12:11f.).

This understanding of letters of recommendation as a "substitute" source of authority or credibility, which allows Paul to bring the two questions in 3:1 together, is not idiosyncratic to Paul. It is the common function of such letters in the ancient world in general, as evidenced not only by the letters of recommendation written by Paul himself,[12] but also in non-Pauline letters of recommendation known to us from antiquity.[13] To need such letters is to admit that one lacks that evidential accreditation from one's own life which is already evident or available to those whose acceptance is being sought. That is to say, since someone in this situation can only recommend himself or herself, the need consequently exists for someone *else* to speak on one's behalf in order to substantiate the claim being made. Hence, although a valid and at times necessary means of attestation in and of themselves, the

---

of the stress on "from you" in 3:1, see Roloff, *Apostolat,* 78; Georgi, *Gegner,* 230 n. 3, 243-245; Barth, "Eignung," 233f.; Bultmann, *Exegetische Probleme,* 22f. See Acts 15:23-29 for an example of a letter of recommendation sent out from the church in Jerusalem and Acts 18:27 for a letter sent from one mission congregation to another. It is enough to say that the individuals or communities who wrote these letters had to have been influential, or to have some sort of readily recognizable credibility with the Corinthians, as Lietzmann, *An die Korinther,* 110, points out.

12. Cf. Philemon; Rom. 16:1f.; I Cor. 16:10f.; II Cor. 8:16-24; Col. 4:7-9. In each case, Paul writes on behalf of someone who cannot recommend himself or herself and offers one or more *reasons* why the person being recommended ought to be readily accepted (this is also true of the letters listed by Keyes; see next note). Of special interest in this regard is the report in Acts 18:27f. that Apollos was sent to Corinth from Ephesus with just such a letter of recommendation from the church there. Thus Schlatter, *An die Korinther,* 502, was correct in pointing out that "nothing unusual took place when those who also went to Corinth possessed such letters."

13. As listed and reproduced in part by Keyes, "Greek Letter of Introduction," 32-38. Keyes lists only Rom. 16:1f. from the Pauline corpus. There are no doubt more examples now available. Unfortunately, I was not able to consult the treatment of "recommendation" as a common social practice intended to initiate a reciprocal friendship or the letter of recommendation practice itself by Peter Marshall in his *Enmity and Other Social Conventions in Paul's Relations with the Corinthians,* unpublished Ph.D. dissertation, Macquarie University (1980), 141-202, 398-426 (referred to in his article "Metaphor," 309 n. 40 and 313 n. 52).

very need for letters of recommendation points to a "credibility-deficiency" among those being addressed in the one carrying such letters.[14]

Paul's second question in II Cor. 3:1 is best understood therefore as a further explication or interpretive restatement of the first. Just as Rom 3:1b defines more closely what is meant by 3:1a, so II Cor. 3:1b also defines what is meant by 3:1a, so that to ask the former question *is* to ask the latter one and vice versa. Taken together, the two questions in II Cor. 3:1 thus raise the issue of whether or not Paul must adduce, like his opponents, any outside corroboratory evidence (i.e., letters of recommendation) in order to support his claim to sufficiency in 2:17. Paul's answer is an unqualified no. For if he were to capitulate to such a demand, he would be denying the significance of his assertion in 2:17 that his own work in Corinth commends him.[15] Or in the terms of 3:1 itself, he would be drawing the false conclusion that his argument in 2:17 was, in fact, an exercise in "self-recommendation."

In addition, Paul's insistence that he does not need letters of recommendation *from* the Corinthians is the counterpart to his statement in 5:12 that he is not commending himself *to* the Corinthians. For as we have seen in chapter four, Paul does not seek or need the approval of the Corinthians in order to give credibility to his ministry, as if he were on trial before them, since Paul's only judge is God himself. Rather, from Paul's perspective, it is the Corinthians' genuineness which is now being tested by their response to those who are presently challenging Paul's authority in Corinth (see 13:3-9). For Paul is confident of his own calling from and standing before God (cf. 2:17; 5:11; 10:7; 13:2, 6, 10).

14. To say more than this concerning the function of these letters or to speculate about their content would be to overstep the limits of our evidence. For this caution, see Hickling, "Sequence of Thought," 381f. For the suggestion that the letters actually recounted the pneumatic deeds of those who carried them, cf. Vos, *Traditionsgeschichtliche Untersuchungen,* 133; Georgi, *Gegner,* 245; for the less likely supposition that they carried a declaration of an obligatory institutional authority, cf. Käsemann, "Legitimität," 45. The most that can be said is that they probably pointed to some quality or accomplishment which was intended to support the opponents' claim to authority in Corinth.

15. Paul's present argument in II Cor. 2:17–3:1 thus makes the idea improbable that "again" in 3:1 indicates that Paul had indeed recommended himself in the past, but now refused to do so again, as Marshall, "Metaphor," 302-314, suggests.

Paul's point in II Cor. 3:1 can now be summarized. Paul anticipates the charge that his argument for his sufficiency in 2:17 is merely an exercise in "self-recommendation," so that what Paul really needs in order to demonstrate his sufficiency is letters of recommendation to verify his claim. But Paul reminds the Corinthians, by denying this false conclusion, that it is his divine call and the ministry in Corinth which resulted from it (also publicly recognized by Jerusalem: see Gal. 2:7-9) that supports his claim. II Cor. 2:17 itself is all the "recommendation" Paul needs to commend himself. For this "primary evidence," being the "divine attestation" of his calling and ministry presented to the Corinthians themselves, is adequate to support his claim to sufficiency.[16]

The rhetorical questions of 3:1 can thus be transposed into two indicative statements in the following way:

3:1a   My argument in 2:17 is not an exercise in "self-recommendation";

3:1b   *in other words,* I do not need, as some do, letters of recommendation to you or from you to speak on my behalf.

"Self-recommendation" in the negative sense and "letters of recommendation," from Paul's point of view, are not two different modes of recommendation, both of which are denied, but rather two aspects of the same type of recommendation, i.e., a recommendation necessitated by a lack of evidence from one's *own* work which is already present and known among those to whom one is recommended.

B. THE LETTER OF PAUL AS
THE LETTER OF CHRIST: II COR. 3:2f.

1. The Transitional Function of 3:1

It is the identification in Paul's thinking between "self-recommendation" and "letters of recommendation" in II Cor. 3:1 that provides the

16. One thing that cannot be said on the basis of II Cor. 2:17–3:1, therefore, is that Paul is "without personal concern . . . for the establishment of his reputation . . . ," as Kasch, συνίστημι, 898, maintains.

connecting link in his argument between what first appears to be two unrelated themes, namely, between his reference to his practice of self-support in 2:17 and his reference to his role as the founder of the Corinthian church in 3:2f.[17] This same connection is also reflected in II Cor. 10–12, where Paul moves from a discussion of his authority over the Corinthians, with its corresponding "canon" of one's "founding function" in 10:12-18, to a discussion of the genuineness of his apostleship as such, with its "canon" of "weakness" in chapters 11–12. For as 10:1-11 illustrates, Paul's opponents were using his weakness as an apostle to call into question his authority over the Corinthians, thus bringing the two aspects together (cf. especially 10:8-11).

In II Cor. 2:14–3:3 the order is reversed. Paul moves from a discussion of his "weakness" as *the* "canon" of his apostolic calling and his sufficiency for it in 2:14-16 to a discussion of his relationship to the church in Corinth as its founder in 3:2-3. But the concept which binds together these two distinct aspects of Paul's ministry as an apostle is once again his opponents' criticism as anticipated and reflected in 3:1. Moreover, here too Paul argues that on both fronts it is his ministry in Corinth itself which recommends him, whether it be his decision to support himself on the one hand (2:17), or his role as the church's spiritual father on the other hand (3:2f.). Therefore, although the subject matter in 3:2f. is different from that of 2:17, the basic issue of the nature of Paul's recommendation nevertheless remains the same. 3:1 thus functions as the transition between these two themes by presenting the negative counterparts to Paul's recommendations. This transitional function can best be seen when it is diagrammed in the following manner:[18]

17. Hickling, "Sequence of Thought," 382f., regards the transition from the "relatively trivial starting point" in 3:1 to the "intensely theological" issue of the relationship among Christ, the Corinthians, and Paul in 3:2f. to be so great as to be a "transformation into another species." But given Paul's view of his own suffering as stated in 2:14-16a and the connection between the divine attestation in 2:17 and the argument in 3:1 discussed above, Paul's argument does not appear to be such "a sudden leap from the relatively trivial to the heights" (p. 383). Cf. Prümm, *Diakonia Pneumatos* I, 99: "The sudden nature of the introduction is only a sign of a close, inner connection with what precedes."

18. Since having come to this conclusion concerning the transitional function of 3:1, I am pleased to have discovered that my understanding of the nature of this transition, even to the point of suggesting a similar form of diagram to represent it,

2:17:   Paul's practice of self-sup-
        port grounds his claim to
        sufficiency

3:1a: This is not, therefore,   = 3:1b: I.e., Paul does not need
        a matter of "self-recom-   letters of recommenda-
        mendation" in the nega-   tion
        tive sense

                              3:2:   The church itself is
                                      Paul's letter

2. The Corinthians as Paul's Letter of Recommendation

The meaning and function of Paul's basic affirmation in 3:2f., "you are our letter," is thus readily apparent. Paul does not need letters of recommendation in order to corroborate his primary evidence in support of his claim to sufficiency for the apostolic ministry in general, or for his authority in Corinth in particular (3:1), *because* the Corinthians themselves fulfill this function. As the result of Paul's apostolic work, the church in Corinth *is* Paul's letter of recommendation. The argument implicit in II Cor. 3:2 is therefore the same as we have already seen in I Cor. 9:1f. (cf. II Cor. 10:14):[19] it is Paul's own missionary work as the founder of the church in Corinth which recommends his authority as an apostle over the Corinthians.

---

has also been presented by Parunak, "Transitional Techniques," 540-542. Parunak refers to this type of transition as a "direct hinge," i.e., as

> a transitional unit of text, independent to some degree from the larger units on either side, which has affinities with each of them and does not add significant information to that presented by its neighbors. The two larger units [in our case 2:14-17 and 3:2-3] are joined together, not directly, but because each is joined to the hinge.

For this description and his diagram, see p. 541.

19. Contra Oostendorp, *Another Jesus*, 34, who argues that it is misleading to interpret II Cor. 3:2 as a parallel to I Cor. 9:2 because of the distinction between Paul's attempt to prove that he was called by Christ in I Cor. 9:2 and his defense of his upright performance of the ministry in 3:2. Nevertheless, even though this distinction is a valid one, the structure of the argument is the same in both texts.

Moreover, given the polemical situation behind II Corinthians, Paul's assertion that the Corinthians are his "letter of recommendation" also carries a very distinct implication for his readers. For inasmuch as the church in Corinth is a direct result of Paul's ministry, to deny Paul's apostleship would be tantamount to a denial of their own existence as Christians. As a result, Paul's basic assertion in II Cor. 3:2 not only grounds 3:1b, and in so doing furthers Paul's apologetic on behalf of his sufficiency for the apostolic ministry, it also makes clear to the Corinthians the implication of their willingness to side with those who call Paul's sufficiency into question. Morna Hooker is therefore fully justified in declaring that 3:2 is a "brilliant metaphor."[20]

Having made his basic point, Paul then goes on to develop it by means of a series of participial phrases which, upon closer examination, fall into two distinct groups syntactically, and as I will argue below, logically as well. The demarcation is indicated syntactically by the change in number and gender from the feminine singular participles "having been engraved," "being known," and "being read" modifying "letter" in 3:2 to the masculine plural participle "being revealed" with its subordinate finite proposition "that you are a letter of Christ" in 3:3a. All this is dependent upon the initial finite predicate "you are" in 3:2. The remaining feminine singular participles in 3:3b then relate to the predicate nominative "letter of Christ." From the syntax it is clear, therefore, that Paul intends to make *two* distinct statements concerning the Corinthians:

1. You are our letter
2. (You) are a letter of Christ

with the second assertion being syntactically dependent upon the first. Each assertion is then further defined by its own set of participial modifiers.

Hence, although the participle "being revealed" (*phaneroumenoi*, v. 3) is dependent upon the initial proposition "you are our letter," so that 3:2f. comprises only one sentence grammatically, the versification preserved in our text, which makes a break beginning with "being revealed," faithfully reproduces Paul's intention. We will return to the

20. Hooker, "Beyond the Things," 296.

significance of these observations below. For the moment it is enough to point out that on the basis of the syntax alone we are justified in considering the two assertions separately before trying to relate them. For only in this way can the question of the interconnection between these two statements, which presents such a problem to exegetes, be resolved.

Paul's initial development of his basic assertion in 3:2 that the Corinthians are *his* "letter" confronts us with two exegetical difficulties. The first surrounds the question of the textual variant "our"/ "your." The second, though not unrelated problem is the apparent internal contradiction which many commentators have suggested is inherent in the conception of a letter which is written on the "heart," but which is, at the same time, "known and read by all men." In other words, on whose heart is Paul's letter of recommendation actually written and how can it be known to all in spite of its internal character?

In answer to this first question it must be emphasized that those recent commentators who argue that *hymōn* ("your") is the better reading are able to do so *only* on internal grounds, since, as C. K. Barrett himself admits, this reading is "weakly attested" externally.[21] Indeed, as Bruce Metzger points out, the "overwhelming textual support" is in favor of *hēmon* ("our"),[22] so much so that the editors of the 26th edition of the Nestle-Aland *Novum Testamentum Graece* chose to omit altogether the evidence in its favor.[23] The burden of proof clearly lies with those who would deny this reading.

It is surprising, therefore, that the internal reasons adduced for doing so actually argue strongly for the very position they are said to disprove, namely, that "our" is the better reading. For on the one hand, Bultmann and Barrett both suggest that "your" is to be preferred because it makes more sense in the context. In Bultmann's view, because the idea of a letter written in Paul's heart

21. Barrett, *Second Corinthians*, 96 n. 3. Barrett nevertheless opts for this reading.

22. Metzger, *Textual Commentary*, 577.

23. See their explanation of this policy on p. 47: "The evidence for the text is not given in full only when the variants have such poor support that they can *in no way be considered as alternatives for the text,* but are of interest only for the history of the text" (emphasis added).

is certainly in the context entirely unmotivated. A letter written in the heart of Paul can certainly not be valid as a letter of recommendation, and "being known and read" cannot be said by him, and the exegesis given in verse 3 ("revealed that") does not fit.[24]

In Barrett's view, because "*your* both gives the required sense, that the Corinthians themselves are—even though unwillingly—Paul's commendation, and leads to the next stage in the argument,"[25] this reading is to be accepted. On the other hand, "if 'our' is accepted instead of *your* the plural *hearts* becomes difficult, though not impossibly so. . . ."[26]

But it is precisely for these very reasons that "our" is to be considered the *more difficult,* and therefore preferred, reading internally as well. For given the contextual difficulties which this reading poses for understanding Paul's argument, it is easier to imagine a scribe looking to v. 3b and altering "our" to "your" for the sake of clarity in the argument, than to posit a textual emendation which makes Paul's thought even more difficult to follow.[27]

On the other hand, it has been argued that "our" is a later assimilation, either to 7:3 ("you are in *our* hearts"),[28] or to the immediately preceding phrase, "*our* letter."[29] These parallels, however, can just as easily be used to support the authenticity of this reading,[30] not to

---

24. Bultmann, *Zweiter Korintherbrief,* 74f.

25. Barrett, *Second Corinthians,* 96 n. 3.

26. Barrett, *Second Corinthians,* 107. Provence, "Who Is Sufficient?" 60, follows Bultmann and Barrett, arguing that

> It is the mixture of the two metaphors [i.e., between 3:2 and 3] which supplies the strongest argument for understanding the proper reading of the disputed text in v. 2 to be "your." The epistle is written upon the hearts of the Corinthian Christians "by the Spirit of the living God."

27. So too Georgi, *Gegner,* 246 n. 3; Windisch, *Zweiter Korintherbrief,* 105; Baird, "Letters," 167. This same point also extends to Weiss's suggestion that the entire phrase be struck as a gloss (cf. Bultmann, *Zweiter Korintherbrief,* 75 n. 18), for which there is no textual support.

28. Barrett, *Second Corinthians,* 96 n. 3.

29. So Rissi, *Studien,* 20; Hickling, "Sequence of Thought," 382 n. 2.

30. Especially 7:3, e.g., Schlatter, *An die Korinther,* 502; Lietzmann, *An die Korinther,* 110; Baird, "Letters," 170; Lambrecht, "Structure and Line of Thought," 351 n. 18; Friesen, *Glory,* 35.

mention the fact that some commentators have maintained that it is questionable to assume that 7:3 is determinative one way or the other for our present context.[31]

This same ambiguity also surrounds the attempt to argue on a theoretical level for one of the respective alternatives. For example, Oostendorp proposes that "your" is to be preferred because Paul must be able to provide proof to the Corinthians *in Corinth*.[32] But given the nature of a letter of recommendation itself, it can just as easily be argued, *theoretically,* that Paul himself must be the one to carry this letter, since he is the one being recommended.[33] Thus, in the light of the inconclusive nature of the internal evidence,[34] and the fact that "our" is commonly agreed to be the more difficult reading, there is no compelling reason to decide against the vast majority of the textual witnesses.

This brings us to the question of the logical relationship, or lack thereof, between a letter of recommendation which has been engraved (perfect passive *engegrammenē*)[35] on Paul's heart,[36] and his corresponding assertion that this letter is known and read by all. The apparent tension between these two statements, as already seen above in Bultmann's comments, lies in the assumption that a letter written on Paul's heart, being internally concealed, cannot be publicly known and read, let alone "by all men."

In reality, however, this problem probably owes its origin more to

---

31. As emphasized by both Bultmann, *Zweiter Korintherbrief,* 75, and Rissi, *Studien,* 20 n. 30.

32. Oostendorp, *Another Jesus,* 34.

33. This is one of Baird's main points in his attempt to argue for the authenticity of the reading "our"; cf. "Letters," 169-171.

34. The two-sided nature of the internal arguments can readily be seen in that Barrett, *Second Corinthians,* 96, 107, uses the same two arguments to support his decision to follow "your" that Lietzmann, *An die Korinther,* 110, uses to support "our."

35. Following the translation suggested by Schrenk, γράφω, 770. For the justification of this translation, see below.

36. Taking the plural "our hearts" as a reference to Paul himself as a continuation of the "apostolic plural" begun in 2:14; see above, pp. 12ff.; Kümmel's addition to Lietzmann, *An die Korinther,* 199; and Wendland, *An die Korinther,* 177f. As such, the plural presents no difficulty for the reading "our," contra Barrett, *Second Corinthians,* 107.

commentators' convictions concerning the "non-objective" and "non-verifiable" nature of Paul's apologetic elsewhere in II Corinthians,[37] than to the impossibility of understanding the inner connection between these two statements. If 3:2 is approached without this assumption and analyzed in the light of what Paul says in the Corinthian correspondence concerning his relationship to the Corinthians as their "father," the inner connection becomes transparent. For as we have already seen, Paul's basic assertion in 3:2a ("you are our letter") is based on his self-understanding as the founder of the Corinthian community. Thus, when Paul goes on to assert that this letter of recommendation, i.e., the Corinthians, *has been written* on his heart, the use of the perfect tense of the participle is best explained as a reference to this very fact. In other words, the Corinthians were written on Paul's heart at the point in time at which the church was founded and have continued to be in his heart ever since.[38] As such, the relationship between Paul and his church indicated by the perfect participle "having been written/engraved" in 3:2 corresponds to his understanding of himself as the Corinthians' "father" developed throughout I and II Corinthians.[39]

37. See above, p. 51 for Käsemann's view, which is the classic representation of this position in our day. Käsemann's position is supported by his fundamental understanding of the non-objective nature of faith and the gospel, as distinctly formulated in the concluding paragraphs to his two essays, "Begründet?" and "Nichtobjektivierbarkeit." For a more recent presentation of this view, cf. Klaiber, *Rechtfertigung und Gemeinde*, 162f. Klaiber too supports his position by pointing to, among other things, the doctrine of justification by faith (cf. p. 163) understood against the traditional Lutheran view of the law/gospel contrast (cf. pp. 185-187).

38. This is my attempt to express the basic significance of the perfect tense in this instance. Cf. Blass-Debrunner-Funk, *Grammar*, §340; Robertson, *Grammar*, 893, 895.

39. Paul's portrayal of himself as the Corinthians' "father" in I and II Corinthians corresponds to his ability to portray himself as a result of this same "founding function" as the "mother" of the Christians in Galatia in Gal. 4:19, while in I Thess. 2:7f. and 11 Paul reflects this same self-understanding by referring to himself in the same context as the Thessalonians' mother *and* father. It is significant to note, in addition, that in this latter passage Paul's use of this corresponding parental image is introduced in order to convey what we will see below is also the main thrust of Paul's "fatherhood" image in the Corinthian correspondence, namely, that his parental relationship to his churches implies a love for his church which expresses itself openly in his commitment to suffer on its behalf (cf. I Thess. 2:8). This, in

The significance of this correspondence for understanding Paul's train of thought in II Cor. 3:2 is brought to the fore as soon as the implications of Paul's "fatherhood" for his ministry in regard to the Corinthians are outlined. On the one hand, it is precisely because Paul is their "father" that he refuses, out of his fatherly love (cf. 12:14f.), not to burden them with his support since, in his words, "children are not responsible to save up for their parents, but parents for their children" (12:14). Moreover, as we have pointed out above, Paul's decision to support himself in Corinth is merely one specific aspect of his suffering as an apostle on behalf of the Corinthians (cf. I Cor. 4:11f.; II Cor. 11:7ff.). Thus, in II Cor. 6:4ff., Paul can list his "catalog of sufferings" not only as that which commends his ministry as such (cf. 6:3), but also as that which provides evidence of his fatherly love for the Corinthians, specifically that of his acceptance of them as his children. In 6:11, the second conclusion[40] which Paul draws from his suffering is that his "heart" is "opened wide" toward the Corinthians. The further development of this theme in 6:12f.[41] (see my discussion of I Cor. 9 above) makes it evident that by this expression Paul is once again conceiving of his suffering as an outworking of his love for the Corinthians. For in 6:12-13 Paul appeals to the Corinthians to reciprocate his *feelings* for them. The basis of this appeal, as the parenthetical statement in 6:13 makes clear, is Paul's conception of his relationship to the Corinthians as that of a parent to his children. In other words, the unexpressed premise for Paul's argument in 6:11-13 is that children are obligated to return the affection of their parents—an affection which Paul has amply demonstrated.

On the other hand, Paul attributes his *continuing concern* for the Corinthians to his parental role as their "father." In I Cor. 4:15 the fact

turn, testifies to the legitimacy of his gospel and the genuine nature of his apostolic ministry (cf. I Thess. 2:10f.).

40. Following Bultmann, *Zweiter Korintherbrief,* 177, and Plummer, *Second Corinthians,* 203, in seeing 6:11 as relating back to Paul's previous discourse.

41. Taking 6:11b as more than merely a synonymous repetition of 11a, as Bultmann, *Zweiter Korintherbrief,* 177, does. Instead, I follow Barrett, *Second Corinthians,* 191; Plummer, *Second Corinthians,* 201; Kümmel, addition to Lietzmann, *An die Korinther,* 206; Schlatter, *An die Korinther,* 575, in seeing this important second phrase as a reference to Paul's affection for the Corinthians.

that Paul is their "father" is the motivation Paul expresses for his decision to write to the Corinthians concerning his suffering in verses 7-13, albeit not "to shame" them, but "to admonish" them "as beloved children" (v. 14; cf. v. 16). In the same way, Paul's zeal on behalf of the Corinthians in II Cor. 11:2 is based on the fact that he was the one who "betrothed" them to Christ, a clear reference to his "founding function" as their apostolic father. Since Paul was the one who initiated this relationship, he feels responsible to preserve the Corinthians' purity until their marriage to Christ can be consummated (11:2). It is this concern, therefore, which motives Paul's "foolishness" in II Cor. 10-13 (cf. 11:1), since the Corinthians are now in danger of being led astray from Christ (cf. 11:3f.).

Paul's expressions of concern for the Corinthians in I Cor. 4:14f. and II Cor. 11:2-4, derived from his parental relationship to them and occasioned by the danger of sin which besets them, is thus another specific example of the *suffering* Paul undergoes for their sake, i.e., of the "daily pressure upon (him) of concern for all the churches," explicitly identified as one of Paul's tribulations in II Cor. 11:28. It is this "anxiety" over the Corinthians which has determined his behavior toward them in the past, whether that entailed writing the "sorrowful letter" mentioned in II Cor. 2:4 and 7:8ff. as an expression of his love for them, changing his travel plans in order "to spare" them his wrath (cf. 1:15f., 23 in the light of 13:2f., 10), or even giving up other possibilities for ministry because of his overbearing concern and fear for their welfare (cf. 2:12f.; 7:5). Thus, no matter how severe and threatening Paul's letters are, they too are expressions of Paul's *concern* and *suffering* on their behalf. The Corinthians need only to remember Paul's decision to support himself in Corinth and the results of his concern for their spiritual well-being to be assured that his attitudes and actions, even when he must "test" their faith and obedience (see 2:9; 7:12; 13:5, 7), are grounded in his fatherly love and concern for his children. For as Paul himself summarizes it in II Cor. 7:3,

> I do not speak to condemn you; for I have said before that you are in our hearts to die together and to live together.

When Paul says in II Cor. 3:2 that the Corinthians, as his letter of recommendation, have been written on his heart, this reference to his parental role in regard to the Corinthians therefore carries the very concrete connotation of his continuing concern and commitment to suffer on their behalf. Once this is realized, Paul's further assertion that this letter of recommendation, i.e., that he is the founding "father" of the Corinthian church, is "known and read by all men" follows logically from his previous affirmation. For the suffering which Paul undergoes as an apostle, precisely because he was the one who was called to establish the church in Corinth, can be readily seen by all. In fact, as Paul himself puts it in I Cor. 4:9, in his suffering he has become "a spectacle to the world." Or, in our own context, Paul's being "led to death" is said to manifest the knowledge of God "in every place" (II Cor. 2:14). One need only look at Paul's way of life to see that the Corinthians are in his heart!

Once again, therefore, the "internality" of Paul's corroboratory evidence in II Cor. 3:2 is not to be equated with an inability to be known, so that an inherent contradiction must be posited to exist in Paul's thinking, either consciously or unconsciously. Rather, what is "written on Paul's heart" is manifest for all to see, since the suffering in view is a direct result of his apostolic calling to be the founder of the Corinthian church.

The structure of Paul's argument in II Cor. 3:2 thus parallels the structure of his prior argument in 2:17, both of which are based upon Paul's understanding of his suffering as an apostle. What can be known and read by all in Paul's suffering on behalf of the Corinthians is that he is their "father through the gospel" (cf. I Cor. 4:15). As such, his decision to support himself, his change in travel plans, and his "weighty letters," rather than being aspects of his ministry in Corinth which call his apostleship into question,[42] are in reality attestations of that very apostleship. For they are a direct result of Paul's incontrovertible parental relationship to the Corinthians. Far from being part of an attempt to use the Corinthians for his own ends, Paul's suffering testifies not only to the divine sincerity of Paul's ministry (II Cor. 2:17; cf. 1:12), but also to his genuine fatherly affection for the Corinthians (3:2; 7:3). And in the light of II Cor. 10:13 and Paul's parallel statement concerning Titus in 8:16, this affection is equally God-given.

---

42. Based on Paul's explicit references to these criticisms in II Cor. 1:17; 10:1f., 9f.; 11:7; 12:12f., 17; 13:3.

Understood in this way, Paul's positive statement concerning his own ministry in II Cor. 3:2 contains the same critique of his opponents that we saw implied in 2:17. This becomes especially apparent when Paul's assertion concerning himself in 7:2 is compared with his accusation against his opponents in 11:20. Paul's refusal in 3:1f. to "recommend himself" therefore fulfills the same purpose as that stated in his corresponding denial in 5:12. By pointing to the Christian existence of the Corinthians themselves as his corroborating evidence, which can be known and read by all in his *suffering* on their behalf (cf. 4:12), Paul is giving the Corinthians the support they need to be proud of their apostle, and from which they can respond to those who are questioning his apostleship because of his very suffering. "In heart" in 5:12 does not refer to that which cannot be seen per se,[43] but to the mode of Paul's ministry, i.e., to the fact that as an apostle he suffers (cf. 4:7ff.) because of his "heart." In the context, "in heart" thus refers to that behavior motivated and determined by the love of Christ controlling Paul (5:13f.). In contrast, "in face/appearance" refers to that outward strength in which those false apostles boast whose ministry is not controlled and shaped by the cross as an expression of the love of Christ.

Finally, this interpretation of II Cor. 3:2 makes it unnecessary to posit an allusion either to Prov. 7:3, as Windisch and C. Wolff have suggested,[44] or to Jeremiah 38:33 (LXX), as suggested by Earl Richard,[45] in order to explain Paul's thinking at this point. For the "heart"-motif, as we have seen, is part of the larger theme of Paul's "fatherhood" running throughout the Corinthian correspondence. As such, its introduction at this point is a natural development of the "self-recommendation" theme in 3:1f.

Moreover, the use of the verb "to engrave" *(engraphein)* in conjunction with this motif is also a natural one, given Paul's desire to express the fact that the letter of recommendation is located in his heart. The use of this verb to refer to something placed in the heart or soul is

---

43. Contra, e.g., Luz, *Geschichtsverständnis,* 127.

44. Windisch, *Zweiter Korintherbrief,* 104; C. Wolff, *Jeremia,* 135.

45. Richard, "Polemics," 345f. He points to Kümmel and Jewett as further representatives of this view (p. 346 n. 20), though he notes that Kümmel refers to both Jeremiah and Proverbs as the backdrop.

a common idiom in the ancient world, being attested in a variety of contexts and periods, both Jewish and non-Jewish.[46] Thus, although by the first century *engraphein* can simply mean "to write" or "to put in writing,"[47] when it is associated with the heart (or soul), as in our context, it is best to give it its distinctive sense of "to engrave" or "inscribe," which entails the appropriate idea of having to embed what is being written into the substance being written upon, as suggested by the prefix *en-graphein*.[48]

Given the existence of this common idiom, together with the internal logic of Paul's argument, there is no reason to suppose, therefore, that Paul is deriving his thought *specifically* from Prov. 7:3 or Jer. 38:33 (LXX), especially when in both OT contexts that which is written on the heart is the law, which up until now has not been introduced into our context. If Paul was already alluding to either of these texts in particular in verse 2, which is of course possible, the indications are too slight to detect from our distance. The question must also be posed concerning the rationale behind choosing one of these passages over the other, as Windisch, Wolff, and Richard all do, since II Cor. 3:2 itself offers no such indication and the allusions in 3:3 indicate that the closest parallel to the heart motif in this verse is Ezek. 11:19 and 36:26f. rather than either Jer. 38:33 or Prov. 3:3 and 7:3.

Hence, rather than importing the OT allusions from II Cor. 3:3 back into 3:2, it seems more appropriate to suppose that once Paul

46. Cf., besides Jer. 38:33 (LXX) and Prov. 7:3, Plutarch, *Moralia* 779B and the references from Philo, Josephus, Aeschylus, Xenophon, and the Testament of Judas listed by Schrenk, γράφω, 770.

47. Cf., e.g., Lucian, *The Lover of Lies* 38; Plutarch, *Aristides* VII.5; Sophocles, *Traxiniai* 157; Josephus, *Ant.* XVI.324; P. Lond 358, 15 (mentioned by Moulton-Milligan, *Vocabulary*, 178); the use of *engraphein* for that which is written in a letter in Josephus, *Ant.* XI.271; XVII.137; Thucydides I.132; in books in Josephus, *Ant.* X.35; in the "book of God" in Philo, *Quod. det.* 139; and in a petition in *Oxy. Pap.* 3273, 5 (first century). Schrenk, γράφω, 770, also lists examples of the opposite situation, i.e., where *graphein* is used to mean "to inscribe in the heart or soul" as an equivalent to *engraphein*.

48. For this meaning, "inscribe" or "engrave," cf. Philo, *Leg. all.* I.19; Josephus, *Ant.* I.70-71; III.166; IV.308; VIII.261; XI.331; XII.416; XIV.188; XIX.291; XII.89 (on leather books, hence the need to be "inscribed"); Epictetus III.16, 9 (for writing notes on wax tablets); Herodotus I.203; II.102; IV.91; VIII.82; VIII.23; Plutarch, *Moralia* 873B.

was compelled by the polemical situation in Corinth to respond to the possible "false conclusion" that he was in need of letters of recommendation, the motifs in 3:2 developed organically by making use of a common idiom, of which Jer. 17:1; 38:33; Prov. 3:3 and 7:3 are *all* examples. Paul could then fill this idiom with his own particular content. H. Räisänen's statement that the "somewhat odd image" in 3:2 "is used by Paul . . . without any OT reminiscences"[49] is therefore too radical. The point is that there are OT examples of this idiom, but they are not determinative for Paul's thought in 3:2. Instead, the natural development of Paul's argument in 3:2, which resulted in the association of motifs "engraved in the heart," then led to Paul's further assertions in 3:3, where Paul develops his second major point concerning his "letter of recommendation." That is to say, it is Paul's statement that his letter of recommendation has been engraved in his heart which provides the transition to the OT imagery in 3:3, rather than the other way around as Windisch has suggested.[50] The important, but difficult, question of the intrinsic relationship between the motifs of 3:2 and 3, as well as that of the meaning of 3:3 itself, still remain, however, to be considered. It will be necessary to take up the latter question first.

3. The Corinthians as the "Letter of Christ" (II Cor. 3:3)

a. The Meaning of 3:3 and Its Function within Paul's Argument

The meaning of Paul's second assertion concerning the Corinthians in II Cor. 3:1-3, "you are a letter of Christ" (3:3), as well as its relationship to the first assertion, "you are our letter," in 3:2, are both dependent upon the fundamental exegetical decision concerning the meaning to be ascribed to the participial phrase "having been ministered by us." Does Paul intend to say by this that he is the author, in some sense, of this letter of Christ? Or does he merely intend to express the fact that

49. Räisänen, *Paul and the Law,* 243.
50. Windisch, *Zweiter Korintherbrief,* 104.

he is the one who delivers this letter as, in J. D. G. Dunn's words, "Christ's postman?"[51]

On the other hand, in order to understand the force of Paul's argument, i.e., that which makes it work and renders it compelling to his audience, the point of the twofold description of this letter expressed in the antitheses of 3:3b needs to be determined. This entails not only discerning the meaning of the antitheses themselves, but also their relationship to one another. But once again, the answer to this question depends upon whether one perceives Paul to be the writer or deliverer of the letter so described. If the former, then we are faced with a bold assertion on Paul's part concerning the nature of his own apostolic ministry; if the latter is the case, then we are forced to understand Paul's argument in 3:3 as a reference to some sort of "letter from heaven" sent by Christ, which is only tangentially related to Paul himself[52] and which, correspondingly, can only be evaluated by divine criteria.[53]

The strongest presentation of the view that "having been ministered by us" refers to Paul's role as a "courier" of the letter written by Christ is that of W. Baird in his important article "Letters of Recommendation. A Study of II Cor. 3:1-3." Baird's argument for this interpretation is based on his premise that one must begin with the "primary metaphor" of 3:1-3 as the key to its coherence, i.e., with the figure of the letter of recommendation introduced in 3:1. For as Baird points out, "the primary figure of speech in the passage represents the Corinthian community as an epistle of recommendation." He then argues that this metaphor is maintained at least through verse 3a, including the participial phrase "having been ministered by us," because of the use of "you

---

51. Dunn, *Baptism*, 137.

52. For the idea of a letter written by God to man, i.e., a "Himmelsbrief," see the sources and literature listed by Bultmann, *Zweiter Korintherbrief*, 75 (who himself rejects its relevance for this context); the rabbinic references listed by Marmorstein, "Holy Spirit," 143f. and the related notes; and finally, Röhrich, "Himmelsbrief." For examples of commentators holding this view, cf. Windisch, *Zweiter Korintherbrief*, 105; Lietzmann, *An die Korinther*, 110; Wendland, *An die Korinther*, 178; see too Georgi, *Gegner*, 246. For another rejection of this view, cf. Rissi, *Studien*, 21. Rissi's argument, however, is weak, based as it is solely on the fact that Paul does not use the precise terminology of a "letter from heaven."

53. As concluded by Vos, *Traditionsgeschichtliche Untersuchungen*, 136.

are a letter." Since Paul is still developing the idea of the Corinthians as a letter of recommendation in 3:3a, it is this metaphor which provides the interpretive key for understanding Paul's role. It follows, therefore, that since 3:3a is *also* taken to mean "you are a letter of recommendation," Paul must, in Baird's view, be the courier and not the amanuensis of the letter.[54] For in the ancient world the epistle of recommendation was carried by the one being recommended.[55]

Baird thus concludes that, by referring to this function of the courier, the phrase "having been ministered by us" "is not changing the figure to make it refer to his ministry of the gospel, but is still employing the metaphor of the epistle of recommendation."[56] Baird then supports this conclusion by arguing that the interpretation "deliver" or "carry"[57] accords with the probable meaning of the verb *diakoneō* itself, as attested elsewhere in Paul and in Josephus. In Baird's words,

> The change [in metaphor], of course, might seem to be suggested by Paul's use of *diakoneō*. But although he often uses *diakonia* for his ministry of the gospel, he never uses the verb *diakoneō* in that way; it is, however, employed for Paul's collection and delivery of the offering for the saints in Jerusalem (Rom. 15:25; II Cor. 8:19-20). The verb *diakoneō* is found in Josephus (*Ant.* vi,298) with the meaning "to deliver" a message, and, as the RSV indicates, this is the meaning which it probably should have in II Cor. 3:3.[58]

As a result, "Paul is not to be understood as either the writer or the ultimate recipient of the letter." In the same way, Paul's prior statement in 3:2 that the letter of recommendation has been engraved on his heart "is not referring to the receiving of the letter but the carrying of it . . . to be revealed to all men when with open heart (II Cor. 6:11) he declares to them the Corinthians' faith (cf. I Thess. 1:8)." Finally, in order to be consistent with this interpretation, Baird interprets "letter of Christ" to mean "letter *from* Christ," suggesting that Paul has

---

54. Baird, "Letters," 169.
55. Baird bases this point on Keyes; see above, n. 13, and "Letters," 169.
56. Baird, "Letters," 169.
57. Ibid., 170.
58. Ibid., 169.

introduced this idea in order to clarify the letter's authorship and thus prevent the Corinthians from falsely concluding that they had written it (cf. 3:1: "from you").[59] Baird summarizes his position by saying,

> It seems evident that in II Cor. 3:1-3a, Paul is employing the figure of the Greek epistle of introduction with a high degree of accuracy and consistency. He needs no literal letter of recommendation to or from any church. He has a figurative epistle whose content is the Christian of Corinth. That letter is written by Christ. It recommends its courier, Paul, to all men as an authorized minister of the gospel of God.[60]

But although Baird correctly emphasizes the primary role of the motif of the letter of recommendation and the coherence of Paul's thought in 3:1-3, his attempt, as well as that of others, to construe *diakoneō* ("minister") in 3:3 to mean merely "deliver" or "carry,"[61] quite apart from any analogy to letters of recommendation, does not do justice to its Pauline usage elsewhere, nor to the present context. For in II Cor. 8:4; 9:1, 12, 13; and Rom. 15:31 Paul also refers to the collection for Jerusalem as a "ministry" *(diakonia)*, which not only meets the financial needs of the saints, but also itself serves to glorify God (see II Cor. 8:19; 9:12f.). We must be careful, therefore, not to draw a hard distinction between Paul's "ministry of the gospel to the Gentiles," i.e., his *"diakonia"* in this sense (cf. Rom. 11:13; II Cor. 5:18; 6:3; 11:8), and his role in arranging the collection for Jerusalem, which is also a *diakonia* to others and to God.

That this distinction is a false one becomes especially apparent when we keep in mind that according to Gal. 2:10 Paul's mandate to remember the poor was an integral part of his larger mandate to take the gospel to the Gentiles (see Gal. 2:7, 9), and that in II Cor. 8:7-9 Paul grounds his admonition to the Corinthians concerning the collection by an appeal to that same gospel (cf. v. 9). It should also be kept in mind that in II Cor. 4:15 Paul can say exactly the same thing concerning the spread of the gospel, i.e., the "grace" which has come

59. Ibid., 170.
60. Ibid., 170-171.
61. So too, e.g., Lietzmann, *An die Korinther,* 11; Wendland, *An die Korinther,* 178; Richard, "Polemics," 347; Räisänen, *Paul and the Law,* 243.

to the Corinthians, that he says concerning the collection in 9:12f., i.e., the "grace of God" (cf. 8:1).

Surely, then, when Paul uses the verb *diakoneō* in II Cor. 8:19f. and Rom. 15:25 of his activity on behalf of the collection, the terminology he employs *(diakonia/diakoneō)* itself indicates that he regarded his role in the collection as much more than merely being the one responsible for delivering the money. The collection is designated a "ministry" *(diakonia)* and is said to be "ministered" *(diakoneō)* by Paul and his co-workers precisely because it is part of Paul's larger ministry of the gospel. It is only appropriate, therefore, that Paul sees the collection to be a result of the grace of God at work in the various churches (cf. II Cor. 8:1, 6f., 19) and *equates* the Corinthians' participation in this ministry with obedience to their confession "in the gospel of Christ" (II Cor. 9:13).[62]

Thus, there is no reason to doubt on the basis of Pauline usage elsewhere that in our present context the verb "to minister" refers to Paul's gospel ministry as an apostle. This is especially the case when to do so would destroy the seemingly obvious correspondence between Paul's use of this verb in 3:3 and Paul's description of himself in 3:6 as a "minister *(diakonos)* of the New Covenant" on the one hand, and the designation of his corresponding apostolic ministry as a "ministry" *(diakonia)* of the Spirit and of righteousness in 3:8f. (cf. 4:1) on the other. Although only of secondary importance, Baird's reference to Josephus, *Ant.* VI.298 also does not confirm his interpretation, since the use of the verb in this context carries a much more general meaning than "to deliver a message." In the context the messengers do deliver a message as commanded. But the meaning of *diakoneō* itself is more appropriately rendered in the general sense of "fulfilling the task entrusted to them," as frequently found in Josephus's writings.[63]

Second, Baird's view fails to account for the use of the perfect

62. Cf. Georgi, *Die Geschichte der Kollekte,* 76 n. 302, for an analysis of the syntactical structure of this verse. He demonstrates on the basis of the parallel structure between 9:13b and c that "in the gospel" must relate back to "confession," rather than directly to "submission," hence my attempt to bring this out.

63. See *Ant.* IX.25; X.177; XIV.358; XVII.140; XVIII.77, 125, 193, 262, 269, 277, 280, 283, 293, 304; XIX.41, 194. For the use of *diakoneō* for ministering to God, see *Ant.* VII.365; and for priestly service to the people, *Ant.* X.72.

tense "having been engraved" in 3:2 and the aorist "having been ministered" in 3:3. In spite of his insightful observation that these two verbs refer to the same thing, their common punctiliar nature, as well as their shared subject matter, is best explained as a reference to the founding of the Corinthian church. We have already seen above how this sense fits the context and serves to explain the logic of Paul's argument in 3:1f. If, in turn, our decision to take *diakoneō* as a reference to Paul's ministry as an apostle is warranted, then the most natural reference for the aorist "having been ministered" is Paul's ministry of bringing the gospel to Corinth and the resulting conversion of those Corinthians now in Paul's church. In other words, what Paul *implies* in 3:2 in his emphasis on the fact that this letter has been engraved in his heart is now expressed *directly* with the participial phrase "having been ministered by us." In addition, as Baird points out, the recognition of the parallel between these two statements further supports the propriety of reading "our" in 3:2.[64]

Once "having been ministered by us" is understood as a reference to Paul's apostolic ministry of establishing the church in Corinth, the grounding function of the participle "being revealed" becomes apparent and the compelling nature of Paul's argument for his audience can be appreciated. But if those who argue that in 3:3 Paul is merely the courier of the letter written by Christ are right, then Paul's apology, based as it is on the existence of the Corinthians as Christians in 3:2, loses this evidential force in 3:3. For in this view, Paul's assertion in 3:2 that the Corinthians are his letter of recommendation which can be known by all is supported only by the additional assertion that this letter has been written by Christ. Paul's opponents, however, would immediately deny this with their counter-assertion that *they* were, in reality, the true servants of Christ (cf. 11:23). Hence, the third reason for rejecting the position presented by Baird is its failure to correspond to the manner of Paul's apostolic self-defense consistently employed thus far in 2:14–3:2 and confirmed by Paul's "apology" elsewhere in II Corinthians.

This conclusion is confirmed by the fact that Baird's view also cannot adequately explain the meaning and function of 3:3 in relation-

64. Baird, "Letters," 171.

ship to 3:2 as expressed in the participle "being revealed" *(phanerou-menoi)* in 3:3a. The best way to illustrate this point is to present my own summary of the meaning and function of this complex statement.

In II Cor. 3:3 Paul extends the preceding metaphor of the Corinthians as Paul's "letter of recommendation" by stressing that the Corinthians owe their existence as Christians to *Christ* as he was made known to them *by the Spirit in the gospel ministry of Paul* (cf. I Cor. 2:1-16; 4:15; II Cor. 10:13f.). Hence, if not the sole author of this "letter of recommendation," Paul is at least its "co-author" (cf. I Cor. 15:10b; Gal. 2:20). For as the participial phrase "having been ministered by us" indicates, the Corinthians owe their existence as Christians to Paul's ministry in Corinth. As the "letter of Christ," the Corinthians are part of what Christ has accomplished through Paul and therefore can become Paul's letter of recommendation, which, at the same time, is a recommendation from the Lord (see II Cor. 10:18 and above, p. 183 n. 9).

Paul's initial two assertions in 3:3a ("being revealed that you are a letter of Christ which was ministered by us") simply make *explicit* the premises which we have already seen were *implicit* in his first two assertions in 3:2, thus providing the support needed for his prior argument:

1. You are our letter *because* you are a letter of Christ
2. which has been engraved in our hearts *because* it was ministered by us.

The new factor in 3:3, and that which extends Paul's argument beyond what he has already asserted, is then introduced in the two following participial phrases. It is at this point, however, that Paul's development of the second letter motif initiated in 3:3 seems to break down. For it appears to be the universal opinion of recent commentators, even among those who wish to stress the coherence of Paul's basic thought in this passage as a whole, that in introducing the ideas of 3:3b Paul mixes his metaphors to the point of divergence.[65] In fact, for some

---

65. Cf., e.g., Baird, "Letters," 171; Lietzmann, *An die Korinther,* 110f.; Prümm, *Diakonia Pneumatos* I, 104; Wendland, *An die Korinther,* 178; Barrett, *Second Corinthians,* 81f. This consensus has been well summarized by Provence, "Who is Sufficient?" 60.

scholars, the mixed metaphor of 3:3b even renders Paul's thought "a mess."[66]

The reason for this astounding consensus is that the two images of 3:3b are understood as *parallel* to one another, with the first image taken to refer to the second. As a result, Paul ends up drawing a contrast between that which was written with ink on the stone tablets of the law and that which was written with the Spirit on tablets of fleshly hearts. For the sake of the second aspect of the comparison, said to be Paul's controlling interest, the first aspect thus becomes absurd.

But this apparent confusion of categories, i.e., ink on the stone tablets of the law, is eliminated once Paul's twofold thought in 3:3b is seen to develop not in parallel categories, so that Paul's *two* statements in 3:3 are taken to represent merely *one* contrast, but in *succession* to one another, so that Paul's two statements are taken *independently* of one another, thus producing *two* separate comparisons.

In the first contrast "having been engraved not with ink but with the Spirit of the living God," Paul intends to stress the *means* by which this letter belonging to Christ has been written. The letter of Christ has been written not by means of human instrumentality, but by the living God himself through his Spirit. For as I. Hermann has correctly emphasized,

> The phrase "not by ink but by the Spirit" refers to the fact that the Spirit is to be understood in the same sense as the ink: as a means through which and with whose help something is carried out. As a result, the Spirit becomes a *functional concept.*[67]

As a statement about the nature of Paul's ministry in Corinth, this contrast is thus best understood as a summary of Paul's prior description of his apostolic ministry of the Spirit in I Cor. 2:1-5, where the contrast between human instrumentality (2:1) and the power of the Spirit (2:4) is said to have determined both the method and the content of Paul's missionary preaching in Corinth.

66. This is the judgment of Hooker, "Beyond the Things," 296. See too Bultmann, *Zweiter Korintherbrief,* 77.

67. Hermann, *Kyrios und Pneuma,* 28. For the reasons already listed above, however, Hermann's corresponding view of Christ as the "founder" of the church in 3:3 must be rejected, though his observation that the Spirit is "the means through which Christ is active in his church . . ." is certainly right (cf. pp. 27f.).

In the second contrast Paul indicates the *locality* of this "writing." The letter of Christ has not been written on stone tablets, but "on tablets composed of fleshly hearts."[68] Understood in this way, this second contrast, in describing the "material" used for the writing of the letter, does not relate to both elements of the preceding comparison, but only to its main point that the letter has been written with God's Spirit. For having said this, Paul then goes on to describe the sphere in which the Spirit has been active. In other words, the second contrast functions to amplify the first.

Without its metaphorical dress, Paul's thought in 3:3 can therefore be represented as follows:

1. The Corinthians are now Christians
2. *as a result* of Paul's apostolic ministry of the gospel in Corinth.
3. *For* as Christians they owe their existence to the work of the Spirit of God
4. *which* has worked in their hearts (through Paul's gospel).

Paul's statement in 3:3 furthers his argument not only by making explicit the implicit grounds for his assertions in 3:2, but also by reminding the Corinthians of that which they absolutely cannot deny: they owe their existence as Christians to the work of the Spirit which they received *through Paul's ministry.*[69] Hence, as recipients of the Spirit in their hearts, their own visible, pneumatic existence makes it manifest that they are Christians and that Paul's ministry, through which they received the Spirit, is genuinely apostolic. It is the very existence of the Spirit in the Corinthian church which supports Paul's claim to apostolic authority in Corinth, since he was the one through whom the Spirit came.

---

68. This is my attempt to render the difficult phrase *en plaxin kardiais sarkinais.* Because of its strong textual support and the fact that it is obviously the most difficult reading, it appears unwarranted to opt for one of the various emendations often suggested by commentators. Moreover, as Barrett, *Second Corinthians,* 96 n. 4, has pointed out, the text "is probably due to the O.T. allusion"—which explains its awkwardness. For a good discussion of this textual problem, cf. Hughes, *Second Corinthians,* 89f. n. 10.

69. So already Sokolowski, *Begriffe Geist und Leben,* 73, who points to I Cor. 2:5 and 3:5 as the key parallels.

This explains Paul's choice of the verb "to reveal" *(phaneroō)* to introduce this assertion as a continuation of the theme of the open manifestation initiated in 2:14 and then continued as an essential element in Paul's "self-recommendation" in 4:2 and 5:11. For the fact that the Spirit was present in the hearts of the Corinthians, far from being hidden and indiscernible, was publicly recognizable, open and evident to any who joined their worship, as I Cor. 12 and 14 make abundantly clear. By pointing to the Spirit as his supporting proof for his apostolic ministry, Paul was offering an argument which the Corinthians could not deny without denying their own faith and pneumatic experience.[70]

II Cor. 3:2 and 3:3 are thus built upon two different images, each with its own internal logic. The point of connection between the two is the Corinthians themselves (cf. "you are" / "you are" in 3:2 and 3).[71] For it is *as* a letter of Christ, written by the Spirit on their hearts, that the Corinthians function as Paul's letter of recommendation. In addition, the force of Paul's argument in 3:3 lies in the fact that he can point to the visible work of the Spirit in the Corinthians' midst as undeniable evidence for the assertions of 3:1f.

As a result, Paul's suffering, presented in 2:14-17 and pointed to in 3:2, and the charismatic work of the Spirit, introduced in 3:3, are not in tension with one another. Indeed, rather than being at odds with each other as the *loci* of two contrasting theologies, i.e., a theology of the cross vs. a theology of glory (= Spirit), Paul's suffering and the work of the Spirit are brought together in our text as two complementary aspects of Paul's apostolic ministry. Both provide empirical proof for the genuine nature of his ministry, the former known and read by all, the latter clearly manifest. For it must be kept in mind that for Paul it

70. Paul's argument in II Cor. 3:3 thus parallels his argument in Gal. 3:1-5, the force of which has been surprisingly overlooked in previous studies of Galatians. It appears, however, that Gal. 3:1-5 is, in fact, the very heart of Paul's argument in Galatians, rather than a parenthesis, as is often assumed. Cf. Jervell, "Volk," 88, and the full-length study of the argument of Galatians by Charles Cosgrove, *The Cross and the Spirit* (1988).

71. Contra those who regard the letter of recommendation as the link. See most recently, Richard, "Polemics," 349, and following him, Lambrecht, "Structure," 351 n. 19.

is God's power/glory which is revealed through Paul's suffering (cf. II Cor. 4:6f. and see above, pp. 77ff.) and that this power/glory is not a hidden theological assumption or postulate, but an ontological reality experienced by the believer which results in the conversion and transformation of those encountered by it. Believers are created anew, ontologically understood (cf. I Cor. 1:26ff.; 2:5, 12-16; 3:16; 5:4f.; 6:19; II Cor. 3:17f.; 4:6; 5:17). J. D. G. Dunn is therefore certainly right when he emphasizes that "the Spirit, and particularly the gift of the Spirit, was a *fact* of experience in the lives of the earliest Christians," a statement which he says is "too obvious to require elaboration."[72] Dunn is probably also right when he attributes current attempts to deny this fact by "automatically" relegating the Spirit in the NT to the realm of the sacraments, or by psychologizing the Spirit "out of existence," to "the poverty of our own immediate experience of the Spirit."[73]

At the same time, it is significant that Paul chooses to make his point in 3:3 by establishing a contrast between the tablets of the heart and the tablets of stone, two important OT images, the latter of which can only be a reference to the law.[74] For in doing so, it becomes evident that Paul not only intends to make a statement about the locality of his ministry of the Spirit, but that he also wishes to remind the Corinthians of the *nature* of this letter so written, in order to express, by implication, an important point about the nature of his own ministry. The significance of Paul's argument from the Spirit, as well as its implications for Paul's self-understanding as an apostle, will only become clear, therefore, after we have examined the OT allusions in II Cor. 3:3 and have placed them within Paul's view of the Spirit in general.

b. The Significance of 3:3 in the Light of its OT Background

Scholars are divided over the precise identity of Paul's OT allusions in II Cor. 3:3b. The prevailing view has been that Paul's twofold contrast in 3:3b is a collage of those interrelated prophetic texts from the LXX

---

72. Dunn, *Baptism,* 225. See the twenty-one references from the NT which he provides as support.

73. Ibid., 226.

74. See the LXX of Ex. 24:12; 31:18; 32:15; 34:1; Dt. 9:10.

which focus on the promise of the new heart/new covenant, over against the LXX version of the giving of the law on Mount Sinai. The reference to the stone tablets is thus said to recall texts such as Ex. 24:12; 31:18; 32:15; 34:1; Dt. 9:10, while its counterpart, together with its association with the Spirit, reflects Jer. 38:33; Ezek. 11:19; 36:26f. The repetition of the tablet motif in this second element is said to be due to Paul's desire to continue the parallel to the stone tablets of the law.[75]

Within this fusion of texts, the only question has been which of these two prophetic texts, i.e., Jer. 38:33 (LXX) or the two passages from Ezekiel, actually occupied the *determinative* role in Paul's thinking by providing the dominant image, which is then elaborated by the other.[76] In contrast, although all seem to agree that the "stone tablet" imagery refers to the tablets of the law, Schlatter, and more recently H. Räisänen, have argued that Paul's contrasting thought in II Cor. 3:3b does not derive in any substantial way, if at all, from Jer. 38:33 (LXX), but instead refers exclusively to the two parallel passages from Ezekiel.[77] On the other hand, Christian Wolff has maintained that neither Jer. 38:33 (LXX) nor Ezek. 11:19; 36:26f. are in view, but rather Prov. 3:3 and 7:3.[78]

---

75. For various examples of this view, cf. Wendland, *An die Korinther,* 178; Bultmann, *Zweiter Korintherbrief,* 76; Prümm, *Diakonia Pneumatos* I, 104, 202; Lietzmann, *An die Korinther,* 110; Dunn, *Baptism,* 48; Lambrecht, "Structure and Line of Thought," 367.

76. For an example of those who argue that Jer. 38:33 (LXX) is dominant, see Richard, "Polemics," 347-349; Hooker, "Beyond the Things," 296; Hughes, *Second Corinthians,* 89-91; Vos, *Traditionsgeschichtliche Untersuchungen,* 137; for the primacy of Ezekiel, see Richardson, "Spirit and Letter," 210; Hickling, "Sequence of Thought," 388f.; Provence, "Who is Sufficient?" 60f.

77. Schlatter, *An die Korinther,* 503; Räisänen, *Paul and the Law,* 242-245.

78. C. Wolff, *Jeremia,* 135. Wolff's point concerning II Cor. 3:3 is part of his larger thesis that Paul does not refer to the prophecy of a "new covenant" in Jer. 31:31 at all, not even in II Cor. 3:6 or the Lord's Supper tradition in I Cor. 11:25 (pp. 131-133, 136), nor do his letters provide any basis for thinking that the Book of Jeremiah was used at all (pp. 141f.). Even more broadly, Wolff concludes that Jeremiah's prophecy of the "new covenant" played no role in early Judaism as a whole (pp. 117-119, 122-124), including the Qumran writings (pp. 125-130), and is found in the NT only in Heb. 8:8-12 and 10:16f. (pp. 145f.). Räisänen, *Paul and the Law,* 242f., 245, follows Wolff in his judgment regarding II Cor. 3:6ff.

The first thing to be emphasized is that the determination of allusions is by no means easily carried out, especially when biblical terminology has become an essential part of an author's own vocabulary, as it certainly has with Paul. It is virtually impossible, therefore, to decide with certainty whether the terminology of the "tablet of the heart" in Prov. 3:3 and 7:3 and Jer. 17:1 also plays a conscious role in Paul's thinking as part of the origin of his terminology in II Cor. 3:3b,[79] or whether, as is usually suggested, the tablet motif is a carryover from Paul's reference to the law. But it does seem impossible to maintain, as Wolff does, that the passages from Proverbs are the sole and determinative source of Paul's contrast, since in Prov. 3:3 and 7:3 alone we find no reference either to the idea of a "fleshly" heart, or to the main point of Paul's contrast that the Spirit is now active in their hearts. For as has often been pointed out, both of these motifs are too closely paralleled in Ezek. 11 and 36 for these passages to be excluded.[80]

The only question to be determined is whether or not Jer. 38:33 ought to be included as part of Paul's conceptual field at this point. The strongest reason for including it is the reference to the new covenant in II Cor. 3:6, which is understood to be parallel in some way to 3:3. In this view Paul is said to be alluding already in 3:3 to this passage, or to have it "in mind" when he speaks of the letter "having been engraved on tablets composed of fleshly *hearts*" (cf. Jer. 38:33 [LXX], "I will write them [= God's laws] upon their *hearts*").

But there are several good reasons for exercising caution at this point. On the one hand, the motif of "engraving" in 3:3, being a carryover from 3:2,[81] is first used in reference to that which has been "engraved" on the stone tablets of the law. Hence, if it refers specifi-

---

79. Cf. Windisch, *Zweiter Korintherbrief,* 104, 106, and Bultmann, *Zweiter Korintherbrief,* 76, both of whom suggest Prov. 7:3 (Windisch 3:3 as well), though not exclusively.

80. Most recently H. Räisänen, *Paul and the Law,* 243f.: "It is noteworthy that the OT passage Paul undoubtedly alludes to is the promise of a new heart in *Ezekiel*" (p. 244). Räisänen then correctly concludes, "Wolff, op. cit. 135, is not justified in glossing over this reference" (p. 244 n. 86).

81. Contra Richard, "Polemics," 347f., who argues that "having been engraved" *(engegrammenē)* in v. 2 derives from Jer. 38:33, while its use in v. 3 comes from Ex. 31:18.

cally to an OT text at all, it probably picks up the use of the motif of "writing" or "engraving" on the tablets of stone found in the LXX of Ex. 24:12; 31:18; 32:15f.; 34:1; and Dt. 9:10, rather than that of writing in the heart found in Jer. 38:33 (LXX), though it is assuming too much to single out Ex. 31:18 as *the* text in view, as R. Bultmann and E. Richard do.[82] On the other hand, the "fleshly heart" motif found in 3:3 explicitly occurs in both Ezek. 11:19 and 36:26, thus providing a more appropriate explanation for this syntactically awkward expression in 3:3 than to suggest that the "heart" motif is taken from Jer. 38:33 (LXX), quite apart from its modification as found in our context. Räisänen is therefore correct in concluding that "there is at least no clear linguistic connection" between II Cor. 3:3 and Jer. 38:33 (LXX).[83] In addition, the motif of the Spirit, which is so central to Paul's thought in 3:3, is missing altogether in Jer. 38:33ff. (LXX), while the characteristic idea of the law written in the heart from Jeremiah does not occur in II Cor. 3:3.[84] Here it is the letter of Christ which is written on the heart.[85]

Finally, as a matter of exegetical principle, Paul's thought ought to be followed as he himself unfolds it before bringing similar Pauline themes together. Thus, even if the traditions from Jer. 38:33 (LXX) and Ezek. 11:19; 36:26 (cf. 37:26ff.) were closely associated or even collapsed together for Paul[86] in what has now become known as his "rabbinic way of thinking," we nevertheless do an injustice to his *explicit* train of thought in any particular passage when we read his

---

82. Bultmann, *Zweiter Korintherbrief*, 76; Richard, "Polemics," 348. The grammatical and stylistic parallels between Ex. 31:18 and II Cor. 3:3 which Richard points out may simply derive from standard linguistic conventions and from Paul's desire to continue the parallel between the two tablets.

83. Räisänen, *Paul and the Law*, 244.

84. For this latter point, see again Räisänen, *Paul and the Law*, 245. But although Räisänen is correct in stressing that "it is clear that it is *not* the *law* in any sense that has been written in the Corinthians' hearts according to verse 3," his following statement, as I will argue in my forthcoming study, does not reflect Paul's thought in 3:6: "The tablets of stone stand for the *gramma* which is the *opposite* of *pneuma* (v. 6)" (p. 245).

85. Contra those who read the law into this text. Cf., e.g., Hermann, *Kyrios und Pneuma*, 27; Hughes, *Second Corinthians*, 89f.

86. Cf. Hartmann, "Bundesideologie," 108, 112.

mind by maintaining that everything he said about a specific point, including his OT support, is always in view.

Thus, in our context, although I disagree with Wolff and Räisänen that an allusion to Jer. 38:33 (LXX) is also lacking in II Cor. 3:6, this does not mean that we are justified in reading this allusion in 3:6 back into 3:3, when no *explicit* reference to either the "law written on the heart" or the "new covenant" has yet been introduced, even though the characteristic content of the old covenant/new covenant is now certainly in view (tablets of stone/tablets of fleshly hearts).[87] To do so would be to "jump the gun" on Paul's thinking and to run the risk of diminishing the distinctives of Paul's argument in 3:3. For as Paul himself indicates, albeit negatively, his concern in 3:3 is not with the new covenant in relationship to the law, as in 3:6ff., but with a contrast between two "materials" of God's activity as "writer": the stone tablets (of the law) and the fleshly tablets of the heart as the recipient of the Spirit.

It is crucial, therefore, that we do not read the tablet of stone/tablet of fleshly heart contrast in 3:3 in terms of the letter/Spirit contrast of 3:6. Although closely related, Paul's point in these two contrasts is nevertheless not identical. In approaching the significance of Paul's contrast in 3:3, we must content ourselves with looking to the texts of Exodus (and the parallel in Dt. 9:10) and Ezekiel for help in understanding the nature of Paul's contrast before we turn our attention to his further development of this theme in 3:6. In this way, both the distinctiveness of the two contrasts, with their respective OT background, as well as their commonality, will come to light.

What then is the significance of Paul's contrast in II Cor. 3:3b when viewed against the background of Exodus and Ezekiel? Unfortunately, the predominant answer to this question has not taken its starting point from the OT texts in view, except to point out the source of Paul's terminology, but has rather seized upon the contrasts between "ink" and "Spirit" and between "stone" and "heart" as abstract indications of two contrasting qualities. Thus, Paul's contrast in II Cor. 3:3b is taken to be a contrast between the outward and the inward, or

---

87. For the strongest proponent of the need to read 3:3 from the perspective of 3:6, see Bultmann, *Zweiter Korintherbrief,* 76f. For the opposite view, see esp. Hickling, "Sequence of Thought," 386; Hughes, *Second Corinthians,* 89.

externality and internality,[88] which can then be associated with death vs. life,[89] conscious vs. unconscious,[90] that which cannot be enjoyed vs. that which can,[91] ritualism vs. the Spirit, which is equated with a "rule book mentality" vs. spontaneity,[92] stiffness vs. suppleness,[93] eternal compliance vs. harmony of thought and action,[94] etc.

The common denominator which runs through this perspective, regardless of its variations, is that "stone tablets," being made out of *stone*, are therefore negative; while the "*fleshly* heart" is their positive counterpart. Understood in this way, II Cor. 3:3b becomes another form of the traditional law/gospel antithesis: that which is written on stone tablets, i.e., the law, being insufficient because of its nature, is replaced by the work of the Spirit as an expression of the gospel.

At first, this interpretation appears to be supported by the stone imagery used in Ezek. 11:19 and 36:26 to represent the hard, incorrigible heart which refuses to, indeed cannot, keep God's commandments. In contrast, the heart of flesh, filled with God's Spirit, is enabled, even compelled, by God to keep his law (cf. Ezek. 11:20 and 36:27). But it is precisely this contrast between the two conditions of the heart which Paul does *not* introduce in II Cor. 3:3.[95] Moreover, there is no such corresponding negative nuance associated with the fact that the law was written on stone, either in Ezekiel, where the new heart of flesh is given in order that God's law might be kept (*not* done away with),[96] or elsewhere in the OT.[97] On the contrary, the very fact that

88. E.g., Ridderbos, *Paul*, 218-219; Bultmann, *Theologie*, 222f.; Vos, *Traditionsgeschichtliche Untersuchungen*, 137f.

89. Bultmann, *Zweiter Korintherbrief*, 76f.

90. So Theissen, *Psychologische Aspekte*, 146-156.

91. Jeremias, λίθος, 269.

92. Dunn, *Jesus and the Spirit*, 201, 223, and similarly *Baptism*, 137, 146f.

93. Prümm, *Diakonia Pneumatos* I, 105, 107-109.

94. Harrisville, *Concept*, 58.

95. This contrast, though not expressed in the text, is nevertheless often assumed to be there; cf., e.g., Provence, "Who is Sufficient?" 60f.; Hickling, "Sequence of Thought," 388f.; Bultmann, *Zweiter Korintherbrief*, 76.

96. Cf. Zimmerli, *Ezechiel* I, 250f.; II, 879f.; Hahn, "Alttestamentliche Motive," 369; most recently Räisänen, *Paul and the Law*, 244.

97. Besides the texts already mentioned from Exodus and Deuteronomy, cf. Ex. 32:19; 34:4, 28f.; Dt. 4:13; 5:22; 9:9, 11, 15, 17; 10:1-5; I Kgs. 8:9; II Chron. 5:10 for the other OT references to the tablets of the law.

God gave Moses the law on stone tablets seems to be one of the hallmarks of its *glory,* as intimated by the repetition of this motif in connection with the first giving of the law in Ex. 24:12 and 31:18 (cf. Dt. 9:10), the explicit designation of these tablets as the "work of God" in Ex. 32:16, the emphasis on their having been written with "the finger of God" (Ex. 31:18; Dt. 9:10), and the demand by God that they be replaced after the sin with the golden calf in Ex. 34:1.

Furthermore, the development of this theme throughout early Jewish literature confirms the fact that the idea of the law's having been written specifically upon stone tablets did not carry a negative connotation, but instead was understood to be one of its positive attributes. Thus, in Jubilees (2nd century BCE) the tablets of stone which Moses receives on the Mountain of God (cf. Jub. 1:1) can be identified, as their earthly reproduction, with the "heavenly tablets" from which the angel dictates God's words (cf. 1:26f.; 2:1). In fact, the designation "heavenly tablets" becomes a customary way of referring to the law itself throughout the Jubilean commentary on and expansion of Gen. 1:1–Ex. 12:50.[98]

The "heavenly tablets" are also conceived to be the source of information for Jubilees itself as the "second law" revealed to Moses (cf. Jub. 6:22). But the complicated question of the relationship between the Mosaic law and Jubilees itself from the perspective of Jubilees need not detain us here. The important point for our purposes is the unmistakable positive development of the tablet motif encountered in Jubilees in which the OT tradition of the tablets of stone has now been extended into the idea of a heavenly set of tablets as the locus of revelation. In this regard it is also important to point out that the "heavenly tablets" in Jubilees contain more than just the revelation recorded in the OT law and Jubilees, since they are also the depository for recording the divine judgment of all living creatures (cf. 5:13f.; 30:20).[99] The tablet motif can even be used to represent other divine messages as well (cf. 32:21f.).

The purpose of this positive development of the stone tablet motif in Jubilees is to underscore not only the divine origin of the law (and Jubilees), but also its everlasting permanence and certainty as testified

---

98. Cf. Jub. 3:10, 31; 4:5, 32; 6:17 in comparison with 6:11f. and 22; 16:3, 9; 18:19; 19:9; 23:32; 24:33; 28:6; 30:9; 31:32; and 33:10.

99. For a parallel tradition, cf. I En. 98:7f.; 104:7f.

to by its written and engraven nature (cf. Jub. 6:23; 16:30; 32:10f., 15; 49:8).[100] Hence, in Jub. 15:25f. we read concerning the importance of being circumcised on the eighth day that

> this law is for all the generations for ever, and there is no circumcision of the days, and no omission of one day out of the eight days; for it is an eternal ordinance, ordained and written on the heavenly tablets.

Indeed, it is the very fact that the laws have been written on such tablets, both heavenly and earthly, which ensures that the righteousness of God, and especially the calendar advocated in Jubilees, can still be seen and retained in spite of its perversion through the forgetfulness and unrighteousness of Israel.[101] To be written on stone tablets, therefore, far from being a negative sign of its inadequacy, is an essential aspect of the law's value, since it indicates the permanent nature of the law's testimony and commands.[102] It is this conviction which no doubt led to the corresponding picture of the existence of "heavenly tablets" from which the law was dictated and upon which the permanent record of God's ordinances, the status of his creatures, and his plans for the future of the world are recorded.

As an illustration of this same conviction, we read in I En. 81:1f. (2nd century BCE–1st century CE) that Enoch was commanded to

> look at the stone tablets[103] of heaven; read what is written upon them and understand (each element on them) one by one. So I looked at the tablet(s) of heaven, read all the writing (on them), and came to understand everything. I read that book and all the deeds of humanity and all the children of the flesh upon the earth for all the generations of the world.[104]

---

100. For a similar emphasis, this time on the eternality of that which has been "written by the finger of God" in the "book of the most high," cf. Joseph and Asenath, Appendix III (p. 80 of Brooks, *Joseph and Asenath*; = 15:12x).

101. See Jub. 1:5-7, 9f., 14; 6:34-38; 16:29-31; 33:15-18; 50:13.

102. Cf. Jeremias, λίθος, 269, who also observes that the emphasis on the stone tablets reflects the fact that "stone was regarded as the most enduring writing material, hence the stone tablets of the Mosaic law. . . ." He nevertheless reads a pejorative connotation into 3:3; see above, n. 91.

103. At this point I am following the literal translation in Charlesworth, *Pseudepigrapha* I, 59 n. 81b.

104. For this same tradition cf. I En. 93:2; 106:19.

Moreover, in I En. 103:2-4 that the future blessings intended for the righteous are inscribed on the same "tablets of heaven" is once again given as an indication of their surety and permanence, and can thus be pointed to as a source of encouragement for the faithful (cf. 108:7-10).

A third important witness to this positive nature of the tablets of the law is found in the Testament of Levi 5:4 and 7:5 (2nd century BCE), where according to the better textual tradition, the law itself is referred to as the "tablets of heaven."[105] Here the implicit connection found in Jubilees and I Enoch is now made explicit.

But the esteem accorded to the tablets of the law is reflected in the tradition in a variety of other ways as well. For example, in II Baruch 6:7-9 (early 2nd century CE) the two tablets are one of the precious things hidden in the earth by an angel at the time of the destruction of Jerusalem in 587 BCE only to be revealed again at the consummation of the age. This point is also made in *The Lives of the Prophets*, Jeremiah 14 (1st century CE), where we are told that the glory of God abides over the buried tablets since the glory of God will never cease from his law (cf. 9, 11, 12).[106] Although not clear in and of itself, a similar esteem could be reflected in IV Ezra 14:22-26 (late 1st century CE), where in response to Ezra's plea that God inspire him to rewrite the law for his people yet to be born, God once again requires that Ezra, like Moses, prepare tablets for this purpose (cf. IV Ezra 14:24; Ex. 34:1). At least it is evident that an essential aspect of the giving of the law in the tradition consisted in its having been engraven on such tablets, since this is one of the two motifs employed by the author of IV Ezra to indicate his intended parallel between Ezra's writing of the law and its original reception by Moses.[107]

In yet another graphic example of this tendency to glorify the

---

105. I.e., the so-called "b" text group. The other tradition, i.e., the "a" text group, reads *paterōn*. For the evidence, see Charles, *Testaments of the Twelve Patriarchs*, 38. My preference for this reading is based on the evaluation of the textual evidence in DeJonge, *Testamenta XII Patriarcharum* I, xiii-xv. For a reference to the tablets of the commandments, cf. Test. Asher 2:10.

106. For this same tradition of the buried tablets, cf. Ps.-Philo, LAB (Hebrew Fragments) 26:12-13.

107. The other is that Ezra is commanded to come away for 40 days, as was Moses; cf. Ex. 24:18; 34:28; Dt. 9:9, 18; IV Ezra 14:23.

tablets of the law, Targum Ps.-Jon. to Ex. 31:18 describes the "tablets of stone" written with the finger of God in the MT text as "tablets of sapphirestone from the throne of glory, weighing forty sein."[108] This same tradition is also found in the late midrashic compilations of Ex. R. 46.2; Lev. R. 32.2.; Song Sol. R. 5.14, §3; and in b. Ned. 38a, in which the sapphire nature of the stone tablets is taken to be the reason that Moses became rich from the chippings left over from making the second set of tablets (cf. Ex. 34:1). This miraculous nature of the stone is also emphasized in the rabbinic tradition that although they were made of such hard stone, the tablets could nevertheless be rolled up like a scroll, thus explaining why they can be referred to as such in Numbers 5:23 (cf. Num. R. 9.48; Song Sol. R. 5.14, §1).[109] Thus, given the holy nature of the tablets themselves, even the remains of the broken set are said to be kept in the ark in Num. R. 4.20, while in Lev. R. 8.3 the tablets become a canon for that which is "beloved" by God. In Ex. R. 46.3 it is the presence of the tablets, since they are of the utmost holiness, which renders it impossible for the alien to eat of the paschal lamb (cf. Ex. 12:43): for "shall those who serve idols have any connection with the Tablets which are the work of God?"

It is this same conviction concerning the holiness of the tablets which also appears to be behind the earlier mishnaic teaching that the tablets were one of the ten things created on the eve of the Sabbath in the week of creation (Aboth 5.9). And it is certainly reflected in the midrash on Ex. 34:29 which attributes the glory on Moses' face not to his encounter with God, but to his contact with the tablets (cf. Ex. R. 47.6; Dt. R. 3.12).

This glorification of the tablets in later rabbinic tradition reaches its apex in Pirke de Rabbi Eliezer, chapter 45, where the tablets take on a life of their own. For now the tablets themselves are able to see Israel's sin with the golden calf, upon which their letters not only fly off, but once the letters vanish, their weight increases to such a degree that Moses is forced to cast them to the ground.[110]

108. Cf. also A. Díez Macho, *Neophyti 1* II: *Exodo,* 503 n. 8.
109. In Song Sol. R. 5.14, §1 it is even asserted that the tablets were "hewn from the orb of the sun"; cf. Simon, *Esther and Song of Songs,* 245.
110. For this same tradition of the writing flying away from the tablets in response to the golden calf incident, cf. Num. R. 9.48.

Finally, Ex. R. 41.6 offers us an entirely different reflection on the significance of the fact that the tablets were made of stone. Here we read three explanations for the choice of this particular material:

1. because most of the penalties for disobeying the Torah were stoning;
2. because the law was given for Jacob's sake, who is referred to as the "stone of Israel" in Gen. 49:24; and
3. because "unless one hardens his cheeks like stone, he will not acquire the Torah," which in b. Er. 54a is interpreted to mean either that one must receive one's reproach stoically, or that one must never grow tired of studying the law.[111]

But once again, there is no intimation that the stone quality of the tablets is an indication of a negative quality to be associated with the law. If anything, the first and third reasons represent the seriousness with which the law is to be taken as the revelation of God's will *par excellence* and the center of Israel's existence as God's people. Nowhere is this last point more graphically illustrated than in the fact that the ark of the covenant, which was placed within the holy of holies as the focal point of Israel's worship, contained the two stone tablets.[112]

Thus, this representative sample[113] makes clear that there is, to my knowledge, no indication at any period in Jewish tradition that the stone-nature of the tablets of the law ever carried a negative connotation similar to the "heart of stone" imagery in Ezek. 11:19 and 36:26. H. Räisänen's assertion that

> it is a well-known Rabbinic association to establish a connection between the stone heart of the book of Ezekiel and the stone tablets of Exodus: it is proper that stone should watch over stone (the law over the stone heart, identified with the evil inclination)[114]

111. Translation and reference to b. Er. 54a are from Lehrman, *Exodus,* 476 with n. 2.

112. Cf. Dt. 10:1-5; I Kgs. 8:9; II Chron. 5:10; Josephus, *Ant.* VIII.104.

113. For a convenient listing of the numerous midrashic traditions concerning the tablets, cf. Ginzberg, *Legends* V, 109 n. 99; IV, 49f. nn. 258-260; 59f. nn. 302-307.

114. Räisänen, *Paul and the Law,* 244.

must therefore be carefully interpreted. For this association is not made to denigrate the law in any way, but to explicate its function. In fact, as Lev. R. 35.5 makes clear, the link between the stone tablets and Ezek. 36:26 is made in order to show that the law exercises a positive function of safeguarding and protecting one from the evil inclination. Moreover, since there is no indication in the context that Paul himself is making this unique rabbinic association in II Cor. 3:3, the common attempt to read into his reference to the stone tablets any such pejorative connotation or negative nuance is without support.

Consequently, there is also no reason to interpret the contrast between the stone tablets and the tablets of the heart as a contrast between something negative and something positive, as has been done in the past. The reference to the law as "stone tablets" in II Cor. 3:3, if not honorific, as it is elsewhere in both pre- and post-Pauline Jewish tradition, is at least a normal designation of the revelation given to Moses which derives from the biblical account of the giving of the law itself. As such, it is safe to say that the reference to the law as "stone tablets" in 3:3b in no way contradicts Paul's assumption in 3:7-11 that the law came "in glory" (cf. 3:7, 9, 11). In fact, it is an essential aspect of this very glory.

On the other hand, the reference to the "hearts of flesh," derived from Ezek. 11:19 and 36:26, also picks up a biblical tradition with many parallels in extra-biblical Jewish literature. For in view of Israel's history of disobedience, it became common to emphasize the nation's "hard heart," while at the same time expressing hope in God's corresponding eschatological promise to replace this "heart of stone" with a *new* heart of flesh and a new spirit / Holy Spirit in order that his people might keep the law and thus remain faithful to the covenant.[115] Paul's statement in 3:3 that the Corinthians' existence as Christians is a result of the work of the Spirit in their hearts of flesh is thus an expression of his confidence that this very eschatological promise from Ezekiel is now being fulfilled!

115. For various adaptations of this perspective, here formulated in terms of Ezekiel, cf., e.g., IV Ezra 3:19-23, 36; 7:23f., 45-49, 72; 8:6f.; 9:29-37 in comparison with 6:26; Jub. 1:7, 10, 21-23 (cf. 15:33f.); Test. Levi 18:10-11; Test. Judah 24:2f.; Odes of Sol. 4:3; Test. Job 48:2, 4; 49:1; 50:1; Life of Adam and Eve 29:8f.; I En. 108:2; Sib. Or. III, 703, 719; Ps.-Philo, LAB 30:6; Baruch 1:17-21 (cf. 2:8); Ex. R. 41.7.

c. The Meaning of II Cor. 3:3b

In II Cor. 3:3b Paul wishes to affirm that the Corinthians' relationship to Christ has not been established by the Spirit's work in conjunction with the law, but by the Spirit's work in their hearts, pictured in terms of the promise from Ezekiel. Against the background of Ezekiel, the contrast between the two spheres of God's revelatory-salvific activity, i.e., the "law" and the "heart," is best understood, therefore, as a contrast between the two basic ages in the history of salvation, which are represented by these two fundamental rubrics. While in the "old age" the locus of God's activity and revelation was the law, in the "new age," according to Ezekiel, God will be at work in the heart.

Again at this point we must be careful not to read more into this statement than is there. The question of the nature of the law, the "problem" with the law, the function of the law in the history of redemption, or the relationship between the law and the gospel, though important for Paul and treated by him elsewhere (including 3:6ff.), are not the point or focus of Paul's assertion here. Moreover, it should be kept in mind that in Ezekiel itself, the hope for the future work of God in the heart in no way alters the validity of the law. And Paul himself, as is well known, can speak positively of the law in and of itself (see II Cor. 3:7, 9, 11; Rom. 7:10, 12f., 14, 16). Hence, if anything is to be assumed as implicit in Paul's contrast in regard to the law, it is that the law is now being kept by those who have received the Spirit, as Ezekiel prophesied.

When forced to speak of a relationship between these two realms of God's activity, we should not, therefore, transpose the negative/positive contrast which exists between the two *affirmations* in 3:3b (i.e., Paul's negative denial that the Spirit at work in the Corinthians is related to the law = old age, and his corresponding positive affirmation that the Spirit is at work in their hearts = new age) into a contrast between the *nature* of the law and the heart themselves. Nor should we transpose the contrast between the law and the heart into a contrast between the law and the Spirit,[116] thus creating a contrast between

---

116. Contra Kümmel, additions to Lietzmann, *An die Korinther,* 199; Bultmann, *Zweiter Korintherbrief,* 76; Räisänen, *Paul and the Law,* 245; Hermann,

either two conflicting qualities or two diverse ways of salvation. If in view at all, the relationship between these two realms of God's activity is best understood in terms of the same *qal wahomer / a minori ad maius* ("how much more") relationship expressed in 3:7-11, i.e., from something glorious to something even more glorious.

Although it cannot be argued here, the external/internal contrast between the *stone* tablets and the *fleshly* heart which is implicit in 3:3, or explicit in 3:6 between the letter and the Spirit, is not, therefore, a contrast between two qualities or ways of salvation. Rather, it is a contrast between the law as it usually functioned in the old covenant, in its impotency to change one's heart, and the potency of the Spirit in its work in the heart within the new covenant, the result of which is that the law itself is now able to be kept.[117]

In saying this, however, the clear and startling significance of Paul's statement in 3:3b should not be overlooked. For in establishing this contrast, Paul is not merely pointing to the fact that the eschatological promise of Ezekiel is now being fulfilled. He is also asserting that it is being fulfilled through his *own* ministry, since Paul is the one through whom the Spirit came to the Corinthians.

Hence, the significance of Paul's contrast in II Cor. 3:3b, when viewed against the background of Exodus and Ezekiel, is twofold. On the one hand, Paul affirms that the age characterized by the law as the locus of God's revelatory activity is over. Thus, the Corinthians owe their relationship to Christ not to the revelation of God in the law, but to God's work in changing their hearts through his Spirit. Conversely, the conversion and new life of the Corinthians are evidence that the new age has arrived,[118] i.e., the age of the "fleshly heart" prophesied by Ezekiel. Apart from the implications he draws from this concerning the nature of the law and the old covenant, Ridderbos is therefore right in emphasizing that the letter/Spirit contrast in 3:6 is a "redemptive-historical contrast, namely, as the two dominating principles of the

---

Kyrios und Pneuma, 108f.; Käsemann, "Geist und Buchstabe," 255f., to give just a few examples of this widespread view.

117. This will be developed in my future study on the basis of II Cor. 3:6-18 and the parallels in Rom. 2:27-29; 7:5f.; and 8:2-4. See my thesis in chapter six below.

118. So too Jones, *The Apostle Paul: A Second Moses,* 33 n. 2: "The Corinthian Christian Gentiles are demonstrable proof of the gospel of the new covenant."

two aeons marked off by the appearance of Christ";[119] or "two regimes."[120]

This also means, however, that any attempt to argue that since the death and resurrection of Jesus the eschatological coming of the Spirit is still bound together with the old covenant in the law must be rejected.[121] Paul's positive affirmation in II Cor. 3:3 thus provides the foundational premise and unexpressed presupposition for his argument in Gal. 3:1-4: in the new covenant God bestows his Spirit directly in the hearts of his people in response to their faith in the gospel. Hence, to replace or supplement this gospel as the medium of the Spirit with the law as the center of the old covenant becomes a denial of the efficacy of the gospel itself (cf. Gal. 2:18, 21). It thus seems probable that the position of the opponents who attempted to do this in Galatia was also present in Corinth, though no doubt modified to fit the Corinthian situation. This would explain why Paul develops his apologetic for his sufficiency as an apostle in contrast to the law in II Cor. 3:3b and then goes on to extend it in 3:6ff. In affirming that the Spirit comes through the gospel, he denies that the old covenant is still in force and hence robs his opponents of their footing.

On the other hand, the Corinthians are also evidence that Paul now occupies a crucial role in the coming of the new age as its apostle. For as the Corinthians themselves could testify, the Spirit at work in their midst and in their hearts was mediated to them through Paul. Thus, just as the authority of Moses was identified with and supported by the law which he mediated to Israel, Paul's authority is identified with and supported by the changed hearts which come about as he mediates the Spirit as *the* eschatological gift *par excellence*.

Although it seems misleading to describe Paul as a "second Moses," since Paul's allusion in 2:16b and 3:4-6 is not to the expectation of such a figure but to the call of Moses and its development in the OT prophetic tradition (see above, chapter three), Paul's *role* is nevertheless similar to that of Moses in that he too functions as the one

---

119. Ridderbos, *Paul*, 215.

120. Ibid., 216; cf. 221-223.

121. See, e.g., Is. 63:11, where God is said to have put the Holy Spirit in the midst of his people through Moses (cf. Num. 11:17, 25, 29; Hag. 2:5).

through whom God's revelation is brought to his people. If my exegesis of 2:14–3:3 is correct, Paul views himself as an eschatological agent of revelation through whom the Spirit is now being poured out in the gospel. Consequently, Paul's authority, like the authority of Moses, also finds its source of validity precisely in the revelation which he brings as a result of his call.[122] Hence, Paul's authority derives from and is best supported by the gospel which he received from Christ and now embodies in his suffering. For the effect of that gospel, as the *power* of God now being manifested in the lives of the Gentiles through the Spirit of God which has been poured out in their hearts, is clearly evident for all to see. As Nils Dahl put it so well,

> The preaching of the gospel is not simply a report about the new covenant, as performative speech it effectively mediates the covenant promises. The existence of the church at Corinth not only testifies to the success of Paul's work, like a letter of recommendation; it even certifies the validity of the new covenant, *as the stone tablets of the law confirmed the validity of the old.* The Spirit of the living God is the inscription on the Corinthians' hearts.[123]

If it is appropriate to refer to Moses in his ministry as the "law-giver," it is thus certainly appropriate to summarize Paul's apostolic role in the ministry of the *gospel* as the "Spirit-giver." For the emphasis throughout II Cor. 3:1-3 lies on the Spirit of God now present in Corinth. And it is precisely for this reason that Paul's reception and execution of his ministry must take place in the "earthen vessel" of his suffering (cf. 4:7ff.): not because he wishes to combat a "theology of glory" with his own personally embodied "theology of the cross," as in I Cor. 4:6ff., but in order that the glory and power which he himself reveals, i.e., the very Spirit of God, might in no way be associated with his own person and/or talent (II Cor. 12:7ff.). As we have seen, therefore, when Paul must defend his authority as an apostle he need only point to his suffering *and* the work of the Spirit as the concrete,

122. See again Jones, *The Apostle Paul: A Second Moses,* 34: "just as the Law, i.e. the tablets of stone, was Moses' letter of recommendation to Israel for his role as their lawgiver and prophet, so the Corinthian community of believing Gentiles is Paul's authentication for his apostolic role."

123. Dahl, "Promise and Fulfillment," 126.

verifiable evidence for his claims. And defend his claims he must. For Paul's claims are shocking in their magnitude, since they place him on a par with the central figure, apart of course from Christ, in the history of redemption, namely Moses.

Although strictly speaking Paul probably did not conceive of himself as a "second Moses," he certainly did understand his ministry to the "Israel of God" (Gal. 6:16) to be the eschatological counterpart to the giving of the law. This is evident not only in his conception of his ministry of suffering as an embodiment of the cross of Christ (II Cor. 2:14-17), but also in his conviction that his ministry of the Spirit was a fulfillment of Ezek. 11:19 and 36:26 (II Cor. 3:1-3). For in both cases, Paul's argument for his sufficiency to be an apostle of the new covenant is based on a comparison to Moses, the mediator of the old covenant—in the first instance to the call of Moses, in the second to his ministry of the law (cf. 2:16b; 3:3b).

Chapter Six

Conclusion:
Suffering and the Spirit as the Twin Pillars
of Paul's Apostolic Self-Defense

A. PAUL: THE SPIRIT-GIVER WHO SUFFERS

As we have seen, Paul's argument in II Cor. 2:14–3:3 unfolds in three stages. Having occasion to refer to his anxiety over Titus in 2:12f., Paul is forced by the polemical situation in which he now finds himself to remind the Corinthians of the role his suffering (including his anxiety over the churches, cf. 11:28 with 2:12f.) plays within his apostolic ministry. He does so by introducing the imagery of a triumphal procession, with himself as the captive slave of God who is constantly being led to death. With this image Paul graphically portrays that it is through his daily experience of death = suffering that the glory and power of God are being revealed. In 2:15-16a Paul then links this imagery to his understanding of the cross of Christ as the wisdom of God, here pictured as an acceptable sacrifice. 2:15-16a thus supports Paul's statement in 2:14 by asserting that *his own* suffering is now also a vehicle for this same "sacrificial aroma" to God. Rather than calling his apostolic ministry into question, it is precisely Paul's suffering which therefore commends him to the Corinthians within the church, as well as defending him from the attacks of his opponents from outside the church.

Paul's portrayal of his apostolic ministry in 2:14-16a, with its corresponding twofold effect among mankind, then leads to the second stage in his argument in which he raises and answers the question of his own sufficiency for such a high calling. Though left unexpressed, Paul's answer to this question is clear. He not only "asserts" that he is sufficient for this life and death producing ministry, but he also offers as evidence for this assertion the fact that he supported himself financially while in Corinth rather than exercising his right as an apostle to earn his living directly from his preaching of the gospel (2:17). Once again, therefore, it is Paul's ministry of suffering, outlined in 2:14-16a and defined in terms of his practice of self-support in 2:17 (cf. I Cor. 4:12; II Cor. 11:27), which functions to ground the validity of his apostleship.

Finally, in the third stage of Paul's argument, he buttresses his apologetic by presenting in 3:1-3 a second piece of incontrovertible evidence, the Corinthians themselves. As their "father in the gospel" (cf. I Cor. 4:15), the Corinthians cannot deny that they owe their very existence as Christians to Paul. Moreover, the strength of his argument lies in the undeniable fact that the Corinthians have received the Spirit which now dwells in their hearts and is active in their midst through Paul's ministry. As a result, it becomes impossible to pit Paul's suffering against his possession of the Spirit or to argue, as his opponents apparently did, that "weakness" and the power and glory of the gospel in the Spirit, i.e., "strength," cannot co-exist in the apostolic ministry. Paul is weak and suffers as an embodiment of the cross of Christ, but he is also a pneumatic through whom the power and Spirit of God are being manifested and poured out.

In the course of this three-stage argument Paul develops two basic assertions concerning his apostolic ministry. On the one hand, his suffering makes it evident that, as an apostle of the new covenant, Paul stands between, on the one side, the death and resurrection of Christ and, on the other, the "life" of his church (or the death of those who reject his ministry of suffering), in the intermediary role of a revelatory agent. On the other hand, the essential content of his mediation between God in Christ and the Church is the Spirit. Thus, as the "Spirit-giver" with the gospel, Paul's role is parallel to that of Moses, the mediator *par excellence* between YHWH and Israel, whose task it was to give the law. That Paul had this parallel in view in our passage is indicated in two ways: first, by his introduction of the sufficiency theme in 2:16b as an allusion to the call of Moses in Ex. 4:10 (LXX), and second, by the introduction of a contrast between his ministry of the Spirit and the law in 3:3b. Paul's argument in II Cor. 2:14–3:3

consequently finds its most fundamental support in what for the Corinthians was the empirically verifiable fact that they had received the Spirit. In turn, as the "Spirit-giver," Paul is the intermediary agent of the eschatological reality of the new age characterized by the work of the Spirit in the hearts of the flesh prophesied by Ezekiel.

It thus seems almost impossible to exaggerate the significance which Paul attributed to his apostolic ministry in II Cor. 2:14–3:3. For if Paul's suffering and his ministry of the Spirit are, in fact, convincing evidence for the validity of his apostolic authority and ministry, a ministry which he attributes directly to God (cf. 2:14; 2:17b; 3:5f.), then the Corinthians' decision to reject that ministry becomes, from Paul's perspective, a rejection of God as well. It is for this reason that Paul ends his second canonical letter to the Corinthians, of which 2:14–3:6 is the "theological heart," with the severe warning to the Corinthians to test themselves in order to make sure that they are still "in the faith." For upon his arrival, Paul will be forced to use his power, revealed in his weakness, to tear down all those who have failed this test by rejecting his apostleship (cf. 13:5, 10).

B. HYPOTHESES FOR FURTHER RESEARCH

This brings us to the end of our study. It does not, however, bring us to a final conclusion, either in regard to Paul's self-understanding as an apostle in general, or in regard to his corresponding apologetic for his apostolic ministry in II Corinthians. For in emphasizing his call by God to be a revelatory agent of the Spirit in the role of a Moses-like intermediary between God and his people in 2:14–3:3, Paul naturally raises the question of the relationship between his ministry of the Spirit and suffering and Moses' ministry of the law.[1] It is to this question that Paul thus turns his attention in 3:4-18, under the general rubric of the letter/Spirit contrast introduced in 3:6. For in picking up his prior

---

1. On this fundamental point, cf. Davies, "Paul and the People of Israel," 11: "It is important to recognize that in II Cor. 3 Paul is concerned essentially with the contrast between two ministries, not with that between two covenants on which two distinct religions were founded."

reference to the call of Moses in 2:17 in 3:4f. and to his ministry of the Spirit in 3:3 in 3:6, Paul develops these basic assertions in terms of his call to be a "minister of the New Covenant," which he now further defines as a ministry which consists not of the "letter," but of the "Spirit." Finally, he then offers the reason for the spiritual nature of this ministry of the "new covenant": "for the letter kills, but the Spirit remains alive." Paul's following discussion in 3:7-18 is devoted to explaining the meaning of this saying, which, in and of itself, remains so cryptic.

The task which still lies ahead, therefore, is to complete Paul's argument concerning the nature of his apostolic ministry established in 2:14–3:3 by examining how Paul understood this ministry in relationship to the ministry of Moses as presented in 3:4-18. But given the results of our study thus far, it is already possible to present a number of working hypotheses concerning the basic meaning of the letter/ Spirit contrast and its relationship to Paul's self-understanding as an apostle, which for the sake of convenience can be presented in the following six theses:

1. Jeremiah 31:31-34 is the context within which the letter/Spirit contrast is to be understood.

The introduction of the "new covenant" terminology in II Cor. 3:6 to define Paul's "ministry" *(diakonia)* not only repeats the emphasis from Ezek. 11:19 and 36:26 in 3:3, but also provides the necessary transition to what follows. It does so by calling to mind the unique emphasis from Jer. 31:31-34 on the law written on the heart as the foundation for the universal knowledge of YHWH among his people. Against the background of Ezek. 11:19 and 36:26, Jer. 31:31ff. thus provides the starting point and frame of reference for understanding Paul's letter/Spirit contrast in 3:6ff. For as a servant of the "new covenant" pictured in Jeremiah's prophecy, Paul understands himself as having been commissioned to be an "apostle of the Spirit."

2. Paul's statement that the "letter kills" is not a negative statement concerning the law per se.

Taking Jer. 31:31ff. as our starting point, Paul's statement that the letter kills is his attempt to describe the law as it functioned in the "old covenant" whenever it encountered Israel's "heart of stone" referred to by Ezekiel, or the unfaithfulness pictured by Jeremiah. As such, II Cor. 3:6b is not a negative statement concerning the structure or nature of the law itself, but a restatement of the problem inherent in the old covenant from its beginning (cf. Jer. 31:32), i.e., that the hard hearts of the people remained unchanged by the revelation of the law.

This point, stated programmatically in 3:6, is then underscored in two ways in 3:7-18. On the one hand, the *a minori ad maius* argument for the glory of the "ministry of the Spirit" in 3:7-11 presupposes and is based upon the unquestionable glory of the "ministry of death" = law. For in all such arguments, the force of the comparison stands or falls on the truth of the premise, taken to be common ground between the parties in the discussion. In our case, this common-ground assumption is expressed in 3:7a. There is no hint in our text, therefore, that Paul wishes to denigrate the law in any way, despite the fact that its function in Israel's history was to effect death and condemnation (cf. 3:7, 9).

On the other hand, in 3:12-15 Paul explicitly develops the point made in both Ezekiel and Jeremiah concerning the problem with the old covenant by turning to the actual account of the establishment of that covenant in Exodus, especially as it reaches its climax in the golden calf incident and second giving of the law in Ex. 32–34. For in this way he is able to adduce the biblical account itself as support for his assertion in 3:14 that "their minds were hardened" and his corresponding understanding of the killing-function of the law as a "ministry of death." At this point it will also be argued, against the prevailing consensus, that Paul's understanding of the veil of Moses in relationship to both the hardened minds of the sons of Israel (cf. 3:13f.) and the glory of the covenant itself corresponds to what the Exodus narrative as it now stands originally intended to teach. Hence, Paul's point throughout 3:6-18 is to follow Ezekiel, Jeremiah, and Ex. 32–34 (cf. Ex. 32:9f.; 33:3-5) in assigning the problem with the old covenant not to the law as such, but to the fact that the hearts of the people remained hardened to God's will. As a result, the glory of God could not dwell in their midst without utterly destroying them (cf. Is. 63:10).

3. The "Spirit" which "makes alive" represents and refers to the activity of God in changing the heart by means of his Spirit in order that God might dwell in the midst of his people in such a way that his glory is once again manifest for all to see.

This thesis derives from Paul's argument concerning the nature of his "boldness," in contrast to the necessity Moses felt to veil himself. Paul's "boldness" is based on the present work of the Lord = Spirit since the work of the Spirit in removing the veil over the heart is to make it possible for God's people to see his glory. Although not explicitly stated in our context, this understanding of the work of the Spirit in the new covenant also implies that Paul conceived of the work of the Spirit as enabling those whose hearts are changed to keep the law which was broken under the old covenant. For only those who keep God's commandments may enjoy God's presence. This point must be established, of course, in comparison with Paul's teaching concerning the law elsewhere, especially in conjunction with his view of the role of the Spirit in Rom. 7–8 and his understanding of the "new creation" in Christ reflected in I Cor. 7:19; 8:6; 10:23f.; II Cor. 5:17; Gal. 5; 6:15; and Rom. 14:6-14.

4. But the "Spirit" which "makes alive" also represents the activity of God in changing the heart by means of his Spirit in order that the law itself might now be properly understood; and by implication, the Old Testament as a whole.

According to II Cor. 3:14, the veil which still exists over the heart (cf. 3:15) also exists "upon the reading of the old covenant." Thus, the work of the Spirit also carries a corresponding hermeneutical implication based on the important OT unity between the moral and the theoretical/practical spheres of life, epitomized in the maxim that "the fear of the Lord is the beginning of wisdom" (cf. Prov. 1:7; 9:10; 15:33; Job 28:28; Ps. 111:10). This means, in turn, that the barrier to a proper understanding of the law removed "in Christ" is not intellectual, but moral. The importance of this point for Paul's immediate argument is found in the fact that, according to 3:7-11, a proper understanding of the glory inherent in the law is an essential prerequisite for an understanding of the exceedingly glorious nature of the gospel.

Again, therefore, the relationship between the law and the gospel is not one of discontinuity, but of a continuous progression from glory to glory. To remove the barrier to a proper understanding of the law is to remove the barrier to the "glory of God in the face of Christ" (II Cor. 4:6), which is the work of the Spirit as presented in I Cor. 1:18–2:16. It remains to be investigated precisely how this proper understanding of the law is achieved, i.e., how this veil is removed which lies over the reading of the "old covenant." But given both that the barrier to be removed is a moral one and the example of Paul's own reading of the OT in II Cor. 3:7-18 itself, the distinctively Christian OT hermeneutic cannot be said to consist in a new esoteric way of reading the OT, much less in a set of predetermined exegetical presuppositions which are only available to those already within the new covenant relationship to God.

5. The result of this renewed access to the glory of God is the actual transformation of those who are able to perceive it (II Cor. 3:18).

At this point in Paul's argument the theme encountered in 3:2f. is once again picked up as evidence for the validity of Paul's ministry. This explains why Paul's emphasis on the glory of the ministry of the Spirit in 3:7-11 and 3:18 both lead to expressions of confidence in 3:12 and 4:1 respectively. For the fact that the glory of God is present in Paul's ministry is evident for all to see in the transformation of those encountered by it.

6. Finally, as Paul's own statement in 4:1 illustrates, we have never left the apologetic level of argumentation in 3:4-18, despite its seemingly abstract, "theological" character, nor have we departed from a presentation of Paul's self-understanding as an apostle or "minister" of the "new covenant."

The parallel between II Cor. 4:2 and 2:17, as well as the criticism of Paul's gospel in 4:3, demonstrate that the issue still at stake throughout 3:4-18 is whether or not Paul's ministry of suffering can be brought together with his ministry of the Spirit. Moreover, Paul's proof that they can be, and indeed are, is also still the same, namely, the Christian existence of the Corinthians themselves as a result of their own perception of the glory of God in Paul's ministry. This means that

Paul's interpretation of the law also finds its support in the effects it is producing among the Corinthians and that the Christian hermeneutic as such is to be tested against the criterion of its results. Paul's view of the law is built upon his ministry of the Spirit, both of which are part of his apostolic ministry of suffering as the embodiment of the cross of Christ.

These theses remain to be demonstrated. But if they prove to be correct, then we must begin not only to revise our understanding of the nature of Paul's ministry and source of apostolic authority, as suggested by the study now at hand, but also to rethink the law/gospel contrast in a fundamental way only now beginning to take place in Pauline studies.

Bibliography

Commentaries on II Corinthians

Barrett, C. K.: *A Commentary on the Second Epistle to the Corinthians.* Harper's New Testament Commentaries. New York: Harper and Row, 1973.

Bernard, J. H.: *The Second Epistle to the Corinthians.* The Expositor's Greek Testament, 3. Grand Rapids: Eerdmans, 1979 (1903).

Bultmann, R.: *Der zweite Brief an die Korinther.* Kritisch-exegetischer Kommentar über das Neue Testament, Sonderband. Göttingen: Vandenhoeck & Ruprecht, 1976.

Calvin, J.: *The Second Epistle of Paul the Apostle to the Corinthians and the Epistles to Timothy, Titus and Philemon.* Calvin's New Testament Commentaries, 10. Trans. T. A. Smail. Grand Rapids: Eerdmans, 1964.

Heinrici, C. F. G.: *Das zweite Sendschreiben des Apostel Paulus an die Korinther.* Berlin: Hertz, 1887.

Héring, J.: *The Second Epistle of Saint Paul to the Corinthians.* London: Epworth, 1967.

Hodge, Charles: *An Exposition of the Second Epistle to the Corinthians.* Thornapple Commentaries. Grand Rapids: Baker, 1980 (1859).

Hughes, Philip E.: *Paul's Second Epistle to the Corinthians.* The New International Commentary on the New Testament. Grand Rapids: Eerdmans, 1962.

Lietzmann, Hans: *An die Korinther I-II.* Handbuch zum Neuen Testament, 9. Ergänzt von W. G. Kümmel. Tübingen: Mohr, 1969⁵.

Meyer, H. A. W.: *Critical and Exegetical Hand-book to the Epistles to the Corinthians.* Translated from the fifth German ed., 1869. Winona Lake: Alpha, 1979 (1883).

Moule, H. C. G.: *The Second Epistle to the Corinthians*. London: Pickering and Inglis, 1976 (1962).

Plummer, A.: *A Critical and Exegetical Commentary on the Second Epistle of St. Paul to the Corinthians*. The International Critical Commentary. Edinburgh: Clark, 1978 (1925).

Prümm, K.: *Diakonia Pneumatos. Der zweite Korintherbrief als Zugang zur Apostolischen Botschaft*. I: *Theologische Auslegung des zweiten Korintherbriefes*. Rome / Freiburg / Wien: Herder, 1967. II / 1: *Theologie des zweiten Korintherbriefes, Apostolat und christliche Wirklichkeit*. Rome / Freiburg / Wien: Herder, 1960. II / 2: *Die apostolische Macht*. Rome / Freiburg / Wien: Herder, 1962.

Schelkle, K. H.: *Der zweite Brief an die Korinther*. Geistliche Schriftlesung, 18. Düsseldorf: Patmos, 1964.

Schlatter, A.: *Paulus der Bote Jesus. Eine Deutung seiner Briefe an die Korinther*. Stuttgart: Calwer, 1969[4].

Strachan, R. H.: *The Second Epistle of Paul to the Corinthians*. The Moffatt New Testament Commentary, 8. London: Hodder and Stoughton, 1948[5].

Tasker, R. V. G.: *The Second Epistle of Paul to the Corinthians. An Introduction and Commentary*. The Tyndale New Testament Commentaries. Grand Rapids: Eerdmans, 1969 (1958).

Wendland, H.-D.: *Die Briefe an die Korinther*. Das Neue Testament Deutsch, 7. Göttingen: Vandenhoeck & Ruprecht, 1971[13].

Windisch, H.: *Der zweite Korintherbrief*. Kritisch-exegetischer Kommentar über das Neue Testament, 6. Göttingen: Vandenhoeck & Ruprecht, 1970[9].

Texts and Translations

Primary sources referred to but not quoted are not included in this bibliography. LCL refers to The Loeb Classical Library (Cambridge: Harvard University).

Ägyptische Urkunden aus den königlichen Museen zu Berlin. I/4: *Griechische Urkunden*. Berlin: Staatliche Museen, 1912.

Brooks, E. W.: *Joseph and Asenath. The Confession and Prayer of Asenath, Daughter of Pentephres the Priest*. Translations of Early Documents 2 / 7. London: Society for Promoting Christian Knowledge / New York: MacMillan, 1918.

Bury, R. G.: *Plato*. LCL, IX, 1952 (1926).

Cary, E.: *The Roman Antiquities of Dionysius of Halicarnassus*. LCL, I-VII, 1947-1956.

Charles, R. H.: *The Apocrypha and Pseudepigrapha of the Old Testament in English*. I: *Apocrypha*. Oxford: Clarendon, 1978 (1913). II: *Pseudepigrapha*. Oxford: Clarendon, 1977 (1913).

————: *The Greek Versions of the Testaments of the Twelve Patriarchs*. Darmstadt: Wissenschaftliche Buchgesellschaft, 1960².

Charlesworth, J. H.: *The Old Testament Pseudepigrapha*. I: *Apocalyptic Literature and Testaments*. Garden City: Doubleday, 1983.

Colson, F. H. and Whitaker, G. H.: *Philo*. LCL, I-X, 1958-1962.

Conybeare, F. C.: *Philostratus. The Life of Apollonius of Tyrana*. LCL, I, 1948 (1912).

DeJonge, M.: *Testamenta XII Patriarcharum, edited according to Cambridge University Library MS Ff. I.24 fol. 203a-262b with short notes*. Pseudepigrapha Veteris Testamenti Graece, 1. Leiden: Brill, 1964.

Díez Macho, A.: *Neophyti 1. Targum Palestinense Ms de la Biblioteca Vaticana*. II: *Exodo*. Madrid/Barcelona: Consejo Superior de Investigaciones Cientificas, 1970.

Dodds, E. R.: *Plato: Gorgias. A Revised Text with Introduction and Commentary*. Oxford: Clarendon, 1959.

Etheridge, J. W.: *The Targums of Onkelos and Jonathan ben Uzziel on the Pentateuch with the Fragments of the Jerusalem Targum from the Chaldee*. New York: KTAV, 1968 (1862).

Fowler, H. N.: *Plato*. LCL, II, 1952 (1921).

Friedlander, G.: *Pirke de Rabbi Eliezer (The Chapters of Rabbi Eliezer the Great) according to the Text of the Manuscript belonging to Abraham Epstein of Vienna*. London / New York: Bloch, 1916.

Harmon, A. M.: *Lucian*, LCL, IV, 1953.

Kilburn, K.: *Lucian*. LCL, VI, 1959.

Lake, K.: *The Apostolic Fathers*. LCL, I, 1977 (1912).

Lamb, W. R. M.: *Plato*. LCL, IV, 1952 (1924).

Lehrman, S. M.: *Exodus*. Midrash Rabbah, III. London and Bournemouth: Soncino, 1951.

Marcus, R. and Wikgren, A.: *Josephus. Jewish Antiquities*. LCL, VIII, 1963.

Norlin, G.: *Isocrates*. LCL, I and II, 1954 (1928) and 1956 (1929).

Novum Testamentum Graece, ed. E. Nestle and K. Aland et al. Stuttgart: Deutsche Bibelstiftung, 1975²⁵ and 1979²⁶.

Paton, W. R.: *Polybius. The Histories.* LCL, I-VI, 1979 (1922) –1980 (1927).

Perrin, B.: *Plutarch's Lives.* LCL, I-XI, 1961-1971.

Rahlfs, A.: *Septuaginta.* Stuttgart: Deutsche Bibelstiftung, 1935.

Robson, E. I.: *Arrian.* LCL, II, 1958 (1933).

The Septuagint Version of the Old Testament. Grand Rapids: Zondervan, 1970.

Simon, M.: *Esther and the Song of Songs.* Midrash Rabbah, IX. London and Bournemouth: Soncino, 1951.

Thackeray, H. St. J.: *Josephus. The Jewish War.* LCL, II and III, 1961 (1928).

Verrall, A. W.: *The 'Seven Against Thebes' of Aeschylus, with an Introduction, Commentary and Translation.* London/New York: MacMillan, 1887.

White, H.: *Appian's Roman History.* LCL, I-IV, 1958 (1912)– 1955 (1913).

Secondary Literature

The following abbreviations are used:

BJRL	*Bulletin of the John Rylands University Library of Manchester*
CBQ	*Catholic Biblical Quarterly*
EvTh	*Evangelische Theologie*
ExpTimes	*Expository Times*
HTR	*Harvard Theological Review*
JBL	*Journal of Biblical Literature*
JSNT	*Journal for the Study of the New Testament*
NovT	*Novum Testamentum*
NTS	*New Testament Studies*
SBL	Society of Biblical Literature
SNTS	Society for New Testament Studies
TDNT	*Theological Dictionary of the New Testament,* ed. G. Kittel and G. Friedrich, tr. G. W. Bromiley. Grand Rapids: Eerdmans.
ThB	*Theologische Beiträge*
ThLZ	*Theologische Literaturzeitung*
ThZ	*Theologische Zeitschrift*

UTB   Uni-Taschenbücher
ZNW   *Zeitschrift für die Neutestamentliche Wissenschaft*
ZThK   *Zeitschrift für Theologie und Kirche*

Anderson, G.: "Lucian: A Sophist's Sophist," *Yale Classical Studies*, 27: *Later Greek Literature*, ed. J. J. Winkler and G. Williams. Cambridge: Cambridge University, 1982, 61-92.

Ast, F.: *Lexicon Platonicum Sive Vocum Platonicarum Index*, 1-3. Darmstadt: Wissenschaftliche Buchgesellschaft, 1956 (1835-1838).

Badian, E.: "Triumph," *The Oxford Classical Dictionary*, ed. N. G. C. Hammond and H. H. Scullard. London: Oxford University, 1970², 1095.

Bailey, K.: "The Structure of 1 Corinthians and Paul's Theological Method with Special Reference to 4:17," *NovT* 25 (1983) 152-181.

Baird, William: "Letters of Recommendation. A Study of II Cor. 3:1-3," *JBL* 80 (1961) 166-172.

Barrett, C. K.: "Titus," *Neotestamentica et Semitica: Studies in Honour of Matthew Black*, ed. E. E. Ellis and M. Wilcox. Edinburgh: Clark, 1969, 1-14 (= idem, *Essays on Paul*. Philadelphia: Westminster, 1982, 118-131).

————: "Cephas and Corinth," *Abraham unser Vater. Juden und Christen im Gespräch über die Bibel. Festschrift für Otto Michel zum 60. Geburtstag*, ed. O. Betz, M. Hengel, and P. Schmidt. Leiden: Brill, 1963, 1-12 (= *Essays on Paul*, 28-39).

————: "Paul's Opponents in 2 Corinthians," *NTS* 17 (1970/1971) 233-254 (= *Essays on Paul*, 60-86).

————: "Christianity at Corinth," *BJRL* 46 (1964) 269-297 (= *Essays on Paul*, 1-27).

————: "ΨΕΥΔΑΠΟΣΤΟΛΟΙ (2 Cor. 11:13)," *Mélanges Bibliques en hommage au R. P. Béda Rigaux*, ed. A. Descamps and A. de Halleux. Gembloux: Duculot, 1970, 377-396 (= *Essays on Paul*, 87-107).

————: *A Commentary on the First Epistle to the Corinthians*. Harper's New Testament Commentaries. New York: Harper and Row, 1968.

Barth, G.: "Die Eignung des Verkündigers in 2 Kor 2:14–3:6," *Kirche. Festschrift für Günther Bornkamm zum 75. Geburtstag*, ed. D. Lührmann and G. Strecker. Tübingen: Mohr, 1980, 257-270.

Bartling, V.: "God's Triumphant Captive: Christ's Aroma for God (2 Cor 2:12-17)," *Concordia Theological Monthly* 22 (1951) 883-894.

Bates, W. H.: "The Integrity of 2 Corinthians," *NTS* 12 (1965/1966) 56-69.

Batey, R.: "Paul's Interaction with the Corinthians," *JBL* 84 (1965) 139-146.

Bauer, W.: *A Greek-English Lexicon of the New Testament and Other Early Christian Literature*, tr. and adapted by W. F. Arndt and F. W. Gingrich. Chicago: University of Chicago, 1957; revised and augmented by F. W. Gingrich and F. W. Danker. Chicago: University of Chicago, 1979².

Baumann, G.: לוח, *Theologisches Wörterbuch zum Alten Testament*, IV, ed. G. J. Botterweck and H. Ringgren. Stuttgart: Kohlhammer, 1982, 495-499.

Baumert, N.: *Täglich Sterben und Auferstehen. Der Literalsinn von 2 Kor 4:12-5:10*. Studien zum Alten und Neuen Testament, 34. München: Kösel, 1973.

Beker, J. C.: *Paul the Apostle: The Triumph of God in Life and Thought*. Philadelphia: Fortress, 1980.

Berger, K.: "Die impliziten Gegner. Zur Methode des Erschließens von 'Gegnern' in neutestamentlichen Texten," *Kirche. Festschrift für Günther Bornkamm zum 75. Geburtstag*, ed. D. Lührmann and G. Strecker. Tübingen: Mohr, 1980, 373-400.

Betz, O.: "Die Vision des Paulus im Tempel von Jerusalem. Apg. 22:17-21 als Beitrag zur Deutung des Damaskuserlebnisses," *Verborum Veritas. Festschrift für Gustav Stählin zum 70. Geburtstag*, ed. O. Böcher and K. Haacker. Wuppertal: Theologischer Verlag Rolf Brockhaus, 1970, 113-123.

————: "Fleischliche und 'geistliche' Christuserkenntnis nach 2. Korinther 5:16," *ThB* 14 (1983) 167-179.

Bieder, W.: "Paulus und seine Gegner in Korinth," *ThZ* 17 (1961) 319-333.

Blass, F. and A. Debrunner: *A Greek Grammar of the New Testament and Other Early Christian Literature*, tr. and rev. R. W. Funk. Chicago: University of Chicago, 1961.

Bornkamm, G.: *Paul*. New York: Harper and Row, 1971.

Bowie, E. L.: "The Importance of Sophists," *Yale Classical Studies*, 27: *Later Greek Literature*, ed. J. J. Winkler and G. Williams. Cambridge: Cambridge University, 1982, 29-59.

Brown, F., Driver, S. R., and Briggs, C. A.: *A Hebrew and English Lexicon of the Old Testament*. Oxford: Clarendon, 1976 (1907).

Bruce, F. F.: *1 and 2 Thessalonians*. Word Biblical Commentary. Waco, TX: Word, 1982.

————: *Paul and Jesus*. Grand Rapids: Baker, 1974.

Brun, Lyder: "Zur Auslegung von II Kor 5:1-10," *ZNW* 28 (1929) 207-229.

Büchsel, F.: εἰλικρινής κ.τ.λ., *TDNT* II, 1964, 397-398.

Bultmann, R.: ἀναγινώσκω κ.τ.λ., *TDNT* I, 1964, 343-344.

————: *Exegetische Probleme des zweiten Korintherbriefes zu 2. Kor. 5:1-5; 5:11-6:10; 10-13; 12:21.* Symbolae Biblicae Upsalienses, 9. Uppsala: Wretmans, 1947.

————: *Theologie des Neuen Testaments,* ed. Otto Merk. UTB, 630. Tübingen: Mohr, 1980[8.]

Campenhausen, H. F. von: *Kirchliches Amt und geistliche Vollmacht in den ersten drei Jahrhunderten.* Beiträge zur historischen Theologie, 14. Tübingen: Mohr, 1963[2].

Cantor, N. F.: *Medieval History: The Life and Death of a Civilization.* New York: MacMillan, 1969[2].

Conzelmann, Hans: *Der erste Brief an die Korinther.* Kritisch-exegetischer Kommentar über das Neue Testament. Göttingen: Vandenhoeck & Ruprecht, 1981[12].

————: χάρις κ.τ.λ., *TDNT* IX, 1974, 372-415.

Cranfield, C. E. B.: "Changes of Person and Number in Paul's Epistles," *Paul and Paulinism. Essays in Honour of C. K. Barrett,* ed. M. D. Hooker and S. G. Wilson. London: SPCK, 1982, 280-289 (= idem, *The Bible and Christian Life.* Edinburgh: Clark, 1985, 215-228).

Cullmann, O.: *Christ and Time: The Primitive Christian Conception of Time and History.* Philadelphia: Westminster, 1975 (rev. ed.).

Dahl, N. A.: "Promise and Fulfillment," idem, *Studies in Paul: Theology for the Early Christian Mission.* Minneapolis: Augsburg, 1977, 121-136.

————: "Paul and the Church at Corinth According to 1 Corinthians 1:10-4:21," *Christian History and Interpretation: Studies Presented to John Knox,* ed. W. R. Farmer, C. F. D. Moule, and R. R. Niebuhr. Cambridge: Cambridge University, 1967, 313-335 (= *Studies in Paul,* 40-61).

Dahn, K. and H.-G. Link: θριαμβεύω, *The New International Dictionary of New Testament Theology,* I, ed. Colin Brown (translation with additions and revisions of *Theologisches Begriffslexicon zum Neuen Testament*). Grand Rapids: Zondervan, 1975, 649-650.

Dautzenberg, G.: "Der Verzicht auf das apostolische Unterhaltsrecht. Eine exegetische Untersuchung zu 1 Kor 9," *Biblica* 50 (1969) 212-232.

Davies, W. D.: "Paul and the People of Israel," *NTS* 24 (1978) 4-39 (= idem, *Jewish and Pauline Studies.* Philadelphia: Fortress, 1984, 123-152).

————: *Paul and Rabbinic Judaism: Some Rabbinic Elements in Pauline Theology.* Philadelphia: Fortress, 1980⁴.

Delling, G.: ὀσμή, *TDNT* V, 1967, 493-495.

————: πλῆθος, *TDNT* VI, 1968, 274-283.

Demánn, P.: "Moses und das Gesetz bei Paulus," *Moses in Schrift und Überlieferung.* Düsseldorf: Patmos, 1963, 205-264.

Dick, K.: *Der Schriftstellerische Plural bei Paulus.* Halle: Niemeyer, 1900.

Dill, S.: *Roman Society from Nero to Marcus Aurelius.* New York: Meridian, 1964 (1956).

Dinkler, E.: "Korintherbrief," *Die Religion in Geschichte und Gegenwart: Handwörterbuch für Theologie und Religionswissenschaft,* IV, ed. K. Galling, et al. Tübingen: Mohr, 1960³, 7-23.

Dodd, C. H.: "New Testament Translation Problems II," *The Bible Translator* 28 (1977) 110-112.

Dudley, D. R.: *The Civilization of Rome.* New York: New American Library, 1962².

Dungan, D. L.: *The Sayings of Jesus in the Churches of Paul: The Use of the Synoptic Tradition in the Regulation of Early Church Life.* Philadelphia: Fortress, 1971.

Dunn, J. D. G.: *Baptism in the Holy Spirit: A Reexamination of the New Testament Teaching on the Gift of the Spirit in Relation to Pentecostalism Today.* Philadelphia: Westminster, 1970.

————: *Jesus and the Spirit: A Study of the Religious and Charismatic Experience of Jesus and the First Christians as Reflected in the New Testament.* London: SCM, 1975.

————: *Unity and Diversity in the New Testament: An Inquiry into the Character of Earliest Christianity.* Philadelphia: Westminster, 1977.

————: "The Responsible Congregation (1 Cor. 14:26-40)," *Charisma und Agape (1 Ko 12–14).* Rome: St. Paul's Abbey, 1983, 201-236.

Eckstein, H.-J.: *Der Begriff Syneidesis bei Paulus. Eine neutestamentlich-exegetische Untersuchung zum 'Gewissensbegriff.'* Wissenschaftliche Untersuchungen zum Neuen Testament, second series, 10. Tübingen: Mohr, 1983.

Egan, R. B.: "Lexical Evidence on Two Pauline Passages," *NovT* 19 (1977) 34-62.

Ehlers, W.: "Triumphus," *Paulys Real-Encyclopädie der classischen Altertumswissenschaft.* Second series, VII/1, ed. G. Wissowa, W. Kroll, and K. Mittelhaus. Stuttgart: Metzler, 1939, 493-511.

Eichholz, G.: *Die Theologie des Paulus im Umriss.* Neukirchen-Vluyn: Neukirchener, 1977².

Ellis, E. E.: "II Corinthians 5:1-10 in Pauline Eschatology," *NTS* 6 (1959/1960) 211-224.

————: "Christ Crucified," *Reconciliation and Hope: New Testament Essays on Atonement and Eschatology presented to L. L. Morris on his 60th Birthday,* ed. R. Banks. Grand Rapids: Eerdmans, 1974, 69-75 (= idem, *Prophecy and Hermeneutic in Early Christianity: New Testament Essays.* Wissenschaftliche Untersuchungen zum Neuen Testament, 18. Tübingen: Mohr/Grand Rapids: Eerdmans, 1978, 72-79).

————: "Paul and His Opponents: Trends in Research," *Prophecy and Hermeneutic in Early Christianity,* 80-115.

Farrer, A. M.: "The Ministry in the New Testament," *The Apostolic Ministry: Essays on the History and the Doctrine of Episcopacy,* ed. K. E. Kirk. London: Hodder and Stoughton, 1946, 115-182.

Findlay, G. G.: "St. Paul's Use of ΘΡΙΑΜΒΕΥΩ," *The Expositor* 10 (1879) 403-421.

Finkelstein, M. I.: "Ἔμπορος, Ναύκληρος and Κάπηλος: Prolegomena to the Study of Athenian Trade," *Classical Philology* 30 (1935) 320-336.

Finley, M. I.: *The Ancient Economy.* London: Chatto & Windus, 1973.

————: "Aristotle and Economic Analysis," *Studies in Ancient Society.* Past and Present Series, ed. M. I. Finley. London/Boston: Routledge and Kegan Paul, 1974, 26-52.

————: *The Ancient Greeks: An Introduction to Their Life and Thought.* New York: Viking, 1964².

Friedrich, G.: "Die Gegner des Paulus im 2. Korintherbrief," *Abraham unser Vater. Juden und Christen im Gespräch über die Bibel. Festschrift für Otto Michel zum 60. Geburtstag,* ed. O. Betz, M. Hengel, and P. Schmidt. Leiden: Brill, 1963, 181-215.

Friesen, I. I.: *The Glory of the Ministry of Jesus Christ, Illustrated by a Study of 2 Cor. 2:14–3:18.* Basel Theologische Dissertationen, 7. Basel: Friedrich Reinhard Kommissionsverlag, 1971.

Furnish, V. P.: *Theology and Ethics in Paul.* Nashville: Abingdon, 1968.

Gauss, H.: *Philosophischer Handkommentar zu den Dialogen Platos.* III/1. Bern: Lang, 1960.

Georgi, D.: *Die Gegner des Paulus im 2. Korintherbrief. Studien zur Religiösen Propaganda in der Spätantike.* Wissenschaftliche Monographien zum Alten und Neuen Testament, 11. Neukirchen-Vluyn: Neukirchener, 1964.

————: "Corinthians, Second Letter to the," *The Interpreter's Dictionary of the Bible*. Supplementary Volume, ed. K. Crim. Nashville: Abingdon, 1976, 183-186.

————: *Die Geschichte der Kollekte des Paulus für Jerusalem*. Theologische Forschung, 38. Hamburg-Bergstedt: Reich, 1965.

Ginzberg, L.: *The Legends of the Jews*. II, III, V, and VI. Philadelphia: Jewish Publication Society of America, 1954 (1910), 1954 (1911), 1946 (1928), and 1955 (1925).

Goppelt, L.: *Theologie des Neuen Testaments*. II, ed. J. Roloff. UTB, 850. Göttingen: Vandenhoeck & Ruprecht, 1978³.

Grundmann, W.: ἀναγκάζω κ.τ.λ., *TDNT* I, 1964, 344-347.

Gunther, J. J.: *St. Paul's Opponents and Their Background: A Study of Apocalyptic and Jewish Sectarian Teachings*. Supplements to Novum Testamentum, 30. Leiden: Brill, 1973.

Güttgemanns, E.: Review of D. Georgi, *Gegner, Zeitschrift für Kirchengeschichte* 77 (1966) 126-131.

————: *Der leidende Apostel und sein Herr. Studien zur paulinischen Christologie*. Forschungen zur Religion und Literatur des Alten und Neuen Testaments, 90. Göttingen: Vandenhoeck & Ruprecht, 1966.

Hahn, F.: "Die alttestamentlichen Motive in der urchristlichen Abendmahlsüberlieferung," *EvTh* 27 (1967) 337-374.

————: "Bibelarbeit über 2. Korinther 3:4-18," *Erneuerung aus der Bibel*. Die Bibel in der Welt, 19, ed. S. Meurer. Stuttgart: Deutsche Bibelstiftung, 1982, 82-92.

Hanson, A.: "1 Corinthians 4:13b and Lamentations 3:45," *ExpTimes* 93 (1982) 214-215.

Harrisville, R. A.: *The Concept of Newness in the New Testament*. Minneapolis: Augsburg, 1960.

Hartmann, L.: "Bundesideologie in und hinter einigen paulinischen Texten," *Die Paulinische Literatur und Theologie*. Teologiske Studier, 7, ed. S. Pedersen. Arhus: Aros/Göttingen: Vandenhoeck & Ruprecht, 1980, 103-118.

Hauck, F. ἑκών κ.τ.λ., *TDNT* II, 1964, 469-470.

Heiligenthal, R.: *Werke als Zeichen. Untersuchungen zur Bedeutung der menschlichen Taten im Frühjudentum, Neuen Testament und Frühchristentum*. Wissenschaftliche Untersuchungen zum Neuen Testament, second series, 9. Tübingen: Mohr, 1983.

Hengel, M.: "Leiden in der Nachfolge Jesus," *Der leidende Mensch, Beiträge zum unbewältigten Thema*, ed. H. Schulze. Neukirchen-Vluyn: Neukirchener, 1974, 85-94.

Hermann, I.: *Kyrios und Pneuma. Studien zur Christologie der paulin-*

ischen Hauptbriefe. Studien zum Alten und Neuen Testament, 2. München: Kösel, 1961.

Heschel, A. J.: *The Prophets*. New York and Evanston: Harper and Row, 1962.

Hickling, C. J. A.: "The Sequence of Thought in II Corinthians, Chapter Three," *NTS* 21 (1975) 380-395.

———: "Centre and Periphery in the Thought of Paul," *Studia Biblica 1978: III. Papers on Paul and Other New Testament Authors*, ed. E. A. Livingstone. JSNT Supplement Series, 3. Sheffield: University of Sheffield, 1980, 199-214.

Hock, R. F.: "Paul's Tentmaking and the Problem of His Social Class," *JBL* 97 (1978) 555-564.

———: *The Social Context of Paul's Ministry: Tentmaking and Apostleship*. Philadelphia: Fortress, 1980.

Hodgson, R.: "Paul the Apostle and First Century Tribulation Lists," *ZNW* 74 (1983) 59-80.

Hofius, O.: " 'Gott hat unter uns aufgerichtet das Wort von der Versöhnung' (2 Kor 5:19)," *ZNW* 71 (1980) 3-20.

Holmberg, B.: *Paul and Power: The Structure of Authority in the Primitive Church as Reflected in the Pauline Epistles*. Coniectanea Biblica, NT Series, 11. Lund: Gleerup, 1978/Philadelphia: Fortress, 1980.

Holtz, T.: "Zum Selbstverständnis des Apostels Paulus," *ThLZ* 91 (1966) 322-330.

Hooker, M. D.: "Beyond the Things that are Written? St. Paul's Use of Scripture," *NTS* 27 (1981) 295-309.

Hoyle, R. B.: *The Holy Spirit in St. Paul*. London: Hodder and Stoughton, 1927.

Iacobitz, C.: *Lucianus, Accedunt scholia auctiora et emendatiora, index et rerum et verborum*. Leipzig: Koehler, 1966 (1841).

Jastrow, M.: *A Dictionary of the Talmud Babli and Yerushalmi, and the Midrashic Literature*, I. London: Luzac/New York: Putnam, 1903.

Jeremias, J.: πολλοί, *TDNT* VI, 1968, 536-545.

———: λίθος, *TDNT* IV, 1967, 268-280.

Jervell, J.: "Das Volk des Geistes," *God's Christ and His People. Studies in Honour of Nils Alstrup Dahl*, ed. J. Jervell and W. A. Meeks. Oslo: Universitetsforlaget, 1977, 87-106.

Jones, P. R.: *The Apostle Paul: A Second Moses according to II Corinthians 2:14-4:7*. Unpublished Ph.D. diss., Princeton Theological Seminary, 1973.

———: "The Apostle Paul: Second Moses to the New Covenant Community: A Study in Pauline Apostolic Authority," *God's Inerrant Word: An International Symposium on the Trustworthiness of Scripture*, ed. J. W. Montgomery. Minneapolis: Bethany, 1974, 219-241.

Kamlah, E.: "Wie beurteilt Paulus sein Leiden?" *ZNW* 54 (1963) 217-232.

Kasch, W.: συνίστημι κ.τ.λ., *TDNT* VII, 1971, 896-898.

Käsemann, E.: "Amt und Gemeinde im Neuen Testament," idem, *Exegetische Versuche und Besinnungen*, I. Göttingen: Vandenhoeck & Ruprecht, 1970⁶, 109-134.

————: "Begründet der neutestamentliche Kanon die Einheit der Kirche?" *Exegetische Versuche und Besinnungen*, I, 214-223.

————: "Zum Thema der Nichtobjektivierbarkeit," idem, *Exegetische Versuche und Besinnungen*, I, 224-236.

————: "Eine paulinische Variation des 'amor fati,'" idem, *Exegetische Versuche und Besinnungen*, II. Göttingen: Vandenhoeck & Ruprecht, 1970³, 223-239.

————: "Geist und Buchstabe," idem, *Paulinische Perspektiven*. Tübingen: Mohr, 1972², 237-285.

————: "Die Heilsbedeutung des Todes Jesu bei Paulus," *Paulinische Perspektiven*, 61-107.

————: "Die Legitimität des Apostels. Eine Untersuchung zu II Korinther 10–13," *ZNW* 41 (1942) 33-71.

Kent, H. A., Jr.: "The Glory of the Christian Ministry. An Analysis of 2 Corinthians 2:14–4:18," *Grace Theological Journal* 2 (1981) 171-189.

Keyes, C. W.: "The Greek Letter of Introduction," *The American Journal of Philology* 56 (1935) 28-44.

Kim, S.: *The Origin of Paul's Gospel*. Wissenschaftliche Untersuchungen zum Neuen Testament, second series, 4. Tübingen: Mohr, 1981/Grand Rapids: Eerdmans, 1982.

Klaiber, W.: *Rechtfertigung und Gemeinde. Eine Untersuchung zum paulinischen Kirchenverständnis*. Forschungen zur Religion und Literatur des Alten und Neuen Testaments, 127. Göttingen: Vandenhoeck & Ruprecht, 1982.

Kleinknecht, K. T.: *Der leidende Gerechtfertigte. Die alttestamentlich-jüdische Tradition vom 'leidenden Gerechten' und ihre Rezeption bei Paulus*. Wissenschaftliche Untersuchungen zum Neuen Testament, second series, 13. Tübingen: Mohr, 1984.

Klinzing, G.: *Die Umdeutung des Kultus in der Qumrangemeinde und im Neuen Testament*. Studien zur Umwelt des Neuen Testaments, 7. Göttingen: Vandenhoeck & Ruprecht, 1971.

Kremer, J.: " 'Denn der Buchstabe tötet, der Geist aber macht lebendig.' Methodologische und hermeneutische Erwägungen zu 2Kor 3:6b," *Begegnung mit dem Wort. Festschrift für Heinrich Zimmermann*, ed. J. Zmijewski and E. Nellessen. Bonner Biblische Beiträge, 53. Bonn: Hanstein, 1980, 219-250.

Kümmel, W. G.: *Introduction to the New Testament*. Nashville: Abingdon, 1975 (rev. ed.).

Ladd, G. E.: *The Presence of the Future: The Eschatology of Biblical Realism*. Grand Rapids: Eerdmans, 1974.

Lambrecht, J.: "Structure and Line of Thought in 2 Cor. 2:14–4:6," *Biblica* 64 (1983) 344-380.

Lang, F.: "Die Gruppen in Korinth nach 1. Korinther 1–4," *ThB* 14 (1983) 68-79.

Lemke, W. E.: "Jeremiah 31:31-34," *Interpretation* 37 (1983) 183-187.

Liddell, H. G. and Scott, R.: *A Greek-English Lexicon, with a Supplement*, rev. and augmented by H. S. Jones. Oxford: Clarendon, 1978 (1940⁹).

Liebeschuetz, J. H. W. G.: *Antioch: City and Imperial Administration in the Later Roman Empire*. Oxford: Clarendon, 1972.

Lightfoot, J. B.: *Saint Paul's Epistles to the Colossians and to Philemon*. London: MacMillan, 1879³.

————: *Saint Paul's Epistle to the Galatians*. London: MacMillan, 1876⁵.

Lüdemann, G.: *Paulus, der Heidenapostel*. II: *Antipaulinismus im frühen Christentum*. Forschungen zur Religion und Literatur des Alten und Neuen Testaments, 130. Göttingen: Vandenhoeck & Ruprecht, 1983.

Luz, Ulrich: "Theologia crucis als Mitte der Theologie im Neuen Testament," *EvTh* 34 (1974) 116-141.

————: *Das Geschichtsverständnis des Apostels Paulus*. Beiträge zur evangelischen Theologie, 49. München: Kaiser, 1968.

Machalet, C.: "Paulus und seine Gegner. Eine Untersuchung zu den Korintherbriefen," *Theokratia. Jahrbuch des Institutum Judaicum Delitzschianum*, II: *Festgabe für Karl Heinrich Rengstorf zum 70. Geburtstag*, ed. W. Dietrich, P. Freimark, and H. Schreckenberg. Leiden: Brill, 1973, 183-203.

MacMullen, R.: *Roman Social Relations 50 B.C. to A.D. 284*. New Haven/London: Yale University, 1974.

Malherbe, A. J.: "Antisthenes and Odysseus, and Paul at War," *HTR* 76 (1983) 143-173.

Manson, T. W.: "2 Cor. 2:14-17: Suggestions towards an Exegesis," *Studia Paulina. In Honorem Johannis de Zwaan Septuagenarii*, ed. J. N. Sevenster and W. C. van Unnik. Haarlem: Bohn, 1953, 155-162.

Marmorstein, A.: "The Holy Spirit in Rabbinic Legend," *Studies in Jewish Theology, The Arthur Marmorstein Memorial Volume*, ed. J. Rabbinowitz and M. S. Lew. London/New York/Toronto: Oxford University, 1950, 122-144.

Marshall, P.: "A Metaphor of Social Shame: ΘΡΙΑΜΒΕΥΕΙΝ in 2 Cor. 2:14," *NovT* 25 (1983) 302-317.

Maurer, C.: σκεῦος, *TDNT* VII, 1971, 358-367.

McDonald, J. I. H.: "Paul and the Preaching Ministry: A Reconsideration of 2 Cor. 2:14-17 in its Context," *JSNT* 17 (1983) 35-50.

McEvenue, S. E.: *The Narrative Style of the Priestly Writer.* Analecta Biblica, 50. Rome: Pontifical Biblical Institute, 1971.

Meeks, W. A.: *The First Urban Christians: The Social World of the Apostle Paul.* New Haven/London: Yale University, 1983.

Metzger, B.: *A Textual Commentary on the Greek New Testament.* London/New York: United Bible Societies, 1975 (corrected ed.).

Meyer, P. W.: "The Holy Spirit in the Pauline Letters: A Contextual Explanation," *Interpretation* 33 (1979) 3-18.

Moore, G. F.: "Conjectanea Talmudica: Notes on Rev. 13:18; Matt. 23:35f.; 28:1; 2 Cor. 2:14-16; Jubilees 34:4, 7; 7:4," *Journal of the American Oriental Society* 26 (1905) 315-333.

Moulton, J. H. and Milligan, G.: *The Vocabulary of the Greek New Testament Illustrated from the Papyri and other Non-literary Sources.* London: Hodder and Stoughton, 1915-1929.

Moxnes, H.: *Theology in Conflict: Studies in Paul's Understanding of God in Romans.* Supplements to Novum Testamentum, 53. Leiden: Brill, 1980.

Munck, J.: *Paul and the Salvation of Mankind.* Atlanta: John Knox, 1977 (1959).

Nestle, W.: *Platon. Ausgewählte Schriften*, IV: *Protagoras.* Leipzig/Berlin: de Gruyter, 1931[7].

Nock, A. D.: *St. Paul.* London: Butterworth, 1938.

————: *Conversion: The Old and the New in Religion from Alexander the Great to Augustine of Hippo.* Oxford: Clarendon, 1933.

Obrien, P. T.: *Introductory Thanksgivings in the Letters of Paul.* Supplements to Novum Testamentum, 49. Leiden: Brill, 1977.

O'Collins, G. G.: "Power Made Perfect in Weakness: 2 Cor. 12:9-10," *CBQ* 33 (1971) 528-537.

Oepke, A.: κενός κ.τ.λ., *TDNT* III, 1965, 659-662.

Oostendorp, D. W.: *Another Jesus: A Gospel of Jewish Christian Superiority in II Corinthians.* Kampen: Kok, 1967.

Parunak, H. V.: "Transitional Techniques in the Bible," *JBL* 102 (1983) 525-548.

Perlitt, L.: "Mose als Prophet," *EvTh* 31 (1971) 588-608.

Piper, J.: *'Love your enemies.' Jesus' Love Command in the Synoptic Gospels and in the Early Christian Paraenesis. A History of the Tradition and Interpretation of its Uses.* SNTS Monograph Series, 38. Cambridge: Cambridge University, 1979.

Pope, R. M.: "Studies in Pauline Vocabulary: 1. of the Triumph-Joy," *ExpTimes* (1909/1910) 19-21.

Price, J. L.: "Aspects of Paul's Theology and their Bearing on Literary Problems of Second Corinthians," *Studies in the History of the Text of the New Testament in Honor of Kenneth Willis Clark*, ed. B. L. Daniels and M. J. Suggs. Salt Lake City: University of Utah, 1967, 95-106.

Provence, T. E.: " 'Who is Sufficient for these Things?' An Exegesis of 2 Corinthians 2:15-3:18," *NovT* 24 (1982) 54-81.

Räisänen, H.: *Paul and the Law.* Wissenschaftliche Untersuchungen zum Neuen Testament, 29. Tübingen: Mohr, 1983/Philadelphia: Fortress, 1986.

Rengstorf, K. H.: *Apostolat und Predigtamt. Ein Beitrag zur neutestamentlichen Grundlegung einer Lehre vom Amt der Kirche.* Stuttgart/Köln: Kohlhammer, 1954.

———: ἱκανός κ.τ.λ., *TDNT* III, 1965, 293-296.

———: στέλλω κ.τ.λ., *TDNT* VII, 1971, 594-595.

Reumann, J.: "Oikonomia = 'Covenant': Terms for Heilsgeschichte in Early Christian Usage," *NovT* 3 (1959) 282-292.

———: "Οἰκονομία-Terms in Paul in Comparison with Lukan Heilsgeschichte," *NTS* 13 (1966/1967) 147-167.

Richard, E.: "Polemics, Old Testament, and Theology: A Study of II Cor. 3:1–4:6," *Revue Biblique* 88 (1981) 340-367.

Richardson, P.: "Spirit and Letter: A Foundation for Hermeneutics," *Evangelical Quarterly* 45 (1973) 208-218.

Ridderbos, H.: *Paul: An Outline of His Theology.* Grand Rapids: Eerdmans, 1975.

Rissi, M.: *Studien zum zweiten Korintherbrief: Der alte Bund—Der Prediger—Der Tod.* Abhandlungen zur Theologie des Alten und Neuen Testaments, 56. Zürich: Zwingli, 1969.

Robertson, A. T.: *A Grammar of the Greek New Testament in the Light of Historical Research.* Nashville: Broadman, 1934.

Robinson, D. W. B.: "The Priesthood of Paul in the Gospel of Hope," *Reconciliation and Hope: New Testament Essays on Atonement and*

Eschatology presented to L. L. Morris on his 60th Birthday, ed. R. Banks. Grand Rapids: Eerdmans, 1974, 231-245.

Roetzel, C. J.: *Judgment in the Community. A Study of the Relationship between Eschatology and Ecclesiology in Paul*. Leiden: Brill, 1972.

Röhrich, L.: "Himmelsbrief," *Die Religion in Geschichte und Gegenwart: Handwörterbuch für Theologie und Religionswissenschaft*, III, ed. K. Galling, et al. Tübingen: Mohr, 1959, 338-339.

Roloff, J.: *Apostolat—Verkündigung—Kirche. Ursprung, Inhalt und Funktion des kirchlichen Apostelamtes nach Paulus, Lukas und den Pastoralbriefen*. Gütersloh: Mohn, 1965.

Rostovtzeff, M.: *The Social and Economic History of the Hellenistic World*, II and III. Oxford: Clarendon, 1953 (1941) and 1959 (1941). I, second revised ed. by P. M. Fraser. Oxford: Clarendon, 1966.

Satake, A.: "Apostolat und Gnade bei Paulus," *NTS* 15 (1968) 96-107.

Schechter, S.: *Aspects of Rabbinic Theology*. New York: Schocken, 1961 (1909).

Schnackenburg, R.: "Apostles Before and During Paul's Time," *Apostolic History and the Gospel: Biblical and Historical Essays presented to F. F. Bruce on his 60th Birthday*, ed. W. W. Gasque and R. P. Martin. Grand Rapids: Eerdmans, 1970, 287-303.

Schnelle, U.: *Gerechtigkeit und Christusgegenwart. Vorpaulinische und paulinische Tauftheologie*. Göttinger theologische Arbeiten, 24. Göttingen: Vandenhoeck & Ruprecht, 1983.

Schoeps, H. J.: *Paul: The Theology of the Apostle in the Light of Jewish Religious History*. Philadelphia: Westminster, 1961.

Schrage, W.: "Leid, Kreuz und Eschaton. Die Peristasenkataloge als Merkmale paulinischer theologia crucis und Eschatologie," *EvTh* 34 (1974) 141-175.

———: *Ethik des Neuen Testaments*. Grundrisse zum NT. Das Neue Testament Deutsch Ergänzungsreihe, 4. Göttingen: Vandenhoeck & Ruprecht, 1982.

Schrenk, G.: γράφω κ.τ.λ., *TDNT* I, 1964, 742-773.

Schürmann, H.: "Die Apostolische Existenz im Bilde. Meditation über 2 Kor. 2:14-16a," *Ursprung und Gestalt, Erörterungen und Besinnungen zum Neuen Testament*. Kommentare und Beiträge zum Alten und Neuen Testament. Düsseldorf: Patmos, 1970, 229-235.

Schütz, J. H.: *Paul and the Anatomy of Apostolic Authority*. SNTS Monograph Series, 26. Cambridge: Cambridge University, 1975.

Schweitzer, E., et al.: σάρξ κ.τ.λ., *TDNT* VII, 1971, 98-151.

Sokolowski, E.: *Die Begriffe Geist und Leben bei Paulus in ihren Bezie-*

hungen zu einander. Eine exegetisch-religionsgeschichtliche Untersuchung. Göttingen: Vandenhoeck & Ruprecht, 1903.

Stalder, K.: *Das Werk des Geistes in der Heiligung bei Paulus.* Zürich: EVZ, 1962.

Stendahl, K.: "Call Rather than Conversion," idem, *Paul among Jews and Gentiles and Other Essays.* Philadelphia: Fortress, 1976, 7-23.

Stowers, S. K.: *The Diatribe and Paul's Letter to the Romans.* SBL Dissertation Series, 57. Chico, CA: Scholars, 1981.

————: "Social Status, Public Speaking and Private Teaching: The Circumstances of Paul's Preaching Activity," *NovT* 26 (1984) 59-82.

Strack, H. and Billerbeck, P.: *Kommentar zum Neuen Testament aus Talmud und Midrasch,* I, III. München: Beck, 1956² and 1926.

Stuhlmacher, P.: "Erwägungen zum ontologischen Charakter der καινὴ κτίσις bei Paulus," *EvTh* 27 (1967) 1-35.

————: " 'Das Ende des Gesetzes.' Über Ursprung und Ansatz der paulinischen Theologie," *ZThK* 67 (1970) 14-39 (= idem, *Versöhnung, Gesetz und Gerechtigkeit. Aufsätze zur biblischen Theologie.* Göttingen: Vandenhoeck & Ruprecht, 1981, 166-191).

————: "Achtzehn Thesen zur paulinischen Kreuzestheologie," *Rechtfertigung. Festschrift für Ernst Käsemann zum 70. Geburtstag,* ed. J. Friedrich, W. Pöhlmann, and P. Stuhlmacher. Tübingen: Mohr, 1976, 509-525 (= *Versöhnung,* 192-208).

————: "Theologische Probleme des Römerbriefpräskripts," *EvTh* 27 (1967) 374-389.

————: *Das paulinische Evangelium.* I: *Vorgeschichte.* Forschungen zur Religion und Literatur des Alten und Neuen Testaments, 95. Göttingen: Vandenhoeck & Ruprecht, 1968.

————: "Das paulinische Evangelium," *Das Evangelium und die Evangelien. Vorträge vom Tübinger Symposium 1982,* ed. P. Stuhlmacher. Wissenschaftliche Untersuchungen zum Neuen Testament, 28. Tübingen: Mohr, 1983, 157-182.

Stumpff, A.: εὐωδία, *TDNT* II, 1964, 808-810.

Tannehill, R. C.: *Dying and Rising with Christ: A Study in Pauline Theology.* Beiheft zur Zeitschrift für die neutestamentliche Wissenschaft und die Kunde der älteren Kirche, 32. Berlin: Töpelmann, 1967.

Theissen, G.: "Legitimation und Lebensunterhalt. Ein Beitrag zur Soziologie urchristlicher Missionare," idem, *Studien zur Soziologie des Urchristentums.* Wissenschaftliche Untersuchungen zum Neuen Testament, 19. Tübingen, Mohr, 1979, 201-230.

————: "Die Starken und Schwachen in Korinth. Soziologische Analyse eines theologischen Streites," *Studien zur Soziologie des Urchristentums,* 272-289.

————: "Soziale Schichtung in der korinthischen Gemeinde. Ein Beitrag zur Soziologie des hellenistischen Urchristentums," *Studien zur Soziologie des Urchristentums,* 231-271.

————: *Psychologische Aspekte paulinischer Theologie.* Forschungen zur Religion und Literatur des Alten und Neuen Testaments, 131. Göttingen: Vandenhoeck & Ruprecht, 1983.

Thrall, M. E.: "Super-Apostles, Servants of Christ, and Servants of Satan," *JSNT* 6 (1980) 42-57.

————: "A Second Thanksgiving Period in II Corinthians," *JSNT* 16 (1982) 101-124.

Trench, R. C.: *Synonyms of the New Testament.* Grand Rapids: Eerdmans, 1953 (1880).

Versnel, H. S.: *Triumphus: An Inquiry into the Origin, Development and Meaning of the Roman Triumph.* Leiden: Brill, 1970.

Vielhauer, P.: "Paulus und die Kephaspartei in Korinth," *Oikodome: Aufsätze zum Neuen Testament,* II, ed. G. Klein. Theologische Bücherei, 65. München: Kaiser, 1979, 169-182.

Vos, J. S.: *Traditionsgeschichtliche Untersuchungen zur Paulinischen Pneumatologie.* Van Gorcum's Theologische Bibliotheek, 47. Assen: Van Gorcum, 1973.

Wallisch, E.: "Name und Herkunft des römischen Triumphes," *Philologus* 99 (1954/1955) 245-258.

Webster's Seventh New Collegiate Dictionary. Springfield, MA: Merriam, 1972.

Weiss, K.: "Paulus—Priester der christlichen Kultgemeinde," *ThLZ* 79 (1954) 355-364.

Wenschkewitz, H.: "Die Spiritualisierung der Kultusbegriffe Tempel, Priester und Opfer im Neuen Testament," ΑΓΓΕΛΟΣ, *Archiv für neutestamentliche Zeitgeschichte und Kulturkunde* 4 (1932) 70-230.

Wettstein, J. J.: *Novum Testamentum Graecum,* II. Graz, Austria: Akademische Druck und Verlagsanstalt, 1962 (1752).

Wilckens, U.: "Die Bekehrung des Paulus als religionsgeschichtliches Problem," *ZThK* 56 (1959) 273-293.

————: *Der Brief an die Römer.* III, Röm 12–16. Evangelisch-katholischer Kommentar zum Neuen Testament. Zürich: Benziger/ Neukirchen-Vluyn: Neukirchener, 1982.

Williamson, L., Jr.: "Led in Triumph: Paul's Use of Thriambeuō," *Interpretation* 22 (1968) 317-332.

Windisch, H.: καπηλεύω, *TDNT* III, 603-605; also cited from the German original, *Theologisches Wörterbuch zum Neuen Testament* III, 606-609.

Wolff, C.: *Jeremia im Frühjudentum und Urchristentum.* Texte und Untersuchungen zur Geschichte der altchristlichen Literatur, 118. Leipzig: Hinrich, 1976.

————: *Der erste Brief des Paulus an die Korinther. Zweiter Teil: Auslegung der Kapitel 8–16.* Theologischer Handkommentar zum Neuen Testament, VII/2. Berlin: Evangelische, 1982.

Wolff, H. W.: *Anthropology of the Old Testament.* Philadelphia: Fortress, 1974.

Zahn, T.: *Introduction to the New Testament,* I. Minneapolis, Klock & Klock, 1977 (1909).

Zerwick, M.: *Biblical Greek Illustrated with Examples.* Scripta Pontificii Instituti Biblici, 114. Rome: Pontifical Biblical Institute, 1977 (1963).

Zimmerli, W.: *Ezechiel.* Two volumes. Biblischer Kommentar: Altes Testament. Neukirchen-Vluyn: Neukirchner, 1979² and 1969.

Zmijewski, J.: *Der Stil der paulinischen 'Narrenrede.' Analyse der Sprachgestaltung in 2 Kor. 11:1–12:10 als Beitrag zur Methodik von Stiluntersuchungen neutestamentlicher Texte.* Bonner Biblische Beiträge, 52. Köln/Bonn: Hanstein, 1978.

Index of Key Passages

Index of Subjects

Only subjects which do not appear explicitly in the table of contents have been listed in this index. References to page numbers include the footnotes on that page.

Apostle/apostleship: Paul's self-understanding as, 15f., 32, 44-49, 59-62, 69-72, 83; sufficiency as, 83, 98f., 93f., 98, 176-178, 225-227; evidential apologetic for, 99-101, 133, 149-151, 159, 167-170, 173, 175f., 182f., 192-196, 208f., 225f., 227f.; prophetic background to, 139f., 177; slave imagery, 142-144. *See also* Paul: self-support as apostle

Diatribe: use in II Cor. 3:1, 180-182

Epistolary plural: use in I & II Cor., 13; use in II Cor. 2:14ff., 14-16; meaning of, 16

Holy Spirit: wisdom and the Spirit, 43f.; revealed in Paul's ministry, 45f., 48f., 205-207, 221-225, 227f.; relationship to suffering, 46, 48f., (see "suffering"; apologetic significance of, 207-209; and the Law, 213-215, 221-223, 228-233; and the theology of the cross, 57-59, 208f.

Imitation of Paul, 60f., 69-72, 77, 128f., 132f.

Law (OT): see "Holy Spirit"; meaning of "stone tablet" imagery, 214-220

Letter/Spirit contrast, context of, 1f., 7f., 79f., 83, 211-213, 228-233

Letters of recommendation: Paul's lack of need for 14f., 183-186; relationship to "self-recommendation", 177f., 182-186; external nature of Paul's, 190, 192-197

Moses, call of: relationship to II Cor. 2:16, 94-97; Paul not a "second Moses," 96f., 223-225

Opponents of Paul in Corinth, 3, 59-62, 75f., 145-149, 151-165, 169f., 177f., 182, 187, 197

Paul: conversion-call, 14, 32, 140-142, 167-170, 183, 185f., 223f.; significance of his founding the church in Corinth, 14f., 92, 130f., 187-189, 193-197, 199f., 204f., 227f.; identity between Paul/Gospel, 15f., 46-48, 49-59, 75, 78f., 135f., 154, 157, 172f., 228; status "in Christ," 47f.; role in II Cor. 2:14, 32f., 45-47, 58f.; relationship to Corinthians church, 98, 128f., 131f., 171f., 194, 197; revelatory function/mediatory agent, 45-49, 57-59, 62-64, 67f., 71-75, 79-83, 227f.; self-support as apostle, 124-145, 149-158, 175, 177, 182f., 226f.; implication for Corinthians, 127-133, 150f., 194; as expression of love, 128, 133,

260

Paternoster Biblical and Theological Monographs

(Uniform with this Volume)

Eve: Accused or Acquitted?
*An Analysis of Feminist Readings of the
Creation Narrative Texts in Genesis 1–3*
Joseph Abraham

Two contrary views dominate contemporary feminist biblical scholarship. One finds in the Bible an unequivocal equality between the sexes from the very creation of humanity, whilst the other sees the biblical text as irredeemably patriarchal and androcentric. Dr. Abraham enters into dialogue with both camps as well as introducing his own method of approach. An invaluable tool for anyone who is interested in this contemporary debate.

2000 / 0-85364-971-5

Deification in Eastern Orthodox Theology
An Evaluation and Critique of the Theology of Dumitru Staniloae
Emil Bartos

Bartos studies a fundamental yet neglected aspect of Orthodox theology: deification. By examining the doctrines of anthropology, Christology, soteriology and ecclesiology as they relate to deification, he provides an important contribution to contemporary dialogue between Eastern and Western theologians.

1999 / 0-85364-956-1 / 386pp

The Weakness of the Law
Jonathan F. Bayes

A study of the four New Testament books which refer to the law as weak (Acts, Romans, Galatians, Hebrews) leads to a defence of the third use in the Reformed debate about the law in the life of the believer.

2000 / 0-85364-957-X

The Priesthood of Some Believers
Developments in the Christian Literature of the First Three Centuries
Colin J. Bulley

The first in-depth treatment of early Christian texts on the priesthood of all believers shows that the developing priesthood of the ordained related closely to the division between laity and clergy and had deleterious effects on the practice of the general priesthood.

2000 / 0-85364-958-8

Paul as Apostle to the Gentiles
*His Apostolic Self-awareness and its Influence
on the Soteriological Argument in Romans*
Daniel J-S Chae

Opposing 'the post-Holocaust interpretation of Romans', Daniel Chae competently demonstrates that Paul argues for the equality of Jew and Gentile in Romans. Chae's fresh exegetical interpretation is academically outstanding and spiritually encouraging.

1997 / 0-85364-829-8 / 392pp

Parallel Lives
The Relation of Paul to the Apostles in the Lucan Perspective
Andrew C. Clark

This study of the Peter-Paul parallels in Acts argues that their purpose was to emphasize the themes of continuity in salvation history and the unity of the Jewish and Gentile missions. New light is shed on Luke's literary techniques, partly through a comparison with Plutarch.

2000 / 085364-979-0

Baptism and the Baptists
Theology and Practice in Twentieth-Century Britain
Anthony R. Cross

At a time of renewed interest in baptism, *Baptism and the Baptists* is a detailed study of twentieth-century baptismal theology and practice and the factors which have influenced its development.

2000 / 0-85364-959-6 / 530pp

The Crisis and the Quest
A Kierkegaardian Reading of Charles Williams
Stephen M. Dunning

Employing Kierkegaardian categories and analysis, this study investigates both the central crisis in Charles Williams's authorship between hermeticism and Christianity (Kierkegaard's Religions A and B), and the quest to resolve this crisis, a quest that ultimately presses the bounds of orthodoxy.

1999 / 0-85364-985-5 / 278pp

The Triumph of Christ in African Perspective
A Study of Demonology and Redemption in the African Context
Keith Ferdinando

This book explores the implications for the gospel of traditional African fears of occult aggression. It analyses such traditional approaches to suffering and biblical responses to fears of demonic evil, concluding with an evaluation of African beliefs from the perspective of the gospel.

1999 / 0-85364-830-1 / 439pp

Suffering and Ministry in the Spirit
Paul's Defence of His Ministry in 2 Corinthians 2:14 – 3:3
Scott J. Hafemann
Shedding new light on the way Paul defended his apostleship, the author offers a careful, detailed study of 2 Corinthians 2:14 – 3:3 linked with other key passages throughout 1 and 2 Corinthians. Demonstrating the unity and coherence of Paul's argument in this passage, the author shows that Paul's suffering served as the vehicle for revealing God's power and glory through the Spirit.

1999 / 0-85364-967-7 / 276pp

The Words of our Lips
Language-Use in Free Church Worship
David Hilborn
Studies of liturgical language have tended to focus on the written canons of Roman Catholic and Anglican communities. By contrast, David Hilborn analyses the more extemporary approach of English Nonconformity. Drawing on recent developments in linguistic pragmatics, he explores similarities and differences between 'fixed' and 'free' worship, and argues for the interdependence of each.

2001 / 0-85364-977-4

One God, One People
*The Differentiated Unity of the People of God
in the Theology of Jürgen Moltmann*
John G. Kelly
The author expounds and critiques Moltmann's doctrine of God and highlights the systematic connections between it and Moltmann's influential discussion of Israel. He then proposes a fresh approach to Jewish–Christian relations, building on Moltmann's work and using insights from Habermas and Rawls.

2000 / 0-85346-969-3

Calvin and English Calvinism to 1649
R.T. Kendall
The author's thesis is that those who formed the Westminster Confession of Faith, which is regarded as Calvinism, in fact departed from John Calvin on two points: (1) the extent of the Atonement and (2) the ground of assurance of salvation. 'No student of the period can ignore this work' – *J.I. Packer.*

1997 / 0-85364-827-1 / 224pp

Karl Barth and the Strange New World within the Bible
Neil B. MacDonald

Barth's discovery of the strange new world within the Bible is examined in the context of Kant, Hume, Overbeck, and, most importantly, Wittgenstein. Covers some fundamental issues in theology today: epistemology, the final form of the text and biblical truth-claims.

2000 / 0-85364-970-7

Attributes and Atonement
The Holy Love of God in the Theology of P.T. Forsyth
Leslie McCurdy

Attributes and Atonement is an intriguing full-length study of P.T. Forsyth's doctrine of the cross as it relates particularly to God's holy love. It includes an unparalleled bibliography of both primary and secondary material relating to Forsyth.

1999 / 0-85364-833-6 / 323pp

Towards a Theology of the Concord of God
A Japanese Perspective on the Trinity
Nozomu Miyahira

This book introduces a new Japanese theology and a unique Trinitarian formula based on the Japanese intellectual climate: three betweennesses and one concord. It also presents a new interpretation of the Trinity, a co-subordinationism, which is in line with orthodox Trinitarianism; each single person of the Trinity is eternally and equally subordinate (or serviceable) to the other persons, so that they retain the mutual dynamic equality.

1999 / 0-85364-863-8

Your Father the Devil?
A New Approach to John and 'The Jews'
Stephen Motyer

Who are 'the Jews' in John's Gospel? Defending John against the charge of anti-Semitism, Motyer argues that, far from demonising the Jews, the Gospel seeks to present Jesus as 'Good News for Jews' in a late first century setting.

1997 / 0-85364-832-8 / 274pp

Origins and Early Development of Liberation Theology in Latin America

With Particular Reference to Gustavo Gutierrez

Eddy José Muskus

This work challenges the fundamental premise of Liberation Theology: 'opting for the poor', and its claim that Christ is found in them. It also argues that Liberation Theology emerged as a direct result of the failure of the Roman Catholic Church in Latin America.

2000 / 0-85364-974-X

'Hell': A Hard Look at a Hard Question

The Fate of the Unrighteous in New Testament Thought

David Powys

This comprehensive treatment seeks to unlock the original meaning of terms and phrases long thought to support the traditional doctrine of hell. It concludes that there is an alternative – one which is more biblical, and which can positively revive the rationale for Christian mission.

1999 / 0-85364-831-X / 500pp

Evangelical Experiences

A Study in the Spirituality of English Evangelicalism 1918–1939

Ian M Randall

This book makes a detailed historical examination of evangelical spirituality between the First and Second World Wars. It shows how patterns of devotion led to tensions and divisions. In a wide-ranging study, Anglican, Wesleyan, Reformed and Pentecostal-charismatic spiritualities are analysed.

1999 / 0-85364-919-7 / 320pp

Is World View Neutral Education Possible and Desirable?

A Christian Response to Liberal Arguments

(Published jointly with The Stapleford Centre)

Signe Sandsmark

This thesis discusses reasons for belief in world view neutrality, and argues that 'neutral' education will have a hidden, but strong world view influence. It discusses the place for Christian education in the common school.

1999 / 0-85364-973-1 / 205pp

The Extent of the Atonement
A Dilemma for Reformed Theology from Calvin to the Consensus
G. Michael Thomas
A study of the way Reformed theology addressed the question, 'Did Christ die for all, or for the elect only?', commencing with John Calvin, and including debates with Lutheranism, the Synod of Dort and the teaching of Moïse Amyraut.
1997 / 0-85364-828-X / 237pp

The Power of the Cross
Theology and the Death of Christ in Paul, Luther and Pascal
Graham Tomlin
This book explores the theology of the cross in St Paul, Luther and Pascal. It offers new perspectives on the theology of each, and some implications for the nature of power, apologetics, theology and church life in a postmodern context.
1999 / 0-85364-984-7 / 368pp

Constrained by Zeal
Female Spirituality amongst Nonconformists 1825–1875
Linda Wilson
Constrained by Zeal investigates the neglected area of Nonconformist female spirituality. Against the background of separate spheres, it analyses the experience of women from four denominations, and argues that the churches provided a 'third sphere' in which they could find opportunities for participation.
1999 / 0-85364-972-3

Disavowing Constantine
Mission, Church and the Social Order in the Theologies of John Howard Yoder and Jürgen Moltmann
Nigel G. Wright
This book is a timely restatement of a radical theology of church and state in the Anabaptist and Baptist tradition. Dr. Wright constructs his argument in dialogue and debate with Yoder and Moltmann, major contributors to a free church perspective.
2000 / 0-85364-978-2 / 247pp

The Voice of Jesus
Studies in the Interpretation of Six Gospel Parables
Stephen Wright

This literary study considers how the 'voice' of Jesus has been heard in different periods of parable interpretation, and how the categories of figure and trope may help us towards a sensitive reading of the parables today.

2000 / 0-85364-975-8

The Paternoster Press
P O Box 300
Carlisle Cumbria
CA3 0QS UK

Web: www.paternoster-publishing.com